P9-CKX-176

Dante's Fearful Art of Justice

Dante's Fearful Art of Justice deals primarily with the symbolical significance of 'the state of souls after death' in various episodes of the *Inferno*,
the first canticle of Dante's *Divina Commedia*. The fruitfulness of the
Auerbach-Singleton approach to the poem is demonstrated by Professor
Cassell's investigations, which are based on the belief that Dante used
both the theological system of fourfold allegory and the prefiguration-
fulfilment pattern of history found in the Old and New Testaments.

The author first deals with the history of *contrapassum*, 'just retribution,' as it appeared in philosophy and theology, and describes Dante's
use of historical and artistic figuration, both classical and Christian. It is
central to Cassell's aim to show how Dante believed that his portrayal
of the damned revealed the justice of God. Critics have believed that the
relation of sin to the suffering of the shades in Hell was tenuous or
even arbitrary in many cases. Cassell shows, through a close examination of Dante's assimilation of the Classics (and their medieval interpretations), of patristics, and of traditional iconography, that there is an
intimate metaphorical and artistic aptness in the poet's representation. Cassell relies at some points on art history, and thirty-four illustrations of frescoes, statuary, and illuminations from paleo-Christian
times to the fourteenth century are therefore included.

This volume will be of particular interest to medieval specialists,
historians of the Renaissance and Reformation periods, and those con-
cerned with European literature.

ANTHONY K. CASSELL teaches medieval and Renaissance literature at the
University of Illinois at Urbana-Champaign.

ANTHONY K. CASSELL

Dante's Fearful Art of Justice

UNIVERSITY OF TORONTO PRESS

Toronto Buffalo London

©   University of Toronto Press 1984
Toronto Buffalo London
Printed in Canada

ISBN 0-8020-2504-8

Canadian Cataloguing in Publication Data
Cassell, Anthony K. (Anthony Kimber), 1941-
    Dante's fearful art of justice
    Includes index.
    ISBN 0-8020-2504-8
    1. Dante Alighieri, 1265-1321. Divina commedia-
Criticism and interpretation. I. Title.
    PQ4439.C37 1984   851'.1   C84-098127-9

Publication of this book is made possible by grants from the National Endowment
for the Humanities, from the Dr M. Aylwin Cotton Foundation, from the
Research Board of the University of Illinois at Urbana-Champaign, and from the
Publications Fund of University of Toronto Press.

IN MEMORIAM

HARRIET ISABEL FRANSELLA

Contents

Acknowledgments

This inquiry into the sins of Dante's Hell has taken several years to complete, and, as each year passed, so I owed ever more to my family, friends, former teachers, colleagues, associates, assistants, and students. It is an enjoyable task to try to repay some of that accumulated debt here. This study would simply not exist had I not had the privilege, some twenty years ago, of taking the graduate courses offered by Charles S. Singleton at the Johns Hopkins University. I confess that in admiration and emulation I still frankly plunder his thought, and my book might be considered as one long footnote to this confession.

Others too have aided the work's formation: a large part of my debt is due John B. Friedman, my colleague at Illinois, whose very friendship is for me an education. To my friend David Bright goes my deep gratitude for his incredible sense of humour, profound advice, and Latinity. My colleagues, in the History of Art, Philip Fehl, Allen Stuart Weller, Edwin Rae, and Slobodan Ćurčić, have all generously shared their knowledge with me. I sincerely thank my friends in the Dante Society for their kind encouragement and aid, particularly Joan M. Ferrante, Robert Hollander, Rachel Jacoff, Anthony Pellegrini, and Richard Alan Shoaf, who read sections of the book and made valuable suggestions. To Claudio Pescatore, whose culture encompasses both nuclear engineering and more literature than does that of most *litterati*, I owe an especial mention for help and encouragement.

To my faithful graduate research assistants, Nona Flores, Mark Williams, Fred Jenkins, and David Larmour, go my personal and scholarly respect and sincere gratitude; I would especially like to note Miss Flores' aid and wisdom while we were researching the Pier della Vigna-Judas-Ahithophel connections for chapter 3. The Research Board of the University of Illinois has aided me generously, not only in providing funds for these assistants but also for preparing the final manuscript.

As I close, my deepest thanks and love is due, as always, to my wife, Janet Fitch, who not only helped edit and proof the volume in each of its stages, but who also patiently replaced my passives, abolished alliterations, and painstakingly purged my purpling prose.

Anthony K. Cassell
Champaign, 1983

Note on Works Cited and Abbreviations

All quotations from Dante's Poem I have taken from Giorgio Petrocchi's text as reprinted in *The Divine Comedy*, translated with a commentary by Charles S. Singleton, Bollingen Series LXXX (Princeton, NJ: Princeton University Press 1970–5), 6 vols. (Where Singleton's *Commentary* is cited I have noted it thus: *Inferno: Commentary*.) Translations from the *Divine Comedy* are drawn from Singleton's volumes, and from the translation by John D. Sinclair, *The Divine Comedy of Dante Alighieri*, 3 vols. (Oxford: The Bodley Head 1939; reprint with corrections 1948; Galaxy Books, New York: Oxford University Press 1961). For *Il Convivio* I have used the two-volume edition by G. Busnelli and G. Vandelli, as revised by Antonio Enzo Quaglio (Florence: Le Monnier 1964). For other works of Dante, I have used the convenient edition, *Le Opere di Dante*, test critico della Società Dantesca Italiana a cura di M. Barbi, E.G. Parodi, F. Pellegrini, E. Pistelli, P. Rajna, E. Rostagno, G. Vandelli, con indice analitico di Mario Casella (Florence: Bemporad 1921); page references are to this edition, unless otherwise indicated.

I have cited many articles from the *Enciclopedia dantesca*, dir. Umberto Bosco, ed. Giorgio Petrocchi et al. (Rome: Istituto della Enciclopedia Italiana 1970–6).

Charles S. Singleton's two fundamental studies on the *Commedia*, *Dante Studies I: Commedia, Elements of Structure* (Cambridge, Mass.: Harvard University Press 1957; reprint Baltimore: Johns Hopkins University Press 1975), and *Dante Studies II: Journey to Beatrice* (Cambridge, Mass.: Harvard University Press 1958; reprint Baltimore: Johns Hopkins Press 1975), are cited as *Elements* and *Journey* to avoid confusion with the journal *Dante Studies* (Dante Society of America).

I have generally used the Loeb Classical Library for the texts and translations of the classics. St Augustine's *Confessions* are cited from the two-volume *LCL* text with the 1631 translation by William Watts, and his *City of God (De civitate Dei)* from the seven-volume edition in the same series by George E. McCracken, William M. Green, et al. (1957–72). For the convenience of the reader I have cited Migne's edition of the *Glossa Ordinaria* (*PL*, 113–14) but have checked older, more accurate editions, not widely available, for Migne's adequacy at each point. Citations from St Thomas Aquinas' *Summa Theologica* are taken from the edition translated by the English Dominican Province, 3 vols. (New York and Boston: Benziger Brothers 1947–8). St Gregory the Great's *Liber Moralium in Job* is quoted from Migne's edition (*PL*, 75–6) and from the English version, *Morals on the Book of Job* in A Library of Fathers of the Holy Catholic Church, translated by Members of the English Church (Oxford: John Henry Parker 1844–56). The Apocryphal Books of the Old Testament are given in the translation of *The New Oxford Annotated Bible with Apocrypha: Revised Standard Version*, ed. Herbert G. May and Bruce M. Metzger, Expanded Edition (New York: Oxford University Press 1962; reprint 1973). The New Testament Apocrypha are quoted in the edition of Montague Rhodes James, *The Apocryphal New Testament* (Oxford: Clarendon Press 1924). Biblical citations are from the Vulgate and Douay versions.

Where existing translations of foreign works are used, I have so noted them, but I have not hesitated to correct, adapt, or change them to clarify word parallels.

Chapter 2 appeared in slightly different form in *Yale Italian Studies*, 1 (1977), 335–70, and chapter 7, now considerably revised, in *Dante Studies*, 99 (1981); some four pages, now reworked in chapter 8, were published in *Italica*, 56 (1979), 331–51. I would like to thank these journals for their kind permission to republish the items here. My gratitude goes also to Aldo S. Bernardo and Anthony L. Pellegrini for allowing me to reprint material in chapters 3 and 4 that appeared in *Dante, Petrarch, Boccaccio: Studies in the Trecento in Honor of Charles S. Singleton* (Binghamton, NY: Medieval and Renaissance Texts and Studies 1983), 19–76. Credits for the photographs are found in the list of plates, pp. 105–7.

ABBREVIATIONS

DCD	*De civitate Dei* (St Augustine)
De Mon.	*De Monarchia* (Dante)
CSEL	Corpus scriptorum ecclesiasticorum latinorum
LCL	Loeb Classical Library
Moralia	*Liber Moralium in Job* (St Gregory the Great)
Morals	*Morals on the Book of Job* (trans. of *Moralia*)

PG	*Patrologiae cursus completus: Series graeca,* ed. J.-P. Migne (Paris 1857–94)
PL	*Patrologiae cursus completus: Series latina,* ed. J.-P. Migne (Paris 1844–64)
PMLA	*Publications of the Modern Language Association*
ST	*Summa Theologica* (St Thomas Aquinas)

'For God knows how to make souls that forsake Him conform to the Divine Order, and by their justly deserved misery to furnish the lower parts of creation with the most meet and suitable laws of His wondrous dispensation.'

St Augustine, *De Catechizandis rudibus*, I, 18

Dante's Fearful Art of Justice

1 JUSTICE AND THE *CONTRAPASSO*

Dante uses the term *'contrapasso'* or 'the justice of retaliatory punishment' but once in all his works. Bertran de Born, damned in Nether Hell amid the sowers of discord, moans unforgettably as he swings his severed head in his hand like a lantern:

> Così s'osserva in me lo contrapasso.

> Thus is the retribution observed in me.

(Inferno XXVIII, 142)

Although the term occurs quite late in the first canticle, the concept of the *contrapasso* is at the centre of the Poet's whole creation of Hell, philosophically, and artistically. The shocking severity of the punishment and the submissive tone of Bertran, as he bows, headless, to a universal imperative, spur the reader to observe the canon which the term implies in the rest of the *Inferno*. Bertran's words tell us, first, that God's punishment in Hell's realm of second death is strictly reasoned, and second, that it is in the mode of the Old Testament. We understand that it reflects the form of justice which, as Dante believed, obtained before the Coming of Christ who made possible man's reconciliation with heavenly grace and mercy through faith, hope, and the love of God and neighbour. Those who reject these virtues are fittingly condemned to dwell forever in a realm where Christ's merciful New Dispensation and Law hold no place.

Dante's primary source for the idea of the *contrapasso* came through St Thomas Aquinas' *Summa theologica* (II–II, qu. 612, art. 4), where the saint conflates the Aristotelian idea of reciprocal justice with the *lex talionis* of the Old Testament, implicitly contrasting it with the 'turning-the-other-cheek' exhortation of the New Law: 'I answer that, retaliation (*contrapassum*) denotes equal suffering in repayment for previous action; and the expression applies most properly to injurious sufferings and actions, whereby a man harms the person of his neighbor; for instance, if a man strike, that he be struck back. This kind of justice is laid down in the Law (Exodus 21:23–4): He shall render life for life, eye for eye, etc. And since also to take away what belongs to another is to do something unjust, it follows that, secondly, retaliation (*contrapassum*) consist in this also that whoever causes loss to another, should suffer loss in his belongings. This just loss is also found in the Law (Exodus, 21:1).'[1] St Thomas in turn had derived the term '*contrapassum*' from translations of Aristotle's *Nicomachaean Ethics* v, 5, where the Philosopher had used the Greek term 'τὸ ἀντιπεπονθός,' 'the state of suffering something in turn, or, in return,' implying 'the state of suffering in retribution for fault or crime committed.'[2]

The biblical concept of *lex talionis*, in which each individual case is disposed of justly, unrelated to crimes of a different type ('life for life, eye for eye, tooth for tooth, hand for hand, foot for foot, burning for burning, wound for wound, stripe for stripe' [Exodus 21:23–5]), will be squarely at the centre of this inquiry into the view of justice depicted in Dante's first realm of the afterlife.[3] There was no hint of any *hierarchy* of intensity or variance worked out in the seriousness of punishment between differing crimes. In the *Inferno* Dante's punishments likewise do not become apparently harsher as we descend with the poets to the depths. How are the blazing tongues imprisoning Ulysses and Guido da Montefeltro (*Inferno* xxvi and xxvii) milder than the ice encasing Bocca in Cocytus (*Inferno* xxxii)? Or how are they severer than the boiling pitch of the grafters (*Inferno* xxi–xxii), or the smeltering sarcophagi of the heresiarchs (*Inferno* x)? Obviously we are not observing a hierarchy of punishment (*poena*) but the workings of a moral mode of justice through symbolism: punishment as it is exquisitely apt and merited in each discrete case. As we descend from circle to circle, the sins become not more serious in punishment but rather in guilt (*culpa*) humanly acquired.[4] The suffering of Hell, like the joys of Heaven, must, ultimately, be unfathomable to the human intellect and, thus, unutterable.[5] Dante chooses to concentrate on human responsibility, upon the state of souls after death literally as the consequence of their own actions, and, thus, upon man who is 'according as by his *merits or demerits* in the exercise of his free will ... deserving of reward or punishment by justice.' It is perhaps no accident that this phrase is repeated twice in the *Epistola* to Can Grande della Scala.[6]

The following chapters are the product of inductive study and thus they stress poetic and critical practice rather than abstract theory. I have examined several episodes which intrigued me with their puzzles, paradoxes, or other cruxes, trying in each case to understand how that segment of the Poem was intended to *work*. I wanted to discover the pattern which existed – that which joined sinner, sin, punishment, and imagery, in each case, into an artistic whole. In order to do so, I attempted to consider each of those elements within the cultural context of Dante's age, drawing upon any sensible and applicable means of grasping what an educated man of Dante's own time might have made of such perplexities as Farinata's tomb, Bertran's severed head, or Ulysses' tongue of fire. Having deciphered various elements, I tried to understand their interrelationships and to fit them into the larger system of the *contrapasso*.

My examinations are based on certain poetical and critical principles, most of which are commonplaces of present Italian and North American Dante studies. The first assumption is that the *Epistola* to Can Grande, even if it is not authentic, is an essential guide to the author's erudition, method, and intentions in the *Commedia*. In this letter the writer describes the Poem as didactic ('doctrinalis,' para. 6) and he clearly sets forth an aim to effect moral change in the reader: 'The aim of the whole and of the part is to remove *those living in this life* from a state of misery, and to bring them to a state of happiness' (para. 15).[7] A major aim of my own studies therefore is to examine *how* Dante tries to achieve this purpose. In this letter (para. 7), too, Dante (and I will henceforth assume that it is he) takes over the traditional fourfold system of allegorical biblical exegesis, and, by applying it to his Poem, he demonstrates his intention to use it as a poetics:

> For the elucidation, therefore, of what we have to say, it must be understood that the meaning of this work is not of one kind only; rather the work may be described as '*polysemous*,' that is, having several meanings; for the first meaning is that which is conveyed by the letter, and the next is that which is conveyed by what the letter signifies; *the former of which is called literal, while the latter is called allegorical, or mystical*. And for the better illustration of this method of exposition we may apply it to the following verses: 'When Israel went out of Egypt, the house of Jacob from a people of strange language; Judah was his sanctuary, and Israel his dominion.' For if we consider the *letter* alone, the thing signified to us is the going out of the children of Israel from Egypt in the time of Moses; if the *allegory*, our redemption through Christ is signified; if the *moral* sense, the conversion of the soul from the sorrow and misery of sin to a state of grace is signified; if the *anagogical*, the passing of the sanctified soul from the bondage of the corruption of this world to the liberty of everlasting glory is signified. *And although these mystical meanings are called by various names, they may one and all in a general sense be termed allegorical, inasmuch*

> *as they are different (diversi) from the literal or historical;* for the
> word 'allegory' is so called from the Greek *alleon*, which in Latin is
> *alienum* (strange) or *diversum* (different).[8]

Traditionally the literal level of a medieval text both concealed and revealed
the other meanings; as the theory had it, this dual function protected and hid
the holy content from the eyes of the profane, but allowed the wise man to
gaze beneath to see the teaching unveiled. Without the secondary levels the
first physical level could not always be comprehended; its full intent lay not
only in the narrative or in the disparate words, sentences, tropes, allusions, and
episodes taken in their reified state, but in the broader, more global plan of
the interplay *between* the levels of signification. In Dante's canto of the
Idolaters (*Inferno* xiv), for example, the literal punishment of a rain of fire
upon a burning *landa* is an effectively horrifying warning in and of itself,
but the aptness and justice of the *contrapasso* only satisfies when we recall the
extra-textual Sodomites of the Cities of the Plain and St Paul's censures in
Romans 1:23–7, where idolatry is linked to sodomy as a cause to its effect.
Further, the literal modifiers of the *landa*, the similes concerning Alexander
and Cato, as I shall show (chapters 5 and 6) make no sense unless we go
outside of the text to the external literary and historical referent, that is to
pagan history (the classical epics taken as such) and to Christian euhemeristic
and mythographical interpretations of that history. Likewise, no connection
can be made *literally* between these similes and the statue of the Veglio
described by Virgil. At the first level they remain a mere concatenation. To
make sense of the whole episode we must look deeply into the allegorical,
moral, and eschatological significances of the dream of Nebuchadnezzar and
into the Christian interpretation of the birth and death of Jove Cretagenes.
Most emphatically, the literal level of the Poem does not bind these elements
together; only allegory in its broad sense does so.

Dante's art becomes appreciable not only in the reading of the literal but
by a close in-gathering and judicious blending of *all* the various levels of
significance. Even in the earlier, and surpassed, *Convivio* (ii, i, 7–9), Dante
clearly stated that the sense of the letter was 'always *subject* and *material* of
the others, especially the allegorical.' The very beauty of art, of *poetic*
unity, vanishes into a mysterious opacity if the structural, 'secondary,' meanings are ignored.

Dante's theoretical ideas derive principally from the twelfth-century
Victorines and from the thirteenth-century Dominican theologians.[9] But even
this fact is problematic. Medieval theologians generally concurred that
mystical or spiritual senses were found solely in Scriptures and not in other
literature. Particularly, St Thomas applies the fourfold system solely to

Holy Writ[10] since only the Deity had the power to ordain events so that they not only had meaning in and of themselves but could also signify other events. Here, as in many other instances, Dante breaks with St Thomas and clearly means the reader to apply the fourfold method to his own creation.

In the paragraph which follows his exposition of fourfold allegory of the *Epistola* (para. 8), Dante continues his reduction of the four levels of meaning to two:

> This being understood, it is clear that the subject, with regard to which the alternative meanings are brought into play, must be *twofold*. And therefore the subject of this work must be considered in the first place from the point of view of the literal meaning, and next from that of the allegorical interpretation. The subject, then, of the whole work, taken in the literal sense only, is *the state of souls after death*, pure and simple. For *on and about that the argument of the whole work turns*. If, however, the work be regarded from the allegorical point of view, the subject is man, according as by his merits or demerits in the exercise of his free will, is deserving of reward or punishment by justice.[11]

In spite of Dante's initial careful distinctions one must hasten to add a *caveat*. First, the separation between the levels of meaning was seldom closely drawn (we note how easily Dante reduces the mystical senses to one, and the total four to two), and, secondly, it was never thought that all four allegorical levels necessarily resided in *every* passage of the Bible. If some 'secondary' levels were present it did not imply that all the others were there as well. Many biblical passages were held to be merely historical and literal, and others (Christ's parables, for example) were thought to be but a fiction containing a moral lesson.[12] Just so in Dante's Poem: no consistent fourfold exegesis need be intended for *every* passage, nor should, or could, such explanations be imposed (and what an arid and mechanical study would result if it were attempted!).

Dante's two paragraphs appear to differ in their handling of the 'subject' or content of the work. Clearly we have two elements in the signifying, histori- cal or literal, level: first, in paragraph 7, the dynamic historical paradigm of the Exodus (not only reflective of the personal moral progress of the real, historical author, Dante Alighieri, but also typologically reflected in the fictional scribe-Poet's account of the Wayfarer's journey towards conversion in the Poem); and second, in paragraph 8, the 'state of souls after death, pure and simple.' As the journey motif points to other meanings in the process of Dante's personal justification and of the possible justification of another individual (our life's journey here), so the 'state of souls after death' points to the unchanging justice of God. In his *Elements of Structure*, Charles Singleton suggested most usefully that this latter, which we might term the spatial, static element, be termed 'symbolism.'[13] It is with this element that my book principally deals, and I have tried to use the term consistently throughout. My task, then, has been to explore the symbolic level as it concerns the *contrapasso* in nether Hell. Where I treat briefly of the journey motif I do so mainly to set off the contrasting fearful, constant quality of the Deity's implacable Judgment as Dante viewed it. My examinations try to show that 'the state of souls' in Hell is indeed symbolic of the historical consequences of the earthly actions of the damned and the inevitable consequence of mankind's persistence in sinfulness, collectively and paradigmatically.[14]

I have included in my explanations not only the traditions of patristic exegesis of the Bible which Dante absorbed, but also other 'visual' Christian sources, art, iconography, liturgy, and extra-liturgical drama, where each seemed to apply when tested carefully against the text. Where Dante uses pagan classical sources, I have tried as much as possible to show that they were absorbed through, and thus were considerably changed by, medieval moralizers and mythographers. Similarly, where earlier and contemporary medieval chroniclers might be reflected, I have attempted to keep in mind that Dante read even these within the context of his own personal interpretation of Christian history.

My second major assumption, which is a corollary of the first, is that the *Epistola* and the *Commedia* itself demonstrate that Dante is attempting a new form of secular literature, new in the sense that the literal level of the narrative is not reducible merely to its allegorical and symbolic significance and thus negated by it (as in the merely poetical case of Orpheus in the *Convivio* [II, i, 3], who did *not*, as the letter of the legend insisted, make wild beasts tame *or* move rocks and trees), but rather that the literal level of the Poem gains meaning from its secondary senses since it absorbs into itself the historicity of the two Testaments and of the Christian history which sprang from them. Again to cite Singleton, the *Commedia* is an 'imitation of God's way of writing.'

Thirdly, my studies assume that Dante's theory, expounded in the *De Monarchia* II, that pagan history (recorded in classical writers as well as in Christian euhemerists and apologists) was itself directed by God to Christian ends, also holds in the Poem.[15] These inquiries may thus, I hope, prove the fruitfulness of the Auerbach-Singleton school, which holds that the writer used both the biblical or theological system of fourfold allegory and the prefiguration-fulfilment pattern of history, the basis of which consisted in the various temporal epiphanies of Christ.

The experiences of the Wayfarer in Hell, although a fiction, conform to and

reflect events which were firm historical truths for a devout Christian of
1300: Dante's journey through all three realms reflects, obviously, Christ's
own descent to Hell and ascent to Heaven, events which readers of his time
confessed as a tenet of faith each time they recited the Apostles' Creed.
Christ's journey to fulfil man's redemption sat at the centre of human history;
it taught the key to the meaning of all creation. It explained events which
came before, as it prepared for those which came thereafter. Dante works the
matrix of history into his literal narration and descriptions to give them the
'polysemous' texture described in the dedicatory letter to the Lord of
Verona.[16] Dante's personae themselves had repeated in secular history (also
part of Creation written by God) fundamental matrical patterns which the
Poet, as scribe, can copy out (*assemplare*) into the poem which he calls an
assemplo or scribe's copy.[17] The moral truth exposed by the sinners' actions
points to earlier past events, BC and AD, which, in turn, point to historical
Redemption, to the ever-present sacraments, and to the *invisibilia Dei* in
the hereafter. Unlike the 'allegory of poets' in which the literal level is reduced
to its secondary meanings (Orpheus' playing reduced merely to the voice of
the wise man which humbles cruel hearts and moves the unlearned [*Conv.* II,
i, 3]), Dante's narrative 'letter' does not 'disappear' in the face of allegorical
or symbolical interpretation, but gains additional significance by the fact that
it both absorbs them and points to them. As Singleton states succinctly,
Dante's allegory is of a theological 'both-and' significance, in which all levels
hold simultaneously and complement one another, rather than of a poetic
'this-for-that' meaning.[18]

We satisfy our quest to understand the *contrapasso* in the *Inferno* when
we see not only that the 'punishment fits the crime' but that it is, in all cases,
more profoundly, a strict manifestation of the sin as guilt. By tracing the
underlying patristic concepts, we can understand that the suffering represents
an exteriorizing of the wickedness and corruption that lurks within the
souls of the sinners. The images of the damned figure symbolically, icono-
graphically, and theologically the very mystery and complexity of their sins.
The souls are fixed in the guilt and pain of their ultimate, accrued, unrepented
wickedness, as Christian orthodoxy insisted: immediately after death, the
damned are punished by becoming unchangeable in their iniquity; the
disorder of their wills, responsible for their damnation, remains in them
throughout eternity; for them goodness is no longer possible.[19]

Our appreciation of the Poet's portrayal of the horrors of Hell and the
terrible justice of God will be intensified when we realize that the damned still
remain in some way *images* of the Godhead whom they rejected, however
they may have perverted that Image.[20] Just as Dante's journey allegorically
reflects Christ's act of Redemption in its many Old-Testament prefigurations,
so the condition of the various souls whom the Wayfarer finds in punishment

also mystically bodies forth the Deity and, consequently, various biblical and historical personages which typify him. In *Inferno* v, Francesca buffeted like a dove figures a lustful counterpart to the loving symbol of the Holy Spirit which punishes her in another of its configurations as a whirlwind. Farinata's punishment points ironically to Christ upright in his tomb and to Noah standing in his Ark, and that of Pier della Vigna points to Christ as the Mystic Vine and to his prefiguration in the Tree of Jesse. Caiaphas lies crucified like Christ among the hypocrites. The thieves in *Inferno* xxiv–xxv metamorphose into frightening, destructive inversions of the crucified Christ as prefigured, familiarly, by the brazen, healing serpent hung on Moses' staff in the desert (Numbers 21: 8–9 and John 3:14).[21] Even the ridiculous Mastro Adamo, suffering the thirst of dropsy (*Inferno* xxx, 49) 'a guisa di leuto,' inverts the thirsting, crucified Christ (the Second Adam) in his traditional figuration as a lyre. Christ is this instrument, says St Bonaventure, for 'the Cross has the form of the wood and [Christ's] body, in turn, supplied the strings extending over the flatness of the wood.'[22] Even the punishment of classical personae points back and forward to both pagan historical events as well as to biblical parallels and inversions. The condition of the damned, and the accounts of the events which led to that condition, are poetically interpreted as figurations repeating biblical and historical precedents. God's image prevails even to the depths where Satan's triune heads dripping tears and bloody drool are a clear, intentionally banal, parody. In this Dante follows the Augustinian tradition which held that sin itself was but a perverse imitation of the Deity; creatures who set themselves against God were in fact awkwardly attempting to be like him (*Confessions* ii, 6). In the wake of St Augustine, St Bernard, and St Bonaventure, Dante states in the *De Monarchia* i, 8: 'In God's intention, every creature exists to represent the divine likeness in so far as its nature makes this possible. On account of this it is said: "Let us make man after our image and likeness." ... The whole universe is nothing but a kind of imprint of divine goodness.' The same theme of God's omnipresence – even in Hell – is articulated through biblical quotations in the *Epistola* to Can Grande (para. 22):

> For the Holy Spirit says by the mouth of Jeremias (23:24): 'Do not I fill heaven and earth?' And in the Psalm (138:7–8): 'Whither shall I go from thy spirit? Or whither shall I flee from thy face? If I ascend into heaven, thou art there: if I descend into hell, thou art present.'[23]

Dante's sinners do not parody the Godhead in any random way. In each instance Dante alludes to precisely the divine aspect which the sinners in each episode have most perverted or rejected; their imposed caricature of the

Godhead always evokes, allegorically or symbolically, an attribute of the Person which represents the strongest contrast with the sin punished. The *contrapasso* of Bertran de Born (*Inferno* XXVIII), with which we began, provides a perfect paradigm of infernal justice as expressed by Dante's technique. Having, in life, incited the young Prince Henry to rebel against his father, Henry II of England, Bertran is physically sundered in Hell as he once sundered father from son. As Dante describes the two parts of the divided body of the Provençal poet, his choice of vocabulary becomes markedly theological:

> ed eran due in uno e uno in due;
> com' esser può, quei sa che sì governa

> and they were two in one and one in two – how this can be, He knows who so ordains.

> (125–6)

The imperfect 'two in one,' as we immediately realize, evokes the trinitarian Godhead, 'three in one'; the irony is that the union between the head and the body is missing: schism denies the love of God, that is, the Holy Spirit which unites the Persons of the Father and the Son in the doctrine of the Holy Trinity:[24]

> Perch'io parti' così giunte *persone*,
>   partito porto il mio cerebro, lasso!,
>   dal suo principio ch'è in questo troncone.
> Così s'osserva in me lo contrapasso.

> Because I parted *persons thus united*, I carry my brain parted from its source, alas! which is this truncated trunk. Thus is the retribution observed in me.

> (139–42)

Bertran is doomed forever to figure a maimed, twiform inversion of the triune God. The 'figural density' or historicity of the character makes the case of Bertran de Born even more telling.[25] Dante echoes the contemporary conception of Bertran as a refiguration, in recent history, of the ancient Ahithophel who, in the Old Testament, split Absalom from his father, David:

> Io feci *il padre e 'l figlio* in sé ribelli;
>   Achitofèl non fé più d'Absalone
>   e di Davìd coi malvagi punzelli.

I made the *father and the son* rebel against each other. Ahithophel did
not more with Absalom and David by his wicked instigations.

(136–8)[26]

Dante knew that patristic interpretations of the Ahithophel story described
how its events were fulfilled in the New Testament: David, the adumbration of
Christ ('figlio'), is betrayed by Ahithophel, the prefiguration of Judas.[27] We can
therefore see a quadruple pattern of typological repetition involved in Dante's
episode of Bertran de Born, three historical (Old Testament, New Testament,
and a refiguration of the schismatic pattern in recent history), and the
fourth, and last, in the literal level of the Poem, the poetic reflection of schism
in Bertran's punishment in the afterlife.[28] Dante presents his character as
the antitype (that is, fulfilment) of an historical matrix: morally, Bertran did
indeed commit a personal sin of his own free will, but, also, he perpetrated
merely one more act of banal and undistinguished evil. We are not to understand Bertran's sin as one remarkable and isolated act of schism, but, rather,
as just one more human violation of God's divinely ordained pattern for the
whole history of humanity.

Apart from the figuration of God in the divine plan of history, the Poet's
symbolic imagery also reflects the Diety's presence in the two major sacraments, eucharist and baptism. A triform monster gulping dirt, Ugolino's
savage gnawing of Ruggieri's greasy nape, and Satan's eternal meal of three
traitors, all hideously evoke the Mass where more Holy Flesh is eaten.[29] However, the pattern of baptism, the sacrament of initiation, appropriately informs
all three canticles: in the journey, the whole *Commedia* traces the progress of
conversion and initiation into the faith of the medieval Christian.

Dante's journey of initiation into the faith follows the pattern of this
sacrament: it begins with his immersion in the tomb of Hell; then, after Hell,
it continues with his ritual washing by Virgil in *Purgatorio* I, 118–36, and
with his immersion in Lethe and Eunoe presided over by Beatrice come to
judge; and, finally, it culminates with the bathing of his eyes in the River of
Light in *Paradiso* xxx, 85–90, so that he may see the Celestial Rose. Also, in
the symbolism, immersions in fiery fonts, even in ditches of ordure, rivers
of mud, blood, and fire, all allude inescapably to this rite. In his fundamental
essay, 'In exitu Israel de Aegypto,' Charles Singleton traced the allegorical
pattern of the Exodus in the *Commedia*: the crossing of a sea, the coming
forth from the deep, the approach of a desert shore are repeated in the
initial cantos of both the *Inferno* and the *Purgatorio*.[30] The Exodus, however,
was but one biblical prefiguration, albeit the most important, of Christian
conversion and initiation. The central position of this theme in the two pro-
logues signals its importance as an organizing pattern for the rest of the

Poem. To restrict ourselves more narrowly to the purview of this study and its examination of Dante's *contrapasso*, the escape from Egypt is merely the first of a whole series of baptismal allusions and conventional typologies which the Poet will use both openly and obliquely in his symbolism of the punishments in the world of the damned.[31] Both the sacrament of baptism, in which the Holy Spirit descends to the font, and its foreshadowing by Creation itself, in which the Spirit of the Lord floated above chaotic waters, are echoed in *Inferno* IX, 64–99, by the angel who floats above the murkiness of the Styx to silence the proud hosts of nether Hell.[32] Similarly, the wrathful and slothful (*accidiosi*), immersed in second death beneath the slimy waves, repeat the sacrament as it is prefigured by those annihilated in the Flood; their immersion is a judgment and castigation of sin. The immediate evocation of the 'arca' or 'ark' in the next canto, *Inferno* X, recalls the same figure. The heresiarchs invert Noah, the herald of Justice and the type of Christ. The punishment of the simonists upside down in fiery fonts with oily flames licking their feet physically and literally reverses not only chrism, unction, and penance, but also baptism as performed for the sick and moribund: the sprinkling of water upon the head.[33] Even minor prefigurations such as the descent of fire upon the sacrifice of Elijah (3 [1] Kings 18:38) and the leprosy and washing of Naaman (4 [2] Kings 5; cf. *Inferno* XXIX) are used, inverted, and played upon by the Poet in the various episodes of the first canticle. In the realm of the damned, baptism realizes its catechetical definition and Old Testament prolepsis as God's final judgment upon sin.[34] Baptism, as Christian initiation, and the basis for the justification of the individual, is present symbolically in the *Commedia* both in its aspect as the fire of castigation upon iniquity and as the water of the remission of sin. Similarly, from the descent into Hell, through the Exodus of the ascent and purgation of the second realm, to the promised land of Heaven, the Wayfarer's journey is indeed made allegorically in imitation of Christ's baptism, 'to fulfil all justice.'[35]

The literal level of the *Inferno*, though, poses some unique problems, especially when compared to that of the other canticles. Clearly in the *Paradiso*, with its eternal Soul-Lights who record history, teach philosophy and theology, and give prayers, encomiums and confessions, much may be cryptic but all can be believed: the various levels of meaning, communicated by intellectual symbols, add to the profundity of a primal truth. But the case of Hell is quite different, since, here, in imitating God's 'book of the world,'[36] Dante's realism forces him to include the pervasive deceptiveness of the things of the world. In Hell, that ultimate 'earthly city' in Augustinian terms, we cannot always speak of the primacy of the linear, literal level in any but a mere physical sense, in that it must obviously come before other meanings and considerations can be obtained. The literal level of the *Inferno* is not reducible to its secondary senses but is deeply dependent on them; these other levels are not 'lower meanings,' after all, but 'sovrasensi' (*Convivio* II, i, 6), vertical meanings which go *above* and *beyond*. We must heed the lesson of the second canto of the *Purgatorio* and realize that, like Casella's song, the sound or letter of the work must not be rested in as if 'nothing else touched our minds.'[37]

At times, the literal level of Hell has the curious, yet intentional, function of distracting our attention away from the main subject of Dante's Poem, the state of souls after death. The episodes of Francesca, Farinata, Ulysses, and Ugolino draw us back to earth, back to the exciting, passionate, worldly enticements of adventure, romance, and tragedy. The embezzler, Ciampolo (*Inferno* XXII, 77), merely gazes placidly at his tendon as a demon rips it away; Farinata seems to hold all Hell in scorn; Ulysses so enthrals us that we forget his prison of searing flame. As the shades try to dim their own culpability almost to extinction in their *apologiae*, so they almost convince us by their wiles that their punishments also are negligible. The Poet makes God's way of educating the Wayfarer in the *Inferno* significantly different from that in the *Purgatorio* and *Paradiso*. While, in the second realm, the Wayfarer falls into error through his own mistaken conceptions, and, while in Paradise, his misconceptions are directly corrected by heavenly teachers, only in Hell is he led intentionally into error by lying demons and shades.[38] Indeed, the various confrontations with sins and sinners are a tempting of the Wayfarer and an experience *in imitatione Christi*. The Redeemer, as the Bible and the Fathers established, 'was in all points tempted like as we are, yet without sin' (Matthew 4:2). Obviously, as a journey into the desert of temptation and contact 'with beasts' and the Devil initiated Christ's ministry (Mark 1:13), so the terrifying journey across the 'piaggia diserta' and through its counterpart, the upper and 'basso loco' of Hell, must precede Dante's initiation into the new life of a convert. In the sense that the *Commedia* represents 'nostra vita,' 'our life' and journey through the world, the reader also experiences the same temptations in his own initial reactions to the damned, whether drawn in by Francesca and Ulysses or repelled by Filippo Argenti and Bocca degli Abati. Simply put, our experiences as readers of the *Inferno* must first be, as I hope to show, not only an experiencing of the poetry for its sound, for its aesthetic and emotional qualities, but also an appreciation of how deftly Dante presents the Poem as a paradigm of moral lesson, and moral process, an exercise in free will.[39] Though tempted by the perverted 'humanity' of the damned, we are forced to choose between the bewildering, often glossy, image of sin which they conjure up, and the truth, the very justice of the *contrapasso*, which the Poet reveals in the *sovrasensi*.

2 FARINATA

My examination of Dante's view of justice begins with the first episode of lower Hell, that of the heresiarchs buried forever just within the city gates of Dis,[1] since here, particularly, the major substance of the *contrapasso* as a poetic expression of God's sufficient reason has not been tackled satisfactorily. A number of questions still provoke us as we read: how should we interpret Farinata's contentiousness? Why does Dante choose to place the damned in burning *arche*? For what reason does he give the solution to the riddle of the souls' foresight here in the sixth circle? Are only the heretics ignorant of the present or does this apply to all those in Hell? A consideration of the theological, historical, and artistic bases underlying Dante's conception of the state of souls after death may help to solve the moral and anagogical puzzle.

Dante's conception of the City of Dis is informed, as is the rest of Hell, the *città dolente* (and indeed the whole *Commedia*), by St Augustine's division of humanity into two cities, the Heavenly and Earthly. As perceptive critics have seen, the puzzle of the City of Dis is partially solved by taking cantos IX and X not as separate entities but as part of one indivisible experience of the Wayfarer and one unified concept of the Poet.[2] *Inferno* X becomes clear when viewed not as an episode apart – the typical romantic tendency – but as the interior view of the city walls of which we have already seen the exterior. Dante's 'terra' echoes Augustine's 'civitas terrena': the Poet has Farinata himself call this place a 'città.' But the pattern extends beyond vocabulary to concept.

The Wayfarer, led by Virgil through a *secreto calle*,[3] will descend into the bickerings and internecine strife of the earthly *polis* – in this case those of the Guelphs and Ghibellines of his own city, Florence, transported to Hell and used as an exemplum. The subject matter, heresy and wrangling altercation, all reflect the Earthly City 'generally divided against itself.' 'There are litigations; there are wars and battles; there is pursuit of victories that either cut lives short, or that at any rate are shortlived. For whatever part of it has risen up in war against the other part, it seeks to be victorious over other nations though it is itself the slave of vices; and if, when it is victorious, it becomes exceedingly proud and haughty, its victory also cuts lives short ... For it will not be able to rule lastingly over those whom it was able to subjugate victoriously.'[4] The twin sources of sin, avarice its root and pride its beginning, combine in the shades of this circle who still abuse their intellect by seeking material aggrandisement as an end in itself. Their virtue (a proto-Machiavellian 'virtù'), unlike true virtue, came from a desire for dominion, a motive which in itself was not only a vice but which vitiated any good deeds they performed.[5] Farinata and Cavalcante committed the sin of refusing to accept their place as creatures subject to God. They revolted against him to make themselves the centre of the world; through their good works ('ben fare') they are merely 'less base,' not holy.[6] St Augustine identifies the Earthly City with the compulsion to dominate one's fellow man: 'So pride is a perverse imitation of God. For it abhors a society of peers under God, but seeks to impose its own rule, instead of His, on society.'[7] The desire to subject other men perverts God's plan for '[God] did not wish a rational creature, made in His own image to have dominion save over irrational creatures: not over man, but over the beasts.'[8] Those disposed to heresy tend particularly to disturbance of the peace and impatience for supremacy.[9]

As elsewhere in Hell, pride, in this case the pride which leads to the fall of cities, provides the key. Brunetto Latini treated such pride in chapter cxxxi of his *Trésor* under the rubric 'Des criminaux pechiés' ('On Criminal Sins'): 'For pride engenders envy, and envy engenders lying, and lying engenders deception, and deception engenders wrath, and wrath engenders malevolence, and malevolence engenders enmity, and enmity engenders warfare, and warfare sunders the law and lays waste the city.'[10] Farinata's tale recounts how Florence, brought to a pass by her leaders, only through his own efforts escapes razing. It tells of the clash of proud rebels whose compulsion to dominate their fellows can lead the city to destruction. Dante had touched on the theme of the fall of a proud city early in the *Commedia*, in *Inferno* I, where Virgil recalled that 'superbo Ilïón fu combusto' (75), and again in *Inferno* VI, in the factious prophecy of Ciacco. Here cantos IX and X dramatize the turbulence and defeat of a *polis* on the literal level: God, through his Messenger, has again vanquished this city of fire with a mere wand. A fallen city in Hell forms the scene of the action.

Pride and presumption run and maintain Augustine's Earthly City, and Dante makes canto X speak the language of *superbia* in its manifold aspects, boldly underlining the sin in his choice of vocabulary and metaphor. During the whole moving interview between Cavalcante and the Wayfarer, Farinata truly personifies biblical 'stiff-necked' pride: 'Né mosse collo, né piegò sua costa / he neither moved his neck nor bent his side' (75). Dante will later use the same 'neck' image to embody the notion of pride in *Purgatorio* XI, as he has the proud Omberto Aldobrandesco say:

> E s'io non fossi impedito dal sasso
>   che la cervice mia superba doma,
>   onde portar convienmi il viso basso,
>   cotesti, ch'ancor vive e non si noma,
>   guardere' io, per veder s'i'l conosco ...

> And were I not hindered by the stone that subdues my proud neck, so that I must hold my face down, I would look at this man who is yet alive and is not named, to see if I know him ...   (52–6)

There, those purging their pride, are, unlike Farinata, bent double, resembling corbels or caryatids supporting a roof (130–2). The unmovable quality of Farinata's neck is no incidental touch of drama. Patristically the neck itself signifies pride. The *Allegoriae in Sacram Scripturam* defines, 'Cervix est superbia, ut in Deuteronomio [31:27] "Ego ... scio ... cervicem tuam durissimam," id est superbiam tuam rigidissimam / The neck is pride, as in Deuteronomy: "I know thy most stiff neck," that is, your most rigid pride.' Guido da Pisa glosses *Inferno* x, 75, citing Isaias 3:16: 'Ambulant contra Deum extento collo / They walk against God with stretched-out necks.' Further, Dante's description, 's'ergea col petto / he rose upright with chest thrown back,' echoes such definitions of pride as that of Alain de Lille: 'Haec est superbia quae supra se insolenter se erigit / This is pride which insolently raises itself above its station.'[11] In the *Allegoriae* pseudo-Rabanus Maurus again defines '*Pectus*, superbia / Chest: pride.'[12] Pride resounds in the repetition of 'dispitto,' 'disdegno' ('scorn' or 'contempt') and 'disdegnoso' ('scornful'). The effect of the Poet's vocabulary fits perfectly with the pattern of the Earthly City. 'The two cities, then,' states Augustine, 'were created by two kinds of love: the earthly city by love of self carried even to the point of contempt for God.'[13] Such scorn for the Deity particularly besets heresiarchs: 'What else do heretics, than in entertaining false notions of God, contemn Him by their proud conceits?'[14]

The presumption characteristic of heresy also explains the famous problem (solved to satisfaction by Giorgio Padoan) of the term 'magnanimo' twice used to describe Farinata: St Augustine warns, 'Non enim putetis, fratres, quia potuerunt fieri haereses per aliquas parvas animas. Non fecerunt haereses nisi magni homines / For do not think, brethren, that heresies can arise in any small souls. None but great men have caused heresies.'[15] Magnanimity is to be understood in the context of the *terra*. Those who without true belief gain success in the Earthly City do not have true righteousness but merely its resemblance, 'For it is such men who give the appearance of doing something good in order to gain human glory.' They make the virtues the slaves of human pomp as others make them serve bodily pleasure: 'Tam turpiter servire virtutes humanae gloriae quam corporis voluptate / For the virtues to be slaves of human glory is as shameful as for them to be slaves of bodily pleasure.'[16] Yet these Epicureans do not even have the advantage in Augustine's second term of comparison, since they had put their whole lives at the service of *voluptas*. St Gregory the Great allies the effect of heretical preaching to the striving of the rich and powerful for dominion: 'Now very often the preacher of error is allied with the rich of this world, who for this reason, that they strain over earthly employments, are too blind to detect the tricks of the thing delivered, and whereas they go about to be powerful without, they are taken without labor by the noose of froward preachers.'[17] Dante's choice of the two factional leaders now comes into sharper focus: since the mighty and affluent most easily fall victim to heretical error, he selected them so that their social stature would enhance the canto's moral lesson for his reader. Gregory's description of heresiarch's behaviour could almost be a blueprint for the action in *Inferno* x. Their 'excessive warmth of wit sets them on fire, next smartness of speech lifts them up [nitor deinde loquacitatis erigit] and then, finally, dissimulation presents them comely [decorus] to the eyes of men.'[18] The Poet's scene moves dramatically. The Wayfarer, smitten by the presumed moral stature of his great compatriot, falls under the latter's sway and sinks to the very factional quarrelling, which, when habitual, can lead to eternal damnation. Farinata appears comely to Dante's eyes. The Ghibelline's speech (convincingly examined by Petrocchi)[19] provides a fine example of 'eloquio politico'; but let us note the contents:

> O Tosco che per la città del foco
>   vivo ten vai così parlando onesto
>   piacciati di restare in questo loco.

> O Tuscan, who go alive through the city of fire speaking thus modestly, may it please you to stay in this place.   (22–4)

Closer scrutiny reveals the temptation in those beguiling lines – especially their invitation to *stay in this place*, the City of Fire – to remain in Hell. (St Gregory had defined the very 'place of heresy' as pride itself.)[20] 'Come rest with me in the pride of sin' is the substance of Farinata's speech to the living Dante, for those of this circle are not merely heretics but *teachers* and *leaders* of heresy, 'eresiarche' (*Inferno* IX, 127). But the pleasing words jump immediately from Dante's 'parlare onesto' to the topic of cruel dominion:

> La tua loquela ti fa manifesto
> > di quella nobil patrïa natio,
> > a la qual forse fui troppo molesto.

> Your speech clearly shows you a native of that noble fatherland to which
> I was, perhaps, too harmful.   (25–7)

Farinata defines Florence as the homeland of noble adversaries and as the place he molested.

That the 'forse' (27), as some scholars have contended, indicates compunction over his treatment of the city, I cannot agree. De Sanctis saw the speech as a 'confession' – 'a lofty sentiment which purifies and beautifies Farinata in the violence of his passion.' Surprisingly, even Barbi was to write, 'It is true (Farinata realizes), I was guilty.'[21] Eminent as they were, those critics erred: the repentant do not go to Hell. Farinata's is not the 'passione della patria' but a monomania for party strife and personal glory. He had indeed been 'troppo molesto' historically, and one must construe the 'forse' as the false modesty of gloating understatement. Souls are condemned to Hell because they persist in their sin. Those in Limbo, alienated from God not by guilt but by the consequences of the Fall, feel remorse and sadness, and those in Purgatory alone are capable of true repentance. Through Farinata's display of pride we learn of the enduring pertinacity of the sin of heresy. As Francesca's punishment reflects the lustful whirling passion, so the state of this soul reflects the unrepentant obstinacy of overheated, overweening, and obdurate unbelief.[22] In the view of his contemporaries, the factionalism of Farinata was the essence of his heresy.[23] Firm and unbending in his pride, he holds Hell in contempt. Because of his persistence in earthly dissension, the news of his party's failure to return tortures him (or so he claims) more than the hellfire of his eternal tomb: 'Ciò mi tormenta più che questo letto / That torments me more than this bed' (78). But our romantic 'willing suspension of disbelief' must not suffer overextension. To understand this sinner's foolishness, and lest we too be seduced by his spurious show of strength, let us recall that in Christianity fear of Hell, specifically fear of the *flames* of Hell, is the first step to righteousness and to heavenly wisdom.[24] Farinata finally shakes his head; Dante's earthly revelations have truly increased his internal pain.

Just as Farinata's initial speech began not with a challenge but with a respectful vocative, so, in a lesser way, Cavalcante echoes him in flattering address, 'Se per questo cieco / carcere vai per altezza d'ingegno / If you go through this blind prison by reason of high genius' (58–9). In both cases the damned begin with words designed to draw the Wayfarer's sympathetic attention. Only later does Farinata hurl his challenge: 'Per due fiate li dispersi / Twice over I scattered them' (48). He aims to catch the Wayfarer off guard, draw him in, and subject him. Compare, for example, St Gregory's amplification of the technique of heresiarchs: 'For heretics dread to incense their hearers at the outset of their communing with them, lest they be listened to with ears on the watch, and they carefully shun the paining of them, that they may catch their unguardedness, and what they put forward is almost always mild, while that is harsh which they cunningly introduce in going on.'[25] As the scene progresses, the pendulum of aggressive repartee and altercation swings between the Wayfarer and the Ghibelline; each strives for dominance, and the Wayfarer alternately succumbs and overcomes in the master-slave dialogue. Dante's first emotion of 'being eager to obey,' and his open response to Farinata's question reflect the theme incisively. The Wayfarer himself falls into the trap of pride by asserting the importance of his own family and faction, and, descending to the very level of the damned, flings at his interlocutor the kind of *improperium* he fears himself: 'I vostri non appreser bene quell' arte / Yours have not learned that art well.' The teacher of heresy has successfully provoked his victim's own disposition to factionalism and Dante Wayfarer falls for the deceit.

The methods of punishment in Dante's Hell are exquisitely diverse. More often than not the fates of the damned involve something other than penal fire; in spite of the great weight of scriptural authority, it is more the exception than the rule.[26] In fact, in the general plan of lower Hell, from the burning mosques of Dis to freezing Cocytus, the Poet inverts Job 2:19: 'Let him pass from the snow waters to excessive heat: and his sin even to Hell.'

Fire only appears as a punishment inside the city of Dis, on the inner side of the walls of the *città del fuoco* and below. Since there are only five cases (the burning *arche* of these heretics; the fiery rain which falls on the idolaters, sodomites, and usurers; the flames which lick the feet of the simonists; the pheonix-like metamorphoses of the thieves; and the flaming tongues imprisoning the counsellors of fraud),[27] the question of the aptness of punishing fire is not idly put. The concept has perhaps a fourfold inspiration, the first from empirical observation of the fate of contemporary heretics, the second from Scripture and liturgy, the third from artistic convention, and the fourth from patristic doctrine. As we are aware, in Dante's day heretics were burned. Their punishment in the *Inferno* mirrors the civil and criminal sentence meted out to heretics in this life. Though burning alive had been introduced at the Second Council of Constantinople (553 AD), the practice did not become part of ecclesiastical and civil law in the West until the first third of Dante's century, that is, in living memory. Frederick II's infamous law of 1231, included in the *Constitutiones regni Siciliae*, orders obdurate heretics 'ut vivi in conspectu populi comburantur flammarum commissi judicio / that they be burned alive before the populace, committed to the judgment of the flames'; another version adds 'ut animarum incendia patiantur / that they may suffer the fires of the soul.'[28] This law, which at first applied only to the Kingdom of the Two Sicilies, was extended to the whole of the Empire beginning with the Edict of Cremona in May 1238.[29] The legislation came as a recognition of the popular custom of burning suspected heretics, a mob practice previously frowned upon by the Church. Once live cremation entered canon and civil law, the Church sought a defence for 'lighting the tails' of 'the little foxes that spoil the vines'[30] by an appeal to Scripture; it found admirable and soothing authority in John 15:6: 'If a man abide not in me, he is cast forth as a branch and is withered; and men gather them and cast them into the fire where they are burned.'

The first Florentine Inquisitor, although he was not at first officially styled as such, was a contemporary of Cavalcante and of the same noble family, the Dominican Aldobrandino Cavalcanti appointed to the commission against heretics circa 1237–40.[31] In 1283, at the age of eighteen, the young Dante probably joined the crowd to witness the posthumous burning of Farinata and his wife Adaleta by order of one of Aldobrandino's successors, the Minorite Friar Salomone da Lucca.[32] The recentness of such legislation and formal organization against heresy cannot be ignored when we read Dante's lines. It is condign punishment that the Poet places the apostate emperor Frederick here in Hell with his papal antagonist Cardinal Ottaviano. Cavalcante de' Cavalcanti's pain takes on new aptness and significance when we consider his family's intimate ties with the newly founded Inquisition.

However, Dante's austere sense of justice did not always coincide with ecclesiastical and temporal practice. Since we are dealing with a poem and not with history, we must seek further metaphoric and poetic reasons for his choice of punishment if we are to see how Dante portrayed his understanding of God's justice in his poetry. We find such artistic motives in literature and art familiar to the Poet.

In the *Moralia in Job*, St Gregory the Great considers untempered unbelief itself as a metaphoric fire and heat: 'Heretics, as they are over ardent to be wise, study to have heated wits beyond what needs.' And later: 'The restlessness of unrestrained curiosity accords with unabating teeming heat, and so because they long to feel the heat of wisdom beyond what they ought, they are said to come from the south. Paul busied himself to cool the minds of the faithful to this heat of unrestrained wiseness.'[33] Elsewhere in the same work, St Gregory describes the end of stubborn heresiarchs: 'Indeed the fabricators of wrong doctrines springing up against Holy Church, are already made an end of by the heat of truth.'[34] St Bernard echoes the concept in his *Super Cantica Canticorum*: 'Of these men the end is destruction; at last the fire awaits them.'[35] St Gregory even uses the metaphor of refining: 'Whosoever, then is divided from this unity of the Church our Mother ... through heresy in entertaining wrong notions about God ... is bereft of the grace of charity, concerning which Paul saith what we have before given: "And though I give my body to be burned and have not charity, it profiteth me nothing." As if he expressed himself in plain utterance: "Without the bounds of its place, *the fire of fining being applied to me only afflicts me with torment, and does not purify me by its cleansing.*"'[36] Compare Dante's verses 'li avelli ... eran sì del tutto accesi, / che ferro più non chiede verun'arte / The tombs ... were made to glow all over, hotter than iron need be for any craft' (*Inferno* ix, 118–20).

The appropriateness of coupling Farinata and Cavalcante, Frederick ii and the Pope's Legate Cardinal Ottaviano forever in torment seems at once to satisfy a primitive sense of justice: the leaders of opposing factions each will represent eternal and reciprocal bitterness for the other. The aptness leaps to the eye, but even here Dante's concept has full support in dogma. Perhaps Dante found further fittingness recalling the Bishop of Hippo's very definition of the two cities in *De Catechizandis rudibus* (chapter 19): 'Thus there are two cities, one of the wicked the other of the just, which endure from the beginning of the human race even to the end of time, which are now intermingled in body, but separated in will, and which, moreover, are to be separated in body also on the day of judgment. For all men who love pride and temporal dominion together with empty vanity and display of presumption, and all spirits who set their affections on such things and seek their own glory by the subjection of men, are bound fast by one fellowship; and even though they frequently fight one another for these ends, *still are they flung headlong by an equal weight of desire into the same abyss, and are united to one another by the likeness of their ways and deserts* [et sibi morum et meritorum similitudine conjuguntur].' The saint had spoken of Hell's punishments in the same vein in his sermons: 'Ibi tenebrosus ignis et locus horribilis, ibi flamma gehennalis et inextinguibilis ... ibi miseri cum miseris, superbi cum superbis. ... / There the dark fire and fearful place, there the inextinguishable flame of Gehenna ... here the wretched with the wretched, the proud with the proud ...'[37] The Poet's 'simile con simile è sepolto' (*Inferno* ix, 130) surely echoes the saint's conception.

The movements of the sinners in canto x constantly reverse the progression of death to resurrection. Dante emphasizes their actions with synonyms or derivations of the verbs '*erigo*' and '*surgo*' ('*arise*'). Arising is followed by symbols or actions of falling and dying: 'già *son levati* tutt'i coperchi,' 'tutti saran serrati'; 'di Iosafat qui torneranno coi corpi,' 'l'anima col corpo morta fanno'; 'Farinata che *s'è dritto*,' 'el *s'ergea*,' 'com' io al piè de la sua tomba fui'; '*surse* a la vista scoperchiata,' 's'era … *levata*,' '*drizzato*,' 'supin ricadde e più non parve fora,' 'indi s'ascose.' Dante will employ the same verbs '*surgere*' and '*risurgere*' to stress the theme of the Easter Resurrection in *Purgatorio* I, 6, 7, 9.

The Poet's verses, 'La gente che per li sepolcri giace / potrebbesi veder? già son levati / tutt'i coperchi, e nessun guardia face / Might these people who lie within the sepulchres be seen? Indeed, the covers are all suspended, and no one keeps guard' (*Inferno* x, 7–9), and much of the action portrayed in *Inferno* VIII as well as the description of the *avelli* in *Inferno* IX and x reflect and invert Matthew 27 and 28. The earthquake, Christ's death, burial, and resurrection, the open tomb, the sleeping guards, and the appearance of the angel to the holy women are all darkly present. An angel came to allow Virgil and Dante entrance into Dis, and he reminded the Furies of previous triumphal descents into Hell. The open lids of the *monimenti* reflect the result of the earthquake at Christ's death, and must be allied to the various *ruine* we meet during the descent through Hell:

> Et terra mota est et petrae scissae sunt, *et monumenta aperta sunt* et multa corpora sanctorum qui dormierant surrexerunt et exeuntes de monumentis post resurrectionem eius venerunt in sanctam civitatem et apparuerunt multis.

> And the earth quaked and the rocks were rent. And the graves were opened; and many bodies of the saints that had slept arose. And coming out of the tombs after his resurrection, came into the holy city and appeared to many.
>
> (Matthew 27:51–3)

Those who taught that the soul dies with the body, however, will not experience resurrection; the open tomb, the Christian symbol of eternal life, abides as a reminder until its lid will close over them in eternal second death. The damned represent the antithesis of the Easter antiphon 'Surrexit Dominus de sepulcro / The Lord has arisen from the grave.'[38]

From about the ninth century Christ's tomb and the Church altar had been fused in imagery and function. Amalarius of Metz (ca 780–850/1) in the *Eclogae de Officio Missae* states: 'Ecce habes hic tumulum Christi quam conspicis aram / Behold you have here the tomb of Christ which you perceive as an altar.'[39] The joining of altar and sarcophagus was aided by etymological inventiveness which saw 'ara' (altar) as related to the 'arca' (ark), the Tabernacle of the Host which was like Christ's sepulchre. St Gregory the Great spoke of the altar as 'arcam sanctae Crucis / the *arca* of the Holy Cross.'[40] In later times it became the custom to deposit unused consecrated wafers within the altar walls or within the doors of the Tabernacle; since the altar contains the Host, the Body of Christ, it becomes his tomb.

Dante's profound moral parody inverts the action of the liturgical *Visitatio sepulcri*, a ceremony which in many areas of Christendom took place just before the *Te Deum*, at the end of Matins on Easter morning.[41] The drama of the Poem reverses the drama of the Visitation. The infernal sarcophagus, far from being empty, is laden with dead souls. The 'Non est hic sed surrexit / He is not here. For He is risen!' is parodied and reversed in Farinata's appearance ('surrexit sed est hic!'); similarly, Cavalcante arises ('surse a la vista scoperchiata,' *Inferno* x, 52), only to fall back in second death ('supin ricadde').

Medieval Byzantine and Western figurative representations of the Marys at the sepulchre centred on the angel with nimbus and wand pointing to the linen winding sheets in the deserted sarcophagus. In most Western illustrations the angel sits on the tomb's lid as it levitates, floats, or leans at gravity-defying angles (plate 1).[42] Dante's verse, 'Tutti li lor coperchi eran sospesi / Their covers were all raised up' (*Inferno* ix, 121), reflects this tradition.

Dante's view of Farinata 'dalla cintola in su' also follows depictions in Christian painting and sculpture. Early renderings of the Resurrection show a robed Christ standing waist-up in his tomb with the lid 'sospeso.'[43] But the stance of both Farinata and Cavalcante, once the latter too rises to full height (*Inferno* x, 67), parallels a new Gothic vision of a naked Christ, the 'Imago pietatis' or Man of Sorrows (Isaias 52:3; plates 2, 3).[44] In such depictions the dead Redeemer seems already beyond the temporal; flagellated, tortured, and delivered from the cross, he stands 'da la cintola in su,' 'waist-up,' alone and unsupported in his sarcophagus. This new devotional image seems not to be found in the West before the twelfth century, though it may have had a previous tradition which has not come to light or which has not come down to us. Emile Mâle believed that its prototype was a mosaic icon of the Passion preserved in the Church of Santa Croce in Gerusalemme in Rome (plate 4);[45] the work, the original, or a copy of a miraculous image probably brought back from the East in the twelfth century, commanded particular veneration as a pilgrim station especially on Passion Sunday and Good Friday. Together with the Mandylion or Veil of Veronica in Old St Peter's, Mâle thought, it was a major goal of Romer Pilgrims for pardons and indulgences; this fact accounts for the wide dissemination of the figure in European art in the late thirteenth and fourteenth centuries. If Mâle's thesis were right, we could be sure that Dante viewed it on his Roman pilgrimage during the Jubilee Year of 1300, and again, perhaps, in 1302 when he received in Rome the tragic news of his exile. More recently, however, Carlo Bertelli, who directed the restoration of the Santa Croce mosaic in 1961, has disagreed with Mâle's thesis. Bertelli believes that the Roman icon is not a copy of the prototype of the Man of Sorrows image: such depictions were far too wide-spread in Europe previously for us to ascribe such a derivation.[46] But even if Mâle and his followers are not correct in their suppositions concerning the lines of provenance and diffusion, there are certainly enough examples of the 'Imago pietatis' dating close to Dante's time and experience to prove the Poet's most intimate familiarity with it.

In a thirteenth-century Italo-Byzantine panel in the Museum Casa Horne in Florence, the dead Christ stands upright in his tomb with his Mother, the Mater dolorosa, on his right (plate 5).[47] A similar, and very fine, lone figure appears in a Florentine Franciscan prayer book dating from about 1295.[48] In 1320 Simone Martini painted a polyptych now preserved in the Museum of Santa Caterina in Pisa: beneath the central panel of the Madonna and Child, in the predella, stands the poignant Man of Sorrows attended by Saints Mary and Mark (plate 6).[49] A recently excavated fresco by a follower of Giotto in the former cathedral church of Santa Reparata in Florence presents a further example (plate 7).[50] The top of this wall painting was removed during the construction of the new floor of Santa Maria del Fiore sometime after 1375, and the head and neck of Christ are consequently missing, but the fresco still shows vividly the resigned attitude of the dead Christ in the tomb surrounded by the arma Christi[51] or symbols of the passion in the background. The grief-stricken figures of the Virgin and St John flank the figure in the foreground.[52]

The Man of Sorrows was also a favourite theme for contemporary tomb sculpture in Italy; few North Italian churches lack an example.[53] The Bardi Chapel in Santa Croce in Florence contains one version on a tomb dating from the mid-fourteenth century (plate 8). Among several such tomb figures found in the Museo Sforzesco of Milan is an interesting depiction of Christ standing with the traverses of the cross stretching benind him in windmill-like configuration (plate 9; compare Satan as a mill in Inferno xxxiv, discussed below, chapter 8). The 'Imago pietatis' appears in the central panels of the monumental tombs or arche in Verona, notable examples of the Gothic revival of sculptured sarcophagi in imitation of the first Christian pieces of the fourth century. The most significant is the figure of Christ flanked by figures of the Annunciation found on the sarcophagus of Can Grande della Scala, the ruler and patron to whom Dante dedicated the *Paradiso* (plate 10).[54] In depicting the heretics in pain in their *arca*, Dante is clearly inverting this new devotional image of Christ's suffering. Farinata, persistently unbelieving and unredeemed as he sighs and shakes his head (*Inferno* x, 88), fittingly resembles not the living God, the erect, triumphant resurrected Redeemer stepping forth from his tomb, but the dead Man standing within it with his bowed head turned aside.

Dante's scene also reflects related themes suggested by various other meanings of the word 'arca.' Noah's opening of the ark (Latin and Italian 'arca') prefigured the death of Christ, his resurrection from the tomb, and his victory over death, and Noah and his ark commonly appear in the decorations of early Christian sarcophagi and catacombs.[55] The image reflected the prayer of the burial office, the *Commendatio animae*: 'Libera, Domine, animum ejus sicut liberasti Noe de diluvio / Free, O Lord, his soul as you freed Noah from the Flood.' The very name Noah, Isidore tells us, means 'the repose of the dead': 'Noe autem requies interpretatur / Noah then is interpreted as "requiem."'[56] Tombs and crypt paintings depict Noah from the waist up, *orans*, or gesturing toward the returning dove with its olive branch. In most representations from paleo-Christian times on, the ark is extremely small; perhaps through a conflation of the story with the legend of Deucalion, in early illustrations we find it shown as a mere box or chest (again Latin 'arca') with a lock. A far cry from the vast craft of Genesis 6:14–16, the pictured arks could not possibly float upright, much less hold anything more than the figure of Noah (plate 11). The sculptor or painter forgot or ignored Old-Testament details and reduced the ark to a very stylized and conventional cipher or ideogram; he concentrated not on realism or on the literal meaning but on the second, symbolic significance: the fulfilled message of the New Testament. Noah was depicted not only *on* sarcophagi and *in* catacombs, but *in* an *arca* which was figuratively the tomb of Christ. Physically Noah was saved through divine intervention (the dove and the olive branch) and spiritually he was redeemed through Christ's death and the Harrowing of Hell. All details typify the theme of salvation: the patriarch's ark parallels Christ's sepulchre; Noah prefigures Christ; his stance is that of Christ both dead and risen. 'Noe vir justus. Hic per actus suos significat Christum / Noah is the just man. Through his acts he signifies Christ.'[57] Dante has Farinata ironically 'fulfil' this symbolic pattern of history in his Poem.

The quotation from Augustine's *De Catechizandis rudibus* which we cited above concerning the two cities is followed directly and immediately in the saint's work by a consideration of the Flood. He takes Noah's ark (*arca*) to be a symbol of both the Heavenly City and a prefiguration of the Church. The wood of the ark represents the cross; the family of Noah, the blessed. Later, in chapter 27, the saint explains: 'Those who escaped in the Ark were a figure of the Church that was to be, which now floats upon the waves of the world, and is saved from sinking by the wood of the Cross of Christ.'[58] Dante uses the same imagery for the Chariot of the Church in *Purgatory* XXXII, 125–6, 'l'arca del carro' but he transposes the themes in *Inferno* IX and X: the *arche* are an infernal inversion of the figure of the ark; the stone sarcophagi sunk in Hell yet afloat, as it were, amid the flames, inversely parallel the Church and its prefiguration in the tale from Genesis.

In the same work St Augustine gives a further explanation: the ark is the Church because both hold the future blessed and the future damned: 'God was not ignorant of the fact that even from those who had been saved in the Ark there would be born wicked men who would once more cover the face of the whole earth with iniquities.'[59] God foresaw that there would be idolaters and unbelievers. In the *City of God* Augustine explains that the passengers of the vessel and especially the sons of Noah all prefigured things achieved in later times: of Shem's seed, the Jews, Christ was born; of Japheth's, the Gentiles, comes the 'enlargement' of the Church. *Ham (Cham) the middle son, however, is the progenitor of the Earthly City (the damned), the type of the heretic, and the forefather of heresy.* The name 'Cham,' avers Augustine, following Jerome, means 'hot' ('calidus'), and he continues in figurative language which supplies a satisfying analogue, at once doctrinal and metaphoric, to Dante's Poem: 'What does he signify but the *hot breed of heretics?* For heretical hearts are wont to be fired not by the spirit of wisdom, but by that of impatience, and thus disturb the peace of the saints.'[60] For Dante the 'haereticorum genus calidum' is fittingly punished in 'monimenti [che] son più e men caldi / monuments [which] are more and less hot' (*Inferno* IX, 131). As Epicurus, the classical example of heresy, appears on the literal level of the episode, so the biblical *figura* is present in a sunken metaphor. The reader thus may readily idenify the contentious Farinata and his enemy Cavalcante in their fiery *arca* as sons of Ham.

Other symbols of deliverance and redemption surround the sinners. In ecclesiastical art the escape from the Flood contrasted with the escape from destruction by fire. Again art echoed the *Commendatio animae* of the funeral liturgy: 'Libera domine animam servi tui sicut liberasti tres pueros de camino ignis ardentis et de manu regis iniqui / Free O Lord the soul of thy servant as you freed the three children from the furnace of burning fire and from the hand of the wicked king.' The crowded friezes of early Christian sarcophagi frequently present Noah juxtaposed or intermingled with the depiction of the three Hebrew children in the fiery furnace (Daniel 3). The sculptured horizontal waves of the water are identical to the vertical billows of fire surrounding the furnace of Shadrach, Meshach, and Abednego (plate 12).[61] With the ark as a furnace, Dante's inversion and combination of two events, symbolic of God's mercy and man's salvation, throw into relief the implacable nature of divine judgment on the heretics. Dante's scheme of 'burial in second death' in burning sarcophagi repeats God's divine pattern as it echoes both funeral liturgy and catacumbal iconography.

Three times the Poet tells us that the lids of the *arche* are open: 'Tutti li lor coperchi eran sospesi' (*Inferno* IX, 121), 'Già son / levati tutt'i coperchi' (*Inferno* X, 8–9), and 'allor surse alla vista scoperchiata' (*Inferno* X, 52). Such emphasis cannot be without reason. We can find explanation both in the biblical text of the tale of Noah (Gen. 8:13: 'Aperiens Noe tectum arcae aspexit viditque quod exsiccata esset superficies terrae / And Noe opening the covering of the ark, looked, and saw that the face of the earth was dried') and in the explanations of the ark in the Church Fathers. Perhaps the longest disquisition on the subject is Hugh of St Victor's *De arca Noe*, in which the writer gives a full and detailed exposition to each part of the vessel, both those described in the Bible and those of his own imagination. The most interesting parts for our purposes are the chapters on the openings in the craft, especially 'De ostio arcae' and 'De ostio, et fenestra hujus arcae.'[62] The uncovered opening through which the two damned shades make their appearance reflects, in a hellish inversion, the door by which the faithful enter the Church. This portal of the Church-ark should be closed, 'hoc ostium clausum esse debet, ut amplius ad antiquos errores non revertamur / This door should be closed lest we return more vehemently to our ancient errors.' It is the door 'per quam ab infidelitate ingredimur in Ecclesiam ... per quem revocati sumus / through which from our lack of faith we enter the Church ... through which we are recalled.'[63] The rest of Hugh's image, however, parallels the open lids. The evil man, Ham, breaks open the doors of the ark in disobedience: 'Bonum hominem Noe, et malum hominem Cham. Bono homini Deus ostium aperit, malus homo inobedienter exiens ex altera parte valvas frangit. / The good man is Noah, and the evil man is Ham. God opens the portal for the good man; the evil man breaks the hinges by going out disobediently from the other side.'[64] The open state of the arks in Hell symbolizes those who have left the ark of the Church to follow their own error in pride. But Dante's moral and anagogical message is even more complete: God's closing of the arks at the Last Judgment will make the punishment perfect, for as he opens the doors of the ark of the Heavenly City to the blessed, so will he shut the lids of these tombs of the heretics and, metonymically, close the *tomba* of all Hell with its damned forever.

Cantos IX and X begin to come into clearer focus when we examine the

justness of having the limitations of the souls' knowledge revealed at the end
of *Inferno* x. Farinata tells the Wayfarer, Dante:

> 'Noi veggiam, come quei c'ha mala luce,
>   le cose,' disse, 'che non son lontano;
>   cotanto ancor ne splende il sommo duce.
> Quando s'appressano o son, tutto è vano
>   nostro intelletto; e s'altri non ci apporta,
>   nulla sapem di vostro stato umano.
> Però comprender puoi che tutta morta
>   fia nostra conoscenza da quel punto
>   che del futuro fia chiusa la porta.'

> 'Like one who has bad light, we see the things,' he said, 'which are
> remote from us: so much does the Supreme Ruler still shine on us;
> but when they draw near, or are, our intelligence is wholly vain, and
> unless others bring us word, we know nothing of your human state;
> wherefore you can comprehend that all our knowledge will be dead from
> that moment when the door of the future shall be closed.'

(100–8)

Critics have long debated whether Farinata's explanation applies to all souls in
Hell or merely to the heretics.[65] Immediately upon encountering the problem, we are troubled by Ciacco's words earlier in *Inferno* vi, 69, which imply
knowledge of the present. But the Poet has drawn a dividing line at the
Gates of Dis, between Upper and Lower Hell. Below the wall is the 'terra,' the
city, which particularly reflects, as we have seen, the 'civitas terrena.' Beyond
this line, the souls have no knowledge of the present. In this regard one must
keep in mind that the heretics – precisely, *the Epicureans – give the
explanation of their souls' foresight.* Can we see a reflection of God's justice in
this? I would like to offer an answer which not only reflects this justice but
also reveals that Farinata's explanation applies to the heretics alone.[66]

Critics have noted that the Church Fathers disagree about whether or not
departed souls have knowledge of present earthly events. Dante was thus free
to invent and to adopt parts of teachings as he saw fit.[67] All the details
concerning thse Epicureans, however – heretical scorn, their walls and tombs,
and their tendency in life to rest in present things – are concepts joined in
other works outside Dante's poem. The souls in canto x suffer in *arche* within
the walls of a city; these chests, the Poet is careful to say, resemble the
ancient tombs at Arles and Pola, necropoleis which, we might observe, resemble miniature cities of the living.[68] In allying Epicurean doctrine with the

image of a mausoleum to be closed at Judgment Day, Dante's concept seems to recall St Gregory of Nyssa's reaction to the doctrine of those philosophers regarding the soul, and their perception of earthly existence: 'For I hear Epicurus was brought around to this [that the soul does not exist outside the body] by his assumptions that the nature of reality is formed by chance and automatically, inasmuch as there is no providence governing things. ... For to him, the limit of reality was what is perceived and he made perception the measure of the comprehension of everything. He closed his eyes completely to the perceptions of the soul and was unable to recognize anything intelligible and incorporeal, just as someone kept in a little house is excluded from the sight of what is outside. There really are walls which prevent small-souled folk through their own fault from the contemplation of the intelligible ... some who see the universe are blind to what is made clear by it; as a result, *these sophisticated and scornful persons* are cited by those who philosophize about the disappearance of the soul, saying that a body is made up of elements and that the soul cannot exist by itself unless it is one of these and exists in them ... consequently *they are teaching nothing else than that our life is dead.*'[69] After a life of denying the afterlife, enslaved by earthly pleasures and pursuit of earthly reputation at the cost of others, the damned heresiarchs here have real walls which block that narrow earthly perception. Their punishment of blindness to an earthly present in Hell mirrors their blindness to true reality in life.

The 'sepolcri,' then, are particularly apt. Again St Gregory the Great can help us quicken our comprehension in passages which may have inspired Dante, and in which the saint combines the sentences of equal punishment for equal sin, the metaphor of burning graves and the souls' earthly affections and perceptions: 'Those are involved in one and the same punishment who are bound by one and the same guilt in sin. This is well and shortly conveyed by the Prophet [Ezekiel 32:22] when he says, "Asshur is there and all his company; his graves are about him." For who is set forth by the title of Asshur, the proud king, saving that old enemy who fell by pride, *who for that he draws numbers into sin*, descends with all his multitudes into the dungeons of hell? Now "graves" [*sepulcra*] are a shelter for the dead. ... When human hearts admit him in this state of death, assuredly they become his graves. Now "his graves are about him," in that all in whose souls he now buries himself by their affections, hereafter he joins to himself by torments. And whereas the lost now admit evil spirits within themselves by committing unlawful deeds, *then the graves will burn together with the dead.*'[70] The paragraph explains the punishment as symbolic of a general wickedness, and it aids us in seeing how Dante conceived all of the mansions of Hell as one vast *tomba*. The aptness of tormenting heretics and no one

else in this way St. Gregory elucidates in a commentary on a line from Job
15:27, 'Those that remain of him shall be buried in death.' He stresses the
earthly limits of perception of heretics in this life and his gloss casts light on
the justness of the lack of present earthly knowledge on the part of souls
damned in Dante's circle of the heresiarchs: 'Doubtless "the persons left" of
that tribe of heretics "are buried in death," for whereas they return not to the
light of truth *they are sunk down in everlasting punishment by their
earthly perceptions.'*[71]

In the light of Gregory's authority, the justice of Dante's own literal
conception is even more striking and satisfying. Content in life with the
senses' perception of the immediate present and scorning that of the soul, the
heresiarchs find themselves after death entombed amid flames, tortured by
the soul's ignorance, cut off from knowledge of the present, having only the
anguish of dimly foreseeing an inevitable future and the pain of recalling an
unchangeable past. Having rejected 'imitatio Christi' in their life as men, they
ape the Dead Christ in their death. The episode thus provides a didactic
experience for the Wayfarer and an exemplum for the reader. Dante makes
the ideal pun. The tombs are not only 'monuments' but 'monimenti,' 'warn-
ings,' 'admonishments.'[72] For as St Thomas puts it, 'The profit that ensues
from heresy is beside the intention of the heretics, for it consists in the con-
stancy of the faithful being put to the test.'[73] In fact the very cantos show
the historical usefulness of the heresiarchs to the greater body of Christ; they
reflect St Augustine and the other Fathers who had basked in the notion
that the real though unintended lesson taught by the sons of Ham redounded
to the glory of God, recalling 1 Corinthians 11:19: 'For there must also be
heresies: that they also, who are approved may be made manifest among
you.'[74]

3 PIER DELLA VIGNA

Historians and literary critics generally divide into two camps concerning Pier della Vigna.[1] Historians, though giving lip service to the greatness of the *Commedia*, usually see Dante as only a rather poor, somewhat biased, secondary source for the facts of Piero's guilt and death. While *litterati* have often taken Piero's words in the Poem at face value and declared his tragic innocence, historians examine contemporary documents and declare his ignominious guilt.[2] There is, critics must accept, ample historic evidence of the Notary's criminality, not of *lèse majesté*, but of corruption in office, perversion of justice, and self-enrichment at the expense of the innocent and the state. In addition, a close examination of the *contrapasso* through the episode's major images and a new analysis of the iconography of the cantos show that the Poet, far from exculpating his personage, considers him guilty, not only of suicide, but indeed of other crimes which led, in the view of an orthodox Christian, typically, dogmatically, and almost inexorably to it.

Though the greater number of Dante scholars now distinguish between 'Dante Poet' and 'Dante Wayfarer,' earlier critics examining these cantos, almost without exception, ignored this useful separation and missed the moral and anagogical message. They accepted the narrow view of Dante Wayfarer, sympathizing without reflection with Piero's protestation of innocence and with the sense of loss and despair he suffers through eternity. Their opinion sets aside the objective judgment of Dante Poet as a reflection of divine justice, and ignored that this very judgment condemned Piero to the circle of the violent, amidst the horror and repugnance of a trackless waste, a poisonous wood populated with filthy harpies, resounding with moans and cries of despair and pain. The view that Dante celebrated Pier della Vigna as a romantic, great-souled hero is unacceptable in the context of the Poem as a whole and does not square with the Poet's severe concept of divine justice.

Dante was aware that Pier della Vigna's violence toward himself was the historic culmination of an inveterate rapacity and violence against others. Clearly, the Poet believed that Piero's self-righteous view of himself as 'giusto' was not shared by God. No clearer discrepancy between the views of the damned and the divine perspective could be cited than the manner in which Piero praises Frederick II, 'who was so worthy of honour,' and the reality of the place which the Emperor holds in Hell among the burning heretics. In the Poet's view suicides are lower than the animals. Their souls are turned to stocks, sentient but knotted, warped, sterile, and poisonous; the wild boar of the Tuscan Maremma do not inhabit 'thickets so rough or dense.' Piero has lost his human form through lack of Christian virtue and ethics, through shame and despair. The rhetorical brilliance of the episode, particularly Piero's self-serving *apologia*, must not lead us astray. In setting forth the state of this character after death, the Poet presents not some anachronistic facsimile of a Greek heroic tragedy but a vibrant Gothic exemplum for the guidance of his readers' souls: Hell is the fearful place of God's wrath where mercy and pity have no place. Through a close examination of the biblical, patristic, historical, pictorial, and iconographic foundations of the episode's imagery we can delve beyond the surface of the Poem to the moral and anagogical levels. In so doing we shall not only clarify the *contrapasso*, the anagogical revelation on divine retaliation for which the Poet expects us to see the sufficient reason, but also, perhaps, find satisfying solutions to other, secondary cruxes.

As I noted in chapter 1, Dante bases his premise on the axiom that man is made in the image of God, and that this image extends to eternity, though in Hell ghastly changes are wrought upon the creature in torment.[3] The suicides who wickedly tore asunder the image of their Maker also reflect a similarly perverted Christological pattern. Their infernal existence as trees apes Christ as symbolized by the Tree of the Cross in Christian art,[4] and such images as those in the ancient Easter hymn to which Dante ironically refers in the first line of *Inferno* XXXIV, 'Vexilla regis prodeunt inferni / There proceed the banners of the king of Hell.'[5] As once bled the wounds of Christ, the branch of Jesse's Tree, so bleed the wounds of the branches of the damned. In *Inferno* XIII, 107–8 we are told that after Christ's Last Coming as Judge, the bodies of the suicides too will hang upon trees as once did the Redeemer's; thus the deiform image will triumph. We immediately perceive the just and terrifying irony of the punishment. The Poet implicitly invites us to contrast Piero's proud and selfish act of suicide to escape earthly shame and calumny with Christ's willing suffering of similar torture and mockery for the remission of mankind's sin and his submission to death for man's eternal life. The words of the second suicide, the anonymous Florentine, clearly portray the profound, cold egoism of the damned:

> che colpa ho io della tua vita rea?

> What blame have I for your sinful life?   (*Inferno* XIII, 135)

These sinners did not lay down their lives for the love of another but for their own earthly reputation and pride. As in life they contemned God's mercy, so they contemn it in death. The state of their souls in the afterlife is an eternal manifestation of their selfish iniquity.[6] In the symbolism of Christianity which nourished the Poet, the soul's metamorphosis into a thornbush alludes inevitably to the Crown of Thorns and to the Passion. We must see Dante's image in its obvious and blatant figural reversal: a Man crowned with thorns inverted as a thornbush crowned with a human body.

Piero's barren metamorphosis contrasts ironically with his surname, 'della Vigna' or 'de Vinea' ('vineyard' or 'vine'). Indeed, the binary image of the vine and the thorn forms an important unifying factor in the metaphors and symbols of the episode. Although modern commentators have ignored this aspect as, perhaps, too primitive or naive, during Piero's life his family name offered a fertile field for puns of adulation; and after his death it became the source of many a frivolous tale in the chroniclers.[7] Flatterers vied in superlatives comparing the powerful minister to Joseph and even to the Messiah reincarnate. In gushing paeans they described him as the 'vine' which refreshed the state. His friend Nicola della Rocca indulged himself and the Notary with 'O blessed root which hath brought forth such a fruitful branch, O blessed vine ['felix vinea'] who hath produced such precious wine!' and later 'O blessed vine, who refreshest Capua with the abundance of your delicious fruit ... from whose stock the branches differ not!'[8] The stress the Poet placed upon the barrenness of the forest of thorn trees at the opening of *Inferno* XIII thus grows more terrible in the context of the whole and more gruesome in the context of the laudatory word-play which Piero enjoyed.

There are still deeper resonances to the double image of the vine and the thorn. On various allegorical premises, Christian literature and art most commonly related the *arbor crucis* to the vine. In many passages of the Old Testament, such as Micheas 4:4, Zacharias 3:10, and Psalm 79:9 (80:8), the vine figured the promise of redemption, and in late medieval depictions of the Tree of the Cross, Christ is depicted hanging upon a vine.[9] The sinner's metamorphosis into a sterile stock ironically reverses and eschatologically fulfils Jesus' words in John 15:1–8: 'I am the true vine: and my Father is the husbandman. Every branch in me that beareth not fruit, he will take away ... I am the vine: you the branches. He that abideth in me, and I in him, the same beareth much fruit. ... In this is my Father glorified: that you bring forth very much fruit and become my disciples.' St Augustine (cited later by St Thomas in the *Catena aurea*) glossed this passage explaining Christ's own separation from the damned using the very metaphor of the vine and thorn: 'But when he says, "I am the true Vine," he discriminates Himself from that vine to which it is said, "How art thou turned into bitterness, O strange vine!" (Jerem. 2:21). For how should that be the true vine, which, when one "looked that it should bring forth grapes" (Isaias 5:4–6), bore thorns?'[10] Further, Dante's poetic inversion of the damned as the barren 'plants' of Hell is a parody and an intellectual pun on theological vocabulary. The same metaphor appears in St Bernard's *Sermons on the Song of Songs* XXIII, 4, as he asks, 'Who can question that a good man is, as it were, a plant of God?'[11] Particularly, the newly baptized are traditionally said to enter the 'Vineyard' of the Church. The image of the Christian 'planted' as Christ is biblical and is thus common in the Fathers. According to dogma, by the sacrament of baptism every Christian joined in the Vine of Christ, in his Passion and in his Death both by participation and in similitude. St Cyril of Jerusalem explains to his catachumens how the soul is 'planted' in imitation of the Saviour's death and how the righteous shall rise like him in resurrection: 'But so that we may learn that what Christ ... endured for us and our salvation ... and that we are partakers in His sufferings, Paul insists: "If we have been planted together with Him in the likeness of His death [*conplantati* facti sumus similitudine mortis eius], we shall be so in the likeness of His resurrection also" (Romans 6:5). And he is right in saying this; for now that the true Vine has been planted, we also at Baptism have been grafted into His death by participation. Consider this idea most attentively, following the words of the Apostle. He did not say: "If we have been grafted into his death," but "into the likeness of His death." For Christ actually died, His soul was really separated from His body.'[12] Dante's suicides, never to experience the reality of the resurrection of their flesh, are literally 'planted' as thornbushes in a reverse image of Christ's sufferings; by their pain and bleeding they inversely 'participate' in his Passion as punishment.

Perhaps the most striking treatise in the tradition of Christ as the 'mystic vine' is the homonymous work *De vitis mystica*, once attributed to St Bernard and now, by Cavallera and Glorieux, to St Bonaventure.[13] The various metaphors which the saint used of Christ in the treatise recur inversely applied to Pier della Vigna in *Inferno* XIII. The Seraphic Doctor begins with the 'pruning of the Vine,' 'De praecisione vitis'; the Latin word has, ironically, the meaning of 'breaking off abruptly,' the very sense of the verb 'schiantare' employed by Dante.[14] The various occasions upon which Jesus spilled blood are allegorized as a mystical 'pruning,' from the circumcision to the piercing of his side by the lance; even the Incarnation and the cutting off of friends and family are made to serve this metaphor.[15]

In chapter IV, 12, St Bonaventure turns to the various bonds of Christ: the womb of the Virgin, the swaddling bands, and the rope at his captivity are all compared to the binding and staking of the Vine to make it fruitful. The saint, moved by his own parallel, interjects, 'With so many bonds were You all bound up at once, then: You who alone hold the power of binding and loosing!'[16] One immediately recalls the parallel in Piero's boast:

> Io son colui che tenni ambo le chiavi
>   del cor di Federigo, e che le volsi,
>   serrando e diserrando ...

> I am he who held both the keys of Frederick's heart, and turned them,
> locking and unlocking ...   (58–60)

It is rather interesting for this canto in which artful language plays such a large role that after St Bonaventure deals with the Crown of Thorns[17] he glosses lengthily the Seven Last Words of Christ as he hangs upon the cross – those simple utterances so different from Piero's convoluted rhetoric.[18] Even a pun playing on the two significances of the word 'tronco' or 'truncus' is found in Bonaventure's treatise (cf. *Inferno* XIII, 55). The saint glosses John 7:46, applying it to the scourged Christ: '[The servants of the Jews] did not reproach a weakness in the trunk ['non accusaverunt defectum trunci,' or 'they did not reproach weakness in the disfigured man'], seeing the beauty of the leaves; indeed, they sensed that something other than what was seen lay in the broken body.'[19] The metaphors of Christ-as-vine and words-as-leaves continue until the place where the Redeemer utters his words of forgiveness, at which point Bonaventure is moved again to exclaim: 'O folium viride! / O verdant leaf!'[20] Obviously, there is a correspondence between the imagery of the Poem and that of the treatise. The sear barrenness of Piero's thornbush is evoked in the opening anaphora of *Inferno* XIII, 4–7: 'Non fronda verde ... non rami schietti ... non pomi v'eran ... / No green frond ... no smooth boughs ... no fruits were there.' The parallels in Dante's episode suggest that the Poet might well have been acquainted with Bonaventure's treatise and that he used it to create a fitting, figural, inversion.

The words 'vigna' and 'pruno' which Dante uses in *Inferno* XIII he will employ as well for Christ's Church in the *Paradiso* (XII, 86; XVIII, 132). In the last case (*Paradiso* XXIV, 111) Dante echoes Isaias 5:4–6 as he mourns the decay of the Church, 'la buona pianta che fu già vite e ora è fatta pruno / the

good plant which was once a vine and is now become a thorn.' Here in the
Inferno, instead of a vineyard tended by the saints, he creates the image of
an uncultivated trackless wilderness, of a 'della Vigna' wasted by harpies, black
hounds, and the profligate. The Poet concentrates ironically on the lifeless
sterility of the 'pruno' which della Vigna has become (*Inferno* xiii, 4–6). As I
mentioned above, even in the opening lines of the episode the Poet employs
a negative vocabulary of spines and barren branches, calculatedly evocative of
sin and damnation. As St Gregory the Great defines: 'In truth a spine is all
kinds of sinfulness.'[21] The pseudo-Rabanus Maurus' *Allegoriae in Sacram
Scripturam* glosses 'spines' as '*Pride of the heart*, as in the Psalms [31:4,
Douay]: "whilst the thorn is fastened," that is, "whilst pride is humbled in
me." By "thorns" the malice of the heart, as in Isaias [34:13]: "Thorns shall
grow up in his houses," that is, malice will grow in his thoughts.' And
'branches' as ' "*Base men*" as in Job [15:30] "The flame shall dry up his
branches" because eternal damnation will lay waste base men' (my italics).[22]
In Dante's inversion, the soul of 'Petrus de Vinea' is planted randomly in Hell
as the infernal counterpart of the cursed vine of whom it is indeed said in the
Vulgate version of Jeremias 2:21: 'Ego autem plantavi te vineam electam omne
semen verum, quomodo ergo conversa es mihi *in pravum vinea aliena*? / Yet I
planted thee a chosen vine, wholly a good seed; how art thou turned unto me
into one degenerate, o strange vine?'

Piero's description of his soul's fall to the depths and its metamorphosis
evokes other Christological patterns. The manner in which the soul-seeds
sprout randomly into many untidy shoots to form the tangled mass upon
which nest foul hybrid birds (xiii, 10, 97–102) parodies also the genealogy
of Christ conceived as the biblical Tree of Jesse upon which rests the Holy
Spirit: 'And there shall come forth a rod out of the root of Jesse: and a
flower shall rise up out of his root. *And the spirit of the Lord shall rest upon
him*: the spirit of wisdom and of understanding, the spirit of counsel and of
fortitude, the spirit of knowledge and of godliness. And he shall be filled with
the spirit of the fear of the Lord' (Isaias 11:1–3; my italics). The image of
the sinners' bodies hanging from the thorn trees makes an even closer analogy
with this image (*Inferno* xiii, 106–8). Dante's description of harpies nesting
in the 'piante silvestre' and feeding on them also parodies late medieval
(twelfth- to fourteenth-century) artistic depictions of Jesse's Tree, its boughs
laden with the images of the Virgin, Christ, the Patriarchs, and the Prophets, and surmounted by the single dove of the Holy Ghost or by seven doves
representing the Gifts of the Holy Spirit (plate 13).[23] Occasionally a pelican
feeding its nest of young with blood from its own breast replaces the dove or
doves.[24] The Poet's harpies ('quivi le brutte Arpie lor nidi fanno') in their
rapacious feeding reverse the selfless sacrifice of Christ whose bird-symbol

they recall. After the end of the tenth century, often a single artistic representation would combine the Tree of Jesse with the Tree of the Cross (plate 14). Both motifs represented the *salutifera arbor*, the Tree of Salvation; as the Tree of Jesse figured the first step towards redemption, so the Tree of the Cross was its fulfilment.[25] Dante's reversal of both these images of salvation into an image of damnation exemplifies the Christian tradition of employing the same symbols *in bono* and *in malo*.[26] Particularly fitting, as will later become apparent, is the fact that the figure of Christ as the Rod of Jesse also represents the figure of Christ as Judge (Isaias 11:3–5).

Let us now, however, turn briefly to the historical Pier della Vigna and to the intimate relation the facts of his life bear to the poetic and iconographic images of his punishment or *contrapasso* in Dante's episode. The case of the Protonotary was a *cause célèbre*: the Poet need not even mention his name. Piero had been born in Capua towards the end of the twelfth century to an impoverished but well-respected family.[27] His father, Angelo, at least in later life, was a judge, and Piero himself studied both canon and civil law in Bologna. The family's circumstances allowed no support for Piero's education, but a stipend granted by the university or by the Commune of Bologna conceded him at least subsistence. From later demonstrations of talent in Italian rhyme and Latin prose, we can be sure that he also studied *ars dictaminis*. Upon Piero's elegantly written request, Archbishop Berardo of Palermo, an intimate associate of the Emperor, introduced the future minister to Frederick probably in 1221. Piero's extraordinary gifts in linguistic style and his knowledge of the law were grounds for an immediate appointment to the imperial chancery.[28] He developed a close friendship with the Emperor, with whom he shared cultural, philosophical, artistic, and social interests. Piero's climb through the ranks of the imperial civil service was swift. From 1225 until 1247, officially Piero filled only the position of High Court judge, 'judex magnae curiae';[29] but from 1238 to 1247 his real post was that of 'familiaris,' or privy counsellor to the King, since Piero had ceased to function in his office of judge of the court of appeal in 1234.[30] The most significant imperial documents bear Piero's stylistic imprint; of his fashioning is the charter founding the University of Naples in 1224.[31] The most important effect of his tenure in Frederick's service, however, was the imperial constitution promulgated at Melfi in 1231, the *Liber Augustalis*, whose formulation was probably, at least in great part, the work of Piero's own hand.[32] His close association with the Emperor and his primacy among the notaries of the chancery allowed him to hold sway over imperial decisions and privileges granted from about 1239 to 1246. Through him passed all the Emperor's private correspondence and by him were drawn up the edicts and manifestos of the Emperor's virulent quarrel with the Papacy. In May 1247, after the death of his peer and colleague Taddeo da Sessa, Piero was at last given the official title of his full administrative authority, 'Protonotary of the Imperial Court and Logothete of the Kingdom of Sicily.'[33] Though never styled chancellor, he became in effect the head of the imperial chancery, the Emperor's spokesman in all matters legal, diplomatic, social, and political, and director of finances for the Empire. He formed the sole link between the people and their Emperor for petitions and pleas. In the royal palace in Naples, was painted a wall fresco, now no longer extant, which depicted him in this role.[34]

Piero's professional success was coupled with extraordinary personal gain. Some estimates place his fortune at 900,000 Neapolitan ducats and others at 10,000 pounds in gold *Augustales*.[35] Such sums do not include, among other landed properties, his large palace in Naples, his vast gardens outside the city, and his conglomerate of estates near Capua. It is evident, as most historians have seen, that his position presented great temptations for self-aggrandizement at the expense of the public coffers, temptations made even greater by the fact that the monarch allowed him to act upon his own initiative in many matters. The contemporary astrologer Guido Bonatti (punished by Dante as a diviner in *Inferno* xx, 118, and an excellent first-hand source) avers that Piero often subverted the Emperor's orders.[36] Suddenly in February of 1249, under circumstances which remain unclear and which indeed seem to have been intentionally shrouded in mystery by the Crown, Piero fell from favour. He was arrested in Cremona, his eyes were put out, and he was led from town to town to be mocked by the populace until the death sentence was to be executed. In May of the same year, however (accounts differ concerning precise location and method), Piero cheated his prince, and, in despair, dashed his own skull against a stone wall or column in San Miniato.[37]

As we would expect, the fall and death of the Logothete brought with it a flood of unfounded speculation. Various chronicles and commentaries on the *Commedia* present conflicting versions. Contemporaries erroneously linked an earlier poisoning attempt on the Emperor's life to the later ruin of the King's minister. Rumours told that Pier della Vigna had conspired with Frederick's personal physician in a plot with the Pope.[38] Matthew Paris, an otherwise well-respected and informed chronicler, relates that Piero was involved in a poisoning attempt with his *own* physician to murder the King.[39] Fra Salimbene di Adamo, of the Minorite Order which the Pope used so widely to disseminate propaganda and scandal against Frederick II, feigned belief in the innocence of Pier della Vigna: the disloyal Emperor Frederick, in order to ruin Piero with a charge of treason and seize his property, used the calumny that the Logothete had secretly treated with the Pope at the Council of Lyons without imperial witnesses. Historians have shown Salimbene to be totally without credence, for Pier della Vigna did not attend the Council of Lyons.[40] The *Historia anonymi remensis* (ca 1260) tells a different tale: the Emperor had had Piero's coffers searched and had found an incriminating letter.[41] This anonymous chronicler does not specify whether the evidence had been planted or not, but in his account in the *Esposizioni*, Boccaccio leaves no doubt as to the actual falsity of the letter.[42] A Pisan manuscript recounts that Frederick had had Piero blinded and sentenced to death as a fomentor of discord because he had obstinately opposed a reconciliation between the Emperor and the Pope. Again the story is baseless, for the Pope had adamantly opposed all reconciliations after deposing Frederick at the Council of Lyons and had aimed at and eventually succeeded in the destruction of the Hohenstaufen monarchy.[43]

In the fourteenth century the tales were to become more inventive and silly. The Dominican Francesco Pippino relates the rumour that Pier della Vigna had indeed betrayed the Emperor but that the Logothete had had just cause: Frederick had seduced Piero's wife.[44] The Pisan chronicle blithely states the opposite: Piero was punished for coveting the Empress.[45] As the first story is implausible so the second is impossible. The Empress Isabel of England, Frederick's third wife, had died in 1241 long before Piero's fall, and the then-sixty-year-old Emperor had never remarried.

The various conflicting versions reflect the number and type of rumours current in Dante's day. That the Logothete was not involved in a plot to poison the Emperor and that he was not in league with the Pope appears clear. The number of documents which Piero drafted on behalf of his prince, the vehemence with which he defended the imperial cause, and the Pope's implacable treatment of his family and estate after his death make it extremely unlikely that a reconciliation with the Papacy, even in secret, was possible.[46] However, that the Emperor's minister had an avaricious nature and that he was engaged in other crimes just as sinister and thus, ultimately, treasonable is borne out by existing evidence. Piero's greed appears in the methods he used to enlarge his estate in Capua at the expense of a hostel engaged in the care of pilgrims, the poor and the sick, the Ospedale di San Jacopo di Altopascio, the seat of the Order of the Knights of St James situated on the Via Romea, near the Cerbaia or imperial Tuscan hunting preserve.[47] In February 1244, an exchange of property took place between the wealthy monastery and the 'procurator' of the Emperor, Uberto Gangi. In exchange for ceding their rights to an estate including a church and house near Capua, the Master and Brothers received the income and properties of a nearby smaller foundation in Tuscany, the Ospedale di Santa Maria della Trinità. The reasons alleged for the trade were that the Capuan property was too far away for the monastery to administer properly and that the tithes accruing from it had

become too small to be worthwhile. The arrangement would have little historic interest except that the Capuan property ended up in the personal
possession of one whose name appears nowhere in the deed, Pier della Vigna.[48]
After his death, it returned to the control of the crown with the rest of his
confiscated property; and later, as we learn from a letter of Innocent IV, the
exchange was declared null and void.[49] According to the Pope, Pier della
Vigna had used the weight and pressure of the strongest office in the imperial
government to force the Ospedale to relinquish its Capuan property against
its will. We also learn from the papal letter that Piero had made himself feared
by the poor and the powerful rich alike: 'Not only was he the terror of the
humble, but of people of lofty degree' (p. 317). Regardless of the inimical
motives of the Church and regardless of whether the Logothete forced the
exchange with the Emperor's knowledge, ignorance, or connivance, the fact
remains that Piero was capable historically of appropriating for his own use
the possessions of institutions concerned with the sick and needy. With or
without the Emperor he had stolen from Holy Church.

Various fragments of the imperial register published by Huillard-Bréholles
show that Piero was especially involved in imperial finances; many entries
concern the administration of property and the exaction of duties and taxes,
but a great number deal with the prosecution of accused traitors and with
the confiscation of their belongings.[50] Here, too, Piero had much opportunity
to seize property and commandeer it for his own. That he did so is made
clear by the Emperor's letter to his son-in-law, Richard, Count of Caserta,
from which we learn that Piero's years of embezzlement which had led the
state to the brink of destruction had been the subject of other missives from
the Emperor to his lieutenants; the metaphors show that Frederick saw the
crimes as having endangered both his Empire and his person. The document
recommends that the greatest care and secrecy be used henceforth in ascer-
taining the guilt of those accused of treason. It makes clear not only that this
care had not been exercised in the past but that great abuses had been inflicted
upon the innocent. Pier della Vigna is used as the negative example of
the methods previously employed.[51]

Nineteenth- and twentieth-century historians agree on the nature of Piero's
crimes. For Huillard-Bréholles, Piero was guilty of avarice, bribery, and
embezzlement, the sale of justice, and the abuse of power to enrich himself
and his family.[52] Kantorowicz generally concurs but sees the wilful perversion of justice and the enormous misappropriations of state funds as a veritable
betrayal of the Emperor and his trust.[53] The historian and critic Leonardo
Olschki concluded: '[Dante's] representation according to which [Piero] for-
feited peace and life – lo sonno e li polsi – in the faithful discharge of his
function as highest official and confidant of the Emperor, is, in the light of our

knowledge, seen to be a pious fable invented and used by the Poet with definite intentions. The Chancellor was one of the astonishingly large number of high officers of state and dignitaries who unscrupulously exploited their position for their own ends, amassed wealth, and in the end turned treacherously against their lord and benefactor.'[54] Friedrich Baethgen, in an essay which makes convincing changes in the interpretation of major individual documents, comes to the same basic conclusions: Pier della Vigna was not guilty of attempted poisoning but of embezzlement.[55] The American historian Van Cleve concludes: 'His "treasonable acts" consisted in cupidity – the avarice of a man already abundantly wealthy for greater wealth and for greater power, to be obtained from selling justice for his own profit. ... That he was guilty of peculation there can be no reasonable doubt; his trial and the sentence imposed appear to have confirmed his guilt.'[56] Avarice in office, it is agreed, caused the fall of the Emperor's minister.

Just how the christological images and the history of the episode are joined to the traditions of avarice and suicide, we will now explore in chapter 4.

4 AVARICE AND SUICIDE

The literal level of Dante's Poem, at least Piero's own profession of innocence, seems to contradict the consensus of historians. The Wayfarer is left speechless with pity. Dante *poeta*, however, appears, as I will show, to have known the darker sides of the story, since every classical and biblical image which he uses points to a form of violent and rapacious avarice and to its opposite, profligacy. Dante presents two frenzied and unnatural extremes of an Aristotelian mean.

The foul human-faced harpies, who together with the black bitches act as agents of divine wrath in this subdivision of circle seven, form the first composite image. In this metaphor Pier della Vigna plays the role of a classical figure of avarice, Phineus, the harpies' original victim to whom Piero stands in striking parallel even historically. As the greedy Phineus, who had blinded or killed his sons, was blinded by the irate gods in just retaliation, so Piero was blinded in life by Frederick. Fulgentius begins his 'Fabula Finei': 'Phineus is taken as a symbol of avarice,' and he claims that the name Phineus derives from 'fenerando,' 'practising usury.' 'Fittingly he is blind, because all avarice is blind in not seeing what is its own.'[1] The Third Vatican Mythographer and the pseudo-Bernardus Silvestris follow him without originality.[2] In the classics, the harpies are a just infliction upon the avaricious and, indeed, Fulgentius strives hard to etymologize their very names as signifying acts of rapaciousness.[3] The Third Vatican Mythographer cites Fulgentius' explanation, and tells us:

> The Harpies however are called the hounds of Jove, because they are also said to be Furies. Whence also they are said to snatch food from banquets, because this is the work of Harpies. Here also the avaricious are made to suffer the Furies, because they abstain from [using] their share.[4]

'Bernardus' also repeats Fulgentius' explanations for the harpies' names, form, and virginity, but he further allegorizes their swollen bellies: 'A gluttonous belly is a voracious rapacity for money.[5] The aptness of God's *contrapasso* in the *Inferno* is apparent in the smallest detail: the avaricious Piero is tormented by symbols of his shameful greed and rapine. Benvenuto da Imola, in fact, noted in his *Comentum* on the *Comedy*, 'Figuratively a Harpy represents avarice,' and later 'Avarice and prodigality most of all lead a man to despair.'[6]

A second major classical allusion can facilitate an understanding of the structure of the episode. Actaeon, the prototype of the profligate, chased and torn by his own hounds, forms the antithesis of the first image in an Aristotelian balance; for as Dante knew, in the fourth book of the *Nicomachaean Ethics*, the Philosopher had called profligacy a type of self-destruction.[7] Fulgentius interprets the tale as that of the prodigal who wastes his substance on his hounds; though too old for the hunt, Actaeon cannot bear to be parted from his pack and ruins himself to feed them.[8] The allusion also helps us to see that the two bestial agents of torment, the harpies and black hounds of Dante's thirteenth canto, are, in some way, one. They form a unity partly recognized by the early commentators: not only were the harpies the 'hounds of Jove,' but one of Actaeon's bitches was named 'Harpyia.'[9]

Lastly, the central image of the speaking tree, inspired by the Polydorus episode in the *Aeneid*, actually cuts with a double edge, a fact so far unnoticed. In the received interpretation, Pier della Vigna suffers the unjust fate of Polydorus: the innocent son of Priam, entrusted to the care of Polymnestor, King of Thrace, is killed by the latter precisely because of Polymnestor's avarice for Polydorus' riches.[10] The aptness of the parallel is at once apparent. Fra Salimbene, hinting that Frederick II had ruined his faithful minister in order to seize the latter's fortune, twice attributes the following cynical dictum to the Emperor: 'Never did I feed a hog, from which I did not extract lard.'[11] It would appear too that Dante *poeta* would have us see Piero at first as victim and sufferer. That is, until we explore the tradition of allegorization of the Polydorus episode perhaps familiar to the Poet. In the pseudo-Bernardus Silvestris' interpretation of the *Aeneid*, for example, this 'victim' plays quite a different role. Polydorus is seen, bewilderingly, as a grasping entrepreneur wrapped up in his greed, coldly and calculatedly absorbed in his efforts to gain wealth:

> Now Polydorus signifies 'much bitterness,' for 'doris' in Greek is 'amaritudo' in Latin. ... This Polydorus is buried in Thrace because much bitterness is wrapped in avarice: for what can be more bitter

than the avaricious man who 'seeks and like a wretch abstains from what
he has found and fears to use it'? What can be more bitter than that
'he manages everything fearfully and coldly'? Than the fact that 'love of
money grows as the money itself grows,' and that 'the greedy man is
always poor'? Polydorus, then, makes Aeneas flee from Thrace because
the bitterness and toil of seeking and holding on to money often
frighten a man away from the pursuit of money.[12]

May we not see in 'Bernardus'' interpretation some ironical grist for Piero's
profession of devotion to office: 'such that for it I lost both sleep and life'?
Regardless of the overly discussed differences between the Polydorus episode
and Dante's creation, the fact remains that Piero *is* the type of Polydorus.[13]
The Logothete is changed into a tree not only because he may have been the
victim of another's avarice but because he was avaricious himself.

Our appreciation of the aptness of such a transformation is strengthened
further by Bersuire in his *Ovidius moralizatus*. Though this writer is later
than Dante, his view reveals the traditions and significance surrounding this
type of metamorphosis. Discussing the similar fate of the sisters of Phaethon,
he states that the avaricious were regularly turned into trees as a matter of
course![14]

Perhaps independently of its use by the mythographers, the metaphor
of greed as a tree appears in the Church Fathers. St Gregory the Great
discusses the 'root of the juniper' of Job 30:4: the tree, whose root is allegorized as avarice, has thorny spines instead of leaves:

> For the juniper tree has spines instead of leaves, for so bristly are
> those which it puts forth that like thorns they can pierce anyone who
> touches them. Now a thorn is all sorts of sin, because while it draws
> the mind into delight, as it were, by piercing, it wounds it. ... What then
> is there denoted by the 'root of the juniper' but avarice, from which
> the thorns of all the sins are produced? Concerning this it is said by Paul:
> 'For the desire of money [*cupiditas*] is the root of all evils' [1 Timothy
> 6:10, Douay]. For that springs up covertly in the mind, and brings forth
> openly the spines of all sin in practice.[15]

Since Polydorus' bush in *Aeneid* III, 23 is not a naturally bristling thorn but
a myrtle darted with javelins, 'densis hastilibus horrida myrtus,' at least part
of Dante's inspiration may derive from such passages as St Gregory's.

Inescapably and conclusively we begin to perceive that the Poet's images
point to the 'root of all evil,' the love of money, and its consequent out-
growths. The major allusions of the episode of Pier della Vigna are thus in

perfect consonance with contemporary historical records. Both reveal what
Piero's words would hide: a grasping and avaricious nature. The episode in
cantos XIII and XIV, 1–3, in fact possesses a tight artistic unity: violent
avariciousness leading to the destruction of corporal substance is punished
together with violent profligacy engendering the wasting of worldly
substance.

We must now turn to the immediate puzzle of why Dante, having 'disposed' of the misers and squanderers in *Inferno* VII, would place so much
emphasis on covetousness (*cupiditas*) or avarice here. We can find the
answer not only in the biblical and patristic notion of sins engendering more
serious sins, but also in the rhetoric of Frederick's court, in contemporary
opinions about Pier della Vigna, and in the traditional typology of avarice in
the Church Fathers and in Christian art.

The Emperor and his Curia regularly wrote of the concept of sovereignty in
metaphors religious or sacrilegious. The monarch's authority, as Dante
would later echo in the *De Monarchia*, derived solely from the Godhead.[16] As
Kantorowicz has shown, Frederick conceived of himself as 'the fount of
justice,' 'the father and son of Justice,' and, indeed the 'sol iustitiae,' 'the sun
of justice,' the prophetic title of Christ. He frequently spoke of himself as
the Messiah: his birthplace, Jesi, for example, becomes 'Bethlehem' where his
'divine mother gave him life'![17] The Popes' inexorable campaign, including
the deposing of the Emperor, two excommunications, and the proclamation of
a crusade against him, made Frederick feel that he was repeating the very
Passion of Christ. Such imagery consistently reappears in his letters. In March
or April of 1249, most probably from Cremona, Frederick wrote to the King
of France bitterly complaining of the persecution; his kingdom is the Holy
Land; he himself is on the cross.[18] If, in the rhetoric of the King and Court,
Frederick is the Son of God, then the pursekeeper among his ministers, the
breaker of his trust, must be Judas. And thus is Piero styled in the
Emperor's letter to the Count of Caserta referred to above. Here Frederick sees
embezzlement of temporal funds as one with ecclesiastic simony, and he
accuses Piero of the crime. The Logothete's greedy peculations evoke the
avaricious crimes and thefts of the traitor Judas in John 12:6; 'Fur erat et
loculos habens ea quae mittebantur portabat / He was a thief and, having the
purse, carried things that were put therein,' and John 13:29, 'Loculos
habebat Judas / Judas had the purse':

> You will be able to recall through other documents something of the
> base advice and various scandals [*scandali multiformis*] of Petrus, that
> is, of this Simon, still another betrayer, who, *so that he might have the*
> *purse, or that he might enrich himself,* turned the rod of justice into a

serpent, so that he might by means of his usual lies bring this empire
into peril by which we might have perished in the depths of the sea,
one with the Pharaoh's army, like the Egyptians' chariots.[19]

Interestingly, papal documents use similar metaphors. The writer of the *Vita
Gregorii IX*, perhaps Giovanni di Ferentino, refers to Piero as a 'new
Ahithophel.'[20] These same images from rival Church and imperial sources
curiously find a parallel in those forming the iconography of *Inferno* XIII.

Judas Iscariot was more than the betrayer of Christ: he had misap-
propriated money from the poor; and he had taken his own life. The fallen
apostle's descent to betrayal led by degrees from covetousness through
theft and hypocrisy. Of the four Gospels, Matthew (26:15) most emphasizes
the avarice of Judas as the primary motive of his treachery: 'Quid vultis
mihi dare et ego vobis eum tradam ? at illi constituerunt ei triginta argenteos /
What will you give me, and I will deliver him unto you? And they
appointed him thirty pieces of silver.' Describing the anointing at Bethany,
the Gospel of John recounts that the apostle's complaint at the extravagant
'waste' was caused by excessive love of money: when Judas suggested that the
ointment should be sold and the proceeds distributed among the poor, he
did so hypocritically and only as an opportunity for embezzlement (John
12:4–6). The Evangelist calls Judas a thief, 'fur erat,' who would steal what
was put into the common purse entrusted to his safekeeping. St Augustine
glosses:

> Harken to the true witness: 'Now he said this, not because he cared
> for the poor; but because he was a thief and, having the purse, carried
> the things that were put therein (John 12:6).' 'Carried' or 'carried
> off'? Nay, but by office he carried, by theft he carried off. ... Behold
> among the Saints is a Judas! Behold he is a thief, this Judas! And that
> you make not light of that, a thief and sacrilegious, not any common
> kind of thief! A thief who stole from the purse, yea, but from that of
> the Lord! From the purse, yea, but from the sacred purse! If in the courts
> of law a difference is made between the crime of common theft and
> peculation, for it is called peculation when it is the stealing of public
> property and the stealing of private property is not judged so heinous
> as that of the stealing of public property, how much more sternly shall
> that sacrilegious thief be judged who has dared to rob, not in any
> common way, but to rob the Church! *He who steals ought from the
> Church is one with Judas the lost.*[21]

As we would expect, the fallen apostle is thus a familiar *figura* of avarice
in the Fathers of the Church. St John Chrysostomos warns the avaricious to

consider his punishment. Judas lost everything including his immortal soul through greed: 'Judas is set forth as an example to the avaricious.'[22] Regularly in their comments on Judas' sins, the Fathers cite 1 Timothy 6:10: 'Cupidity [love of money] is the root of all evil' (often the passage is cited as 'Radix ... est avaritia'), and Ecclesiasticus [Sirach] 10:9: 'Now nothing is fouler than an avaricious man.'[23] Besides St John Chrysostomos, other Fathers such as Origen, St Cyril of Jerusalem, and Rabanus Maurus all cite avarice as the main motive for Judas' wickedness.[24] St Jerome even extends this view to his gloss on Judas' second name: 'No matter how you interpret it, Iscariot means money and price.'[25] Most illuminating for our purposes, however, is St Thomas Aquinas' treatment of the patristic doctrine of the 'daughters of avarice' (*filiae cupiditatis* or *avaritiae*) in the *Summa Theologica* showing the progression of the sin toward violence and beyond to the sins of Christ's betrayer: 'The daughters of covetousness are the vices which arise therefrom, especially in respect of the desire of an end. Now since covetousness is excessive love of possessing riches, it exceeds in two things. For in the first place it exceeds in retaining, and in this respect covetousness gives rise to *insensibility to mercy*, because, to wit, *a man's heart is not softened by mercy to assist the needy with his riches.* In the second place, it belongs to covetousness to exceed in receiving, and in this respect covetousness may be considered in two ways. First as in the thought (*affectu*). In this way it gives rise to *restlessness, by hindering man with excessive anxiety and care*, for "a covetous man shall not be satisfied with money" (Ecclesiastes 5:9). Secondly, it may be considered in the execution (*effectu*). In this way *the covetous man, in acquiring other people's goods, sometimes employs force, which pertains to violence.*' St Thomas continues listing worse sins until he concludes with treachery 'as in the case of Judas, who betrayed Christ through *covetousness.*'[26]

Most important for a consideration of Dante's episode is Judas' earthly end as described in Matthew 27:3–5. Too late the remorseful apostle, rebuffed by the high priests, tosses his blood money into the temple. In despair he hangs himself from a noose, 'laqueo se suspendit' – tradition said from a tree.[27] This final act was for St Jerome and other Church writers far worse than even his betrayal. Commenting on Psalm 108 [109], the saint writes, 'The repentance of Judas became worse than his sin. How so? He went out and committed suicide by hanging himself; he who became the betrayer of God became his own hangman. In regard to the clemency of the Lord, I say this, that Judas offended the Lord more by hanging himself than by betraying Him.'[28] St Gregory the Great echoes the concept: 'Thus the reprobate Judas, when he inflicted death upon himself to spite sin, was brought to the punishment of eternal death, and repented of sin in a *more heinous way than he had committed sin.*' (My italics.)[29] Evidently for the Fathers of the Church,

Judas was at least as important as an example of avarice and suicide as he was as a symbol of betrayal.

Of the early commentators on *Inferno* XIII, only Dante's son, Pietro Alighieri, mentions Judas in reference to Pier della Vigna and his sin of despair:

> Despair is said to be a sin against the Holy Spirit if it is committed out of contempt and malice, because it is not forgiven in this life – that is, not without difficulty – nor in the life to come, *as in the case of Judas.* It must be construed to mean that such a wood – that is, the state and reputation of those who are desperate – is trackless, because our thought is not able to proceed by consideration of such a case. And the fronds are dry because their memory is dead. Thus he tells how they come to be plants there, and the reason why they will not have their bodies.
> With regard to this it is said in the *Decreta*: '*Judas* sold the Redeemer of all men, and having soon after hanged himself from a noose did not keep that Redeemer's grace – and rightly so, because no one is able to retain that which he has sold.[30]

Maddeningly, Pietro stops here, never to pick up the thread again or to tie his suggestions to the context. And, oddly, no modern commentator has yet thought to take his comparison seriously.

In *Inferno* XIII, it *is* as *Judas*, a body hanging from a tree surrounded by winged demons with human faces, the claws of birds, and swollen stomachs, that Dante has Pier della Vigna visualize himself after the Last Judgment (103–8). For his image, Dante drew not only from Patristics but from the Christian pictorial and sculptural tradition which depicted a lifeless body hanging from a tree to represent both the death of Judas and the more general image of the despair of self-destruction.[31] Such depictions are legion. The suicide of Judas occurs together with the first known realistic portrayal of the crucifixion on an ivory box in the British Museum, made probably in southern Gaul about 400 AD. This first representation is notable especially because of one detail: a bird feeds its young in a nest in the gallows-tree (plate 15). The same hanging figure appears carved on the back of the Brescia Lipsanotheca, a North Italian ivory chest of perhaps the third quarter of the fourth century (plate 16),[32] and on an ivory diptych preserved in the Tesoro del Duomo in Milan (plate 17). Judas with a bird, perhaps plucking out his eyes, is the subject of a miniature in the Stuttgart Psalter (ca 820–30) (plate 18).

Important later variants depict the devil or demons taking the soul of the betrayer: the fiends commonly have human faces and birds' claws and wings, such as those on the cathedral doors of Benevento made towards the end of the twelfth century (plate 19). Most striking is Gislebertus' pilaster capital from Autun Cathedral (ca 1125–1130), which dramatizes the scene vividly: harpies with wings, swollen bellies, and human faces with gaping, hungry mouths surround the lifeless body of the betrayer as it hangs from a heavily foliaged tree (plate 20). An earlier capital in the Church of Saint-Andoche at Saulieu (1115–1120) is similar, showing Judas hanging from a tree with an open-mouthed devil with bird's talons.[33] The sandstone tympanum (ca 1275–1280) of the central west portal of Strasbourg Cathedral includes the death of Judas among other scenes of its Passion Cycle.[34] In another stone relief on the tympanum in the porch of Freiburg Cathedral, almost coeval (ca 1290–1310) with the *Commedia*, Judas hangs with tormenting monsters carved above his head.[35] In about the same period major artisans and artists were creating similar images in contemporary Italy; we find them in the mosaics of the Poet's beloved 'bel San Giovanni' (ca 1271–1300) and in Giotto's frescoes for the Scrovegni Chapel of the Arena in Padua (ca 1305) (plates 21, 22). Clearly such traditional representations influenced Dante's conception of the suicides' state of soul after death.

The artists who drew the early miniatures of the *Divina Commedia* generally limited themselves to depicting the scene and action of the cantos, the thornbushes, the harpies, and their nests, Virgil watching Dante plucking away a branch. In a few cases, however, the actual content of Piero's speech is illustrated. In a manuscript in the Bibliothèque Nationale in Paris (ms. it. 78, f. 66ʳ) we find a sketch of the suicide's body impaled in the branches (plate 23). Another in the Biblioteca Nacional in Madrid (ms. 10057, f. 25ʳ) presents a more interesting drawing of Pier della Vigna hanging from a branch by a rope (plate 24), a clear allusion to the iconographic topos of the sins of despair and suicide based on the death of Judas who, out of grief, hanged himself from a noose.[36]

For the Middle Ages, the Old-Testament traitor and suicide Ahithophel prefigured the New-Testament Judas. In 2 Kings [Samuel] 16–18, we read that, in answer to King David's prayer, the advice of Ahithophel, the chief counsellor to the usurper Absalom,[37] was turned to foolishness and ignored; Ahithophel, seeing that his advice was disregarded, committed suicide in his own house: 'But Achithophel seeing that his counsel was not followed, saddled his ass, and arose and went home to his house and to his city. And putting his house in order, he hanged himself' (2 Kings [Samuel] 17:23).

The traditional interpretation of the so-called 'Judas' Psalm 108 [109] linked the two suicides, Judas and Ahithophel: David's plea and curse upon Absalom and Ahithophel was interpreted verse by verse as being that of Christ upon the Betrayer. In his *Breviarium in Psalmos*, St Jerome begins his exegesis on Psalm 108 thus: ' "Unto the end, a psalm of David." "Unto the end" is a sign that the message of the psalm pertains not to the present but the future. If, moreover, the prophet speaks of the future, the prophecy concerns Christ. "O God, be not silent in my praise." Christ is saying: "Judas betrayed me, the Jews persecuted and crucified me and thought that they were putting an end to me, but you, O God, be not silent in my praise." '[38] St Augustine echoes the theme in his *Enarrationes*: 'Everyone who faithfully reads the Acts of the Apostles (1:15–26), acknowledges that this Psalm contains a prophecy of Christ; for it evidently appears that what is written here, "let his days be few, and let another take his office," is prophesied of Judas, Christ's betrayer.'[39] Rabanus Maurus in his gloss on 2 Kings [Samuel] continues the tradition.[40]

Many moralized Bibles parallel the two suicides pictorially: Judas is depicted hanging from a tree while Ahithophel, in an architectural setting, makes a gibbet of his house (plate 25).[41] Many manuscripts present both Judas and Ahithophel hanging from halters inside a building (plate 26).[42] In an especially noteworthy example (plate 27), a marginal gloss declares that Judas represents those who are ensnared by the noose of simony, who accept the dignity of office only to lose their souls.[43] A related metaphorical use of Ahithophel's story occurs in Richard of St Victor's *De eruditione hominis interioris* where Ahithophel serves as an example of 'affectatio auctoritatis,' the ambitious and vain striving after authority: 'Affectation of authority is when a man now strives to seem to all to be a man of great advice and sanctity, and that matters which are to be determined or defined depend upon his counsel or opinion. ... He who speaks of Achitophel shows us what ambition for authority can do in such people.'[44] The parallels to the ambitious counsellor Pier della Vigna are obvious. The final words of the second, Florentine, suicide centring upon the concept of 'city' and 'house' and concluding with 'Io fei gibetto a me *de le mie case* I made me a gibbet *of my own house*', bear so close a resemblance to the death of the biblical Ahithophel that they must have drawn from it their inspiration and intended allusion: 'And he went *home* to his *house* and to his *city*. And putting his *house* in order, he hanged himself' (2 Kings [Samuel] 17:23; my italics). The sublime unity of poetry, art, and theme is now apparent.

Seeing Judas as a prototype and pattern for the episode also helps us to explain many other exegetical difficulties, especially that of the Wayfarer's ignorance and the Poet's conviction of Piero's real guilt. The Church Fathers make much of the fact that Judas' avarice was hidden from the other apostles, and, in a special way, hidden also from Christ himself. St Thomas' resolution of the problem of the apparent inconsistency of divine prescience with Jesus' unknowing also permits us to glimpse and grasp the interior workings of the *Commedia*; for Dante's Poem is modelled on that same distinction between the limits of human intellect and the knowledge of God's *invisibilia*: 'The wickedness of Judas was known to Christ *qua Deus*; it was unknown to Him *qua homo*.'[45] Similarly, Piero's guilt is concealed from the Wayfarer and from the reader on the literal level, but revealed when we look beneath to the second, spiritual sense. Within the fiction of the Poem, the Poet who has experienced the sight of God and returns to write of it as a 'scribe of God' knows of Piero's real guilt and hidden avarice; Dante, the Wayfarer, does not.

Just as the discarded minister Ahithophel clearly parallels the discarded minister della Vigna, so Judas' selling the Innocent Blood for money parallels the love of money which led Piero to embezzle from the state and persecute the innocent for gain. The Logothete who, as Guido da Pisa notes, 'was ... a great master and doctor of laws, and first judge in the High Court of Frederick the Emperor,' had, in Frederick II's words, 'turned the rod of justice into a serpent.[46] Piero's judgeship is significant in the context of justice and injustice. We should recall at this point that the image of the Tree of Jesse, parodied in the post-Judgment state of the suicides, *itself figures Christ come to judge*: 'And there shall come forth a rod out of the root of Jesse: and a flower shall rise up and out of this root ... *he shall judge the poor with justice*, and shall reprove with equity for the meek of the earth. And he shall strike the earth with the rod of his mouth: and with the breath of his lips he shall slay the wicked. And justice shall be the girdle of his loins ...' (Isaias 11:1–5).[47]

Further, the seventh circle of Hell, in which the suicides hold central place, marks the beginning of the lower realm of those sins which have injustice as their end:

> D'ogne malizia, ch'odio in cielo acquista,
>   *ingiuria* è'l fine, ed ogne fin cotale
>   o con forza o con frode altrui contrista.

> Of every malice that gains hatred in Heaven the end is injustice; and every such end, either by force or by fraud, afflicts another.

> (*Inferno* XI, 22–4)

The suicides, who have extended their violence even to robbing themselves of the world (*Inferno* XI, 43), view their own sin as an injustice to self:

> L'animo mio ...
> *ingiusto* fece me contra me giusto.

> My mind ... made me unjust against my just self.

> (*Inferno* XIII, 70–3)

The episode's solid context of justice and its perversion provides a possible key to the identity of the second, Florentine, suicide. Given a choice between the traditional identifications, rather than Rocco de' Mozzi, the rich man who hanged himself rather than face poverty, we must choose, for reasons of motive, logic, artistic balance, and unity, the *judge* and avaricious *professor iuris*, Lotto degli Agli, who, as the Ottimo tells us, 'Having given a false sentence for money, he hanged himself to avoid poverty and shame.'[48] We must also point out, however, that by intentionally not mentioning Lotto's name in the verses of the *Commedia*, Dante also meant this character to be widely symbolic of the suicidal turn which Florentine politics had taken.

Recognition of Judas as a vital unifying image underlying Dante's conception of the avaricious Piero can add a new dimension to the question of the tree-souls' speech, so well examined stylistically by Leo Spitzer. Origen was the first Church writer to note that the surname 'Iscariot' meant 'suffocated': 'I heard someone explaining that the town of the betrayer Judas is named according to the Hebrew words "from suffocation." If this is so, a great fittingness can be discovered between the name of his town and the way he died, since indeed, by hanging himself from a noose he fulfilled, through his suffocation, the prophecy of the name of his town of provenance.'[49] Roman B. Halas has traced the allied traditions whereby 'Iscariot' derives from 'as^{e}kara', 'death by strangulation': 'Furthermore, the Rabbis and Jewish medical books claim that 'as^{e}kara' is the same as *mḥnq* (suffocation) mentioned in Job 7:15. Death resulting from this disease is swift and painful, for the narrow cavity situated in the neck tends to obstruct the normal flow of air passages and causes instantaneous suffocation. [Since he was] afflicted with this disease in childhood, his parents began to call [Judas] 'as^{e}karayōṭa'. ... He ended his earthly existence by suffocation as a just punishment from God for the sin of betrayal.'[50] Dante's episode may be, thus, not only a visual but an auditory figuration of the suicide as Judas. The language of the episode with its coughing sibilants and the straining speech of the plants with its painful, hissing issuance might take on a different interpretation: the suicides imitate forever the point of death of the rapacious apostle, the hanging 'man of suffocation.'

The Poet, through the character Piero, places stress on the notion of 'root' ('le nove radici'). This seems merely a grotesque concentration on the souls' metamorphosis until we realize that the 'root' of Piero's sin was the love of money, the *radix malorum*, *avaritia* or *cupiditas*. The soul of the sinner has been reduced essentially to the root of its sequence of sins. Piero thus swears an odd fealty to his lord with a pledge of such ambiguous resonance.

Comparing the language of the Circle of Avarice in the *Purgatorio* substantiates our reading. Hugh Capet, the major representative of the sin in the

fifth *girone*, identifies himself using the same imagery familiar to the reader
from *Inferno* XIII:

> Io fui radice de la mala pianta
>   che la terra cristiana tutta aduggia,
>   sì che buon frutta rado se ne schianta.

> I was the root of the evil plant that overshadows all the Christian land
> so that good fruit is seldom plucked from it.

(Purgatorio xx, 43–5)

In retrospect can we understand even more clearly that Piero's bush reflects
perversely a *genealogical* tree, as we noted above. The various uses in the
Commedia of the verb 'schiantare,' meaning 'to break off' or 'pick' twigs or
fruit, also comfort our typological and iconological interpretation. The word is
used of the fruits of Eden in *Purgatorio* xxviii, 120, and of the Tree of Life and
Justice in *Purgatorio* xxxiii, 58.[51] This last usage puts Piero's inverted state
and outrage ('Perché mi schiante?') into clear perspective. Because he
perverted justice and denied life by casting asunder the image of the Redeemer
in his own person, the Logothete is punished by a metamorphosis into a
barren inversion of Christ as *arbor salutifera*. Piero is torn as he once
figuratively tore the Tree of Justice.

Again, in the purgatorial Circle of Avarice, the major images reappear:
Polymnestor and his victim Polydorus again figure among the examples:

>   ed in infamia tutto 'l monte gira
>   Polinestor ch'ancise Polidoro

> and in infamy the name of Polymnestor who slew Polydorus circles
> all the mountain.

(Purgatorio xx, 114–15)

The figure of Judas returns in reference to the greed of Charles of Valois.
Charles Lackland's ('Carlo Sanzaterra') 'Lance of Judas' is avarice, as the context reveals: his 'lancia' bursts the swollen belly of Florence's greed (compare the swollen paunches of the Harpies):

> Tempo vegg'io, non molto dopo ancoi,
>   che tragge un altro Carlo fuor di Francia,
>   per far conoscer meglio e sé e'suoi.

> Sanz'arme n'esce e solo con la lancia
>   con la qual giostrò Giuda, e quella ponta
>   sì, ch'a Fiorenza fa scoppiar la pancia.

A time I see not long from this present day which brings another
Charles out of France, to make both himself and his own the better
known. Forth he comes unarmed save only with the lance which
Judas tilted, and he so couches it that he bursts the paunch of Florence.

(70–5)

Having suffered bitter consequences himself, Dante was only too grimly
aware that Charles had given free rein to his own cupidity in abetting the
Black leader, Corso Donati, in pillaging and plundering the property of
White Guelphs in 1301.

Most important, avarice also appears as an absorbing sin which leads to
the *neglect of one's own flesh*. Hugh Capet laments:

> O avarizia, che puoi tu più farne,
>   poscia c'ha' il mio sangue a te sì tratto,
>   *che non si cura de la propria carne?*

O Avarice, what more can you do to us, since you have so drawn my
blood to yourself that it has no care for its own flesh?

(82–4)

Bearing in mind the historical facts and the significance of the major images
of the episode, we must reread Piero's protestation of innocence in a different light: that he was not guilty of sheer treachery seems borne out both
inside and outside the Poem, and on both the literal and symbolic levels, for
Dante placed Piero not in the ninth circle of Hell among the traitors but in the
seventh among the violent. However, that the course of his sins led him by
degrees to reflect the earthly end of Jesus' betrayer there can be no doubt, and
it is clear that Judas' other attributes taken collectively form the unifying
basis for the imagery of *Inferno* XIII and *Inferno* XIV, 1–3. The cantos portray
nothing of the near-wholesome greatness and magnanimity that romantic
and neo-romantic readers believe they see in him. Beneath the letter lurks the
Logothete's grasping avarice, a willingness to seize from the weak or
innocent, a readiness to sacrifice the poor and humble for cash. Dante, obviously aware of many of the varied tales told of della Vigna's misdeeds and
death, reflects in his poetry the murky, dubious nature of the Logothete's sins

in the ambiguity and conflict between the different levels of the text itself. What Piero's own protests deny, the symbolism and allegory pitilessly reveal as a negative exemplum: a greedy, violent, tyrannous character who kills himself in shame and despair after having persecuted the innocent and stolen from the common coffers. Dante's didactic subtlety is exquisite. His Piero is indeed a new Judas.

5 THE *GRAN VEGLIO*

Inferno xiv, with its profoundly complicated image of the 'Gran Veglio di Creta,' the Old Man of Crete, continues to puzzle its readers. We see at first only mystery.[1] Questions about the Poet's placement of the description of the statue, about the apparent lack of artistic or theoretical unity in the episode, and, above all, about the relation of the statue to the *contrapasso* have led Dantisti to treat the Veglio and the classical allusions, often rather lamely, as mere pedantic 'digressions,' or as examples of the Poet's alleged 'inconsistency of inspiration.'[2] Other problems are equally vexing. Why does Virgil point to the boiling 'fiumicello' and insist: 'Cosa non fu da li occhi tuoi scorta / notabile com'è'l presente rio / Nothing has been discerned by your eyes so notable as the present stream'? What is the significance of the statue's five parts?

This chapter and the next fill a critical void by demonstrating the thematic, dogmatic, and poetic unity formed by the various allusions and references of *Inferno* xiv. Only when we concentrate on the Veglio di Creta, not in isolation, but in its context in the Poem and in the cultural tradition of Christian euhemerism and typology will the meaning of the entire episode become clear.[3]

As most readers are aware, the major paradigmatic source, and, therefore, a major component of the meaning of Dante's statue, is to be found in commentaries on the dream of Nebuchadnezzar in the Book of Daniel, chapter 2. In two important studies, Giovanni Busnelli contributed most to the interpretation of this facet of the Cretan figure.[4] Examining Dante's description in the light of Richard of St Victor's *De eruditione hominis interioris* and Philip of Harveng's *De somnis Nabuchodonosor*,[5] Busnelli came to some impeccable conclusions. Following Flamini and Pascoli, he saw the fissure (*fessura*) as the 'wounding of nature' (*vulneratio naturae*), the fourfold wound left by the Fall, and he saw that the Veglio represented mankind: 'It is nothing but the "vetus homo," the "old man" which is counterposed to the "new man" regenerated through Christ, since the "vetus homo" represents the old life led in sin.'[6] Busnelli's interpretations are quite convincing for those parts of the episode which he claims to explain. Although we will have much occasion to cite his studies, the eminent Jesuit critic, as he himself admitted, did not grasp the unifying ideology behind Dante's plan, and he continued to insist that the Veglio was something apart and tangential having 'the appearance of being a filler, of mysterious excess, but too obscure and buried for it to shine with that most beautiful poetic light which bathes the other parts of Dante's design.'[7] In spite of Busnelli's careful scholarship, there still remain those problems of interpretation which we listed at the outset of the chapter.

Realizing that a major problem with previous critical views was the failure to address the fact that Nebuchadnezzar's dream statue neither bled nor wept,[8] Theodore Silverstein attempted to trace the origin of the 'weeping statue' through classical sources, particularly Ovid's *Metamorphoses*, and through the Christian image of the bleeding Redeemer on the Cross.[9] He compared the blood and tears dripping from the statue to the iconographic tradition of the stream which flows down the Cross for the redemption of Adam whose skull is buried below. The four rivers of Paradise which flow from the Crucified are inversely reflected in the infernal streams springing from the Veglio's fissures. Though Silverstein, like Busnelli, showed no connection between the Veglio and the concept of blasphemy and thus failed to recognize the artistic integrity of the episode, his essay went far in enriching an understanding of the statue's symbolic ramifications.

The extent to which an inverted Christian baptismal language and typology fuses Dante's imagery in the episode seems not to have been noted before.[10] The parallel image of the rivers flowing from the side of Christ, observed by Silverstein, possesses a multiplicity of meanings far richer and discussed far earlier in the history of Christian theology than he indicated. Contrary to Silverstein's contention, it was not merely St Bernard's circle of friends in the twelfth century who elaborated the concept of Christ's tears forming the Rivers of Paradise but even writers from paleo-Christian times.[11] In John 7:37–9, the Redeemer cries out: 'He that believeth in me, as the Scripture saith: *Out of his belly shall flow rivers of living water [flumina de ventre eius]*. Now this he said of the Spirit which they should receive that believe in him.' The passage had enormous influence on Christian doctrine, liturgy, and iconography from the beginning.[12] As Hugo Rahner has demonstrated, the phrase 'flumina de ventre eius,' often cited as 'flumina de ventre Christi,' was made to refer to the wound inflicted in Christ's side after his death and was thus interpreted as predicting the spread of the Gospels and the sacrament of baptism.[13] Early in the tradition, Hippolytus in his *Commentary on Daniel*, I, 17 made Christ's body the fountainhead of the Gospels. From him 'In this garden [Eden] a stream of everlasting water flows and four streams divide from it flowing over the whole earth as is seen of the Church: Christ who is the stream is proclaimed throughout the world through the fourfold Gospels, and flowing over the whole earth He sanctifies whomsoever believes on Him as the words of the Prophet [that is, the Apostle, John 7:38] says: "Flumina de ventre eius." '[14] According to dogma, Ecclesia is, in fact, the spiritual body of Christ and therefore the source from which the water of the Spirit comes to all believers through baptism. In this sacrament the issue from Christ's wound forms a stream divided among the mass of sinners, the *massa peccatrix*.[15] The Veglio and the rivers can be understood darkly as the earthly and infernal, figural, perversion of these truths. Other aspects bear this out.

The Veglio, the literal source of a river flowing through a desert, temporally and materially inverts the spiritual metaphors used of Christ. The Redeemer is also the source of a stream as he comforts his Church in Isaias 43:19–20. Here the Rock of Horeb struck by Moses prefigures the Saviour: 'Behold I do new things: and now they shall spring forth. Verily, you shall know them: I will make a way in the wilderness and rivers in the desert. ... I have given waters in the wilderness, rivers in the desert, to give drink to my people, to my chosen.'[16] St Paul speaks of these events of Exodus 17 and John 7:38 in 1 Corinthians 10:1–5: 'And all in Moses were baptized in the cloud and in the sea. ... And all drank the same spiritual drink: (And they drank of the spiritual rock that followed them: and the rock was Christ).'[17] Christ as the Rock of Horeb thus became a favourite type for Christian exegesis. In only one among scores of examples that could be cited, St Ambrose in his *Explication of Psalm 45:12* explains the passage from the Psalm, 'The stream of the river maketh the city of God joyful,' as follows:

> Post passionem Domini quid aliud sequi debuit, nisi quia de corpore Domini flumen exivit, quando de latere eius aqua fluxit et sanguis, quo laetificavit (Ps. 45:5) animas universorum, quia illo flumine lavit peccatum totius mundi?

> What else ought to have followed the Lord's passion, but that a river came out of the body of the Lord when from his side there flowed water and blood, by which he made to rejoice the minds of all, since with that stream he washes away the sin of the whole world?[18]

Thus from the Veglio described in the canto of unbelief there flows a sinful river of blood and tears (compared to the Bulicame divided among 'peccatrici'), as from Christ there flows the source of the Water of Life, which washes away all the sins of the faithful.

The rain of fire extinguished by a river of blood also reverses a number of common baptismal traditions and typologies. First it inverts the tradition of the fire which descended on the Jordan at the baptism of Christ.[19] The fact that the river of blood quenches the fire above it ('sovra sé tutte fiammelle ammorta') one must see as a hellish parody of the doctrine of *epiclesis* in which the Holy Spirit descends to the baptismal waters and combines with them to bestow life-giving efficacy.[20] Ironically in *Inferno* xiv, 89–90, 141–2, only above the stream is the divine fire purposefully *ineffective* in Hell. The fiery rain thus both fulfils and inverts the words of St John the Baptist, 'I indeed baptize you with water; but there shall come one mightier than I. ... He shall baptize you with the Holy Ghost and with fire' (Luke 3:16). Doctrinally, Divine Fire, as a figure of the Godhead in Christianity, is identical, whether seen in its punishing or purifying aspects. Here in Hell, Gehenna, which consumes the impious, figures the Spirit which can vivify the faithful.[21] Fire as punishment and vengeance, so often stressed in the canto, reflects inversely the dogmatic principle that baptism is a judgment over sin,[22] a concept best understood through the major prefigurations of that sacrament in the Old Testament. The red, boiling, 'presente rio' and its tributary in the Circle of Tyrants, already crossed dryshod by the Wayfarer astride a Centaur, reflect baptism as the antitype or fulfilment both of the crossing of the Red Sea and of the survival of the Flood.[23] The traditional exegesis of the Exodus interprets the drowning of the Pharaoh's cohorts as a prefiguration of the destruction of sin by baptism: Pharaoh's army figures Satan's minions annihilated in the waters of death.[24] That the exodus is the antitype of the flood and of baptism is, of course, biblical (1 Peter 3:18–21), and the Fathers of the Church used it often: Noah prefigures Christ, the first-born of a new creation: the Flood destroys a sinful world just as Christ's death and Resurrection spells the death of sin and the promise of eternal life.[25] The bloody river which punishes the tyrants in the second death of Hell (*Inferno* xii) performs literally and allegorically the same function as did the Flood in history, and the waters of baptism which destroy sin by washing away the wickedness of the Old Man (Romans 6:3–7) in the fulfilment of sacrament.[26] The river's effluent, the 'presente rio' of *Inferno* xiv, is 'notabile' because it is the negative counterpart of what, to Dante, was the *central fact* of Christian History: the Redeeming Blood of Christ.[27] The Poet, of course, presents these concepts not in their positive and regenerative aspect but in the perverse perspective of the nether world, of those in eternal punishment. The hellish river fulfils *in malo* what the rivers flowing from Christ's side fulfil *in bono*. The earthly Veglio and the rivers issuing from it represent sin not only in its aspect as inherited guilt (*culpa*), the concupiscence of original sin, but also in its aspect as punishment (*poena*).[28] The blood and tears dripping from the Veglio's *fessura* are the agents of God's anger upon the wrathful, the tyrants, the barrators,[29] and the traitors, just as in Nether Hell, fire wreaks torture upon the blasphemers, sodomites, usurers, simonists, thieves, and the counsellors of fraud. For the damned here there can be only a 'baptism by fire,' a judgment unto death: their resurrection can only be unto the second death on the Day of Wrath.

This eschatological meaning of the statue under Ida and the fiery Phlege-thon in the seventh circle of Hell appears also in their collective resemblance to the description in the Book of Daniel 7:9–22 of the *Vetustus* or *Antiquus dierum*, the Ancient of Days, that is of the apocalyptic vision of God the Father at Judgment. From both figures, that is, the Deity and Dante's colossus, there issues a fiery river: 'The Ancient of Days sat. ... A swift stream of fire issued forth from before him. ... The judgment sat and the books were opened' (Daniel 7:10). Carl-Martin Edsman has noted that, early in Christian-ity, the iconographic attributes were transferred from God the Father to Christ as Judge, in obedience to Daniel 7:13–15 and in a reconciliation with other biblical passages such as Apocalypse 5:5–8 and John 5:22: 'For nei-ther doth the Father judge any man: but hath given all judgment to the son.' The river of fire at the feet of Christ became a fixed iconographical element in descriptions and in artistic depictions of the Last Judgment. In the mosaics of Torcello, for example, the fiery stream flows down from the Judge, engulf-ing and torturing the damned below.[30]

As previously noted, Busnelli and other critics have realized that Dante based the Veglio on the Pauline version of the Adamic myth in which the Apostle contrasted the 'old man,' the *vetus homo*, with the 'new Man,' by counterposing the figure of Adam as the inverse of Christ, 'the second Adam.'[31] By expanding on their contention, we can further enrich our appreciation of Dante's poetic meaning.

The images of the *vetus homo* and Christ the *novus homo* appear in explications of the statue of Nebuchadnezzar's dream made by the Church Fathers. St Jerome interprets the stone in Daniel which smashes the figure, breaking the kingdoms of gold, silver, bronze, iron, and clay, as Christ. The Redeemer is the rock (Daniel 3:40) broken off the mountain by unseen hands, since he was born without coition, without human seed, from a virgin's womb. Christ is the great mountain which grows from that rock filling the world.[32] Rupert of Deutz follows Jerome: ' "Lapis abscissus de monte sine manibus" id est Christus sine virili complexu de Virgine natus, factus mons magnus, postquam percussit statuam regnorum mundi hujus / "The rock broken off from the mountain without hands," – that is Christ born from

the Virgin without manly embrace – has become a great mountain and afterwards struck the statue of the kingdoms of this world.'[33] Surely inspired by
such a harmony in the exegetical sources, Dante's Veglio must have a significance similar to that of the statue in Daniel. Plainly, it is implied that what
Nebuchadnezzar's prophetic dream foreshadowed *in aenigmate* will find its
fulfilment here on earth: at the Last Judgment Christ will come again as Judge
to break, figuratively, the Idaean-cum-Babylonian idol of earthly sin. The
typology of Christ as rock thus comes principally from two biblical passages
which became inextricably bound together in the doctrine of baptism,[34] the
sacrament which so dominates the imagery of *Inferno* xiv: in patristic interpretations, Christ is the rock which destroys the *vetus homo* in Nebuchadnezzar's dream, just as in baptismal typology the waters which flow from
Christ's side, that is, from the rock of Horeb, destroy the *vetus homo* in the
sacrament of initiation. The earthly statue, thus, *in malo* represents the
source of all sin, while in another way, it ironically reflects *in bono*, the
bleeding Redeemer, Christ dead and buried, the Godhead so violently rejected by the sinners punished here in Hell.

We can see that the Veglio buried under Ida reflects Christ and the *vetus
homo* even more closely when we examine the exegetical tradition on Nebuchadnezzar's dream as absorbed by Dante.[35] Richard of St Victor boldly
identifies the image in Daniel as an effigy of mankind: 'Quid est statua nisi
effigies umana / What is a statue but a human effigy?' And later: 'Quid
enim aliud est hujusmodi statua nisi umana figura, sive umana vita / What
else is a statue of this sort but the human figure or human life?'[36] The
Veglio represents the very cracked and ruined nature which the Redeemer
deigned to put on to work man's salvation. Though, according to doctrine,
Christ was not conceived in sin and did not contract the defects of man, he
nevertheless chose to assume man's infirmity.[37] St Bernard describes Christ's
experience of incarnation using metaphors close to Dante's conception:
'[Christ] has found many gaps in the walls of our human nature, ruinous and
full of fissures as they are, as He has had experiences in his own person
[during his sojourn on earth] of our infirmity and corruption.'[38] The *vetus
homo* is the material, bodily substance which clothed Christ and which,
through the Redeemer's condescension and death, the Christian puts off at
baptism.[39]

Inquiry into the baptismal and eschatological implications of the Veglio can
also explain the five materials which form it. Here again the Poet's inspiration derives from the biblical model in Daniel and on the patristic commentaries surrounding it. The statue, like its prototype, is formed of five different
materials which the Fathers, expanding on Daniel's own explanation to the
Babylonian King, interpreted as a series of empires preceding the coming of

Christ and the age of true Faith. St Jerome allies the materials to specific pagan realms: the golden head signifies the Babylonians; the silver, the Medes and Persians; the bronze, the Greeks and their successor Alexander of Macedon; the iron symbolizes the Romans.[40]

St Augustine divided the ages of man according to biblical periods, following Matthew 1. In the *City of God* XXII, 30, the Bishop of Hippo explains the ages of creation as follows. First the five ages of the *saeculum*:

> The first age, corresponding to the first day, is from Adam to the flood, the second, from then on till Abraham. These are equal, not in years but in the number of generations, for each is found to have ten. From this point, as the evangelist Matthew marks off the periods, three ages follow, reaching to the coming of Christ, each of which is completed in fourteen generations: one from Abraham to David, the second from then till the deportation to Babylon, the third from then until the birth of Christ in the flesh. *Thus there are five ages in all.*[41]

The sixth age, bound by the two Comings of Christ, incarnate as the Son of Man, and as Judge, has already begun in the present and is of indeterminate length: 'The sixth is now in progress, and is not to be measured by any fixed number of generations, for the Scripture says: "It is not for you to know the times which the Father has fixed by his own power" [Acts 1:7].'[42] In the seventh age, at last, after judgment, God will rest and will cause us also to rest in himself.[43] It was natural that the five ages of the *saeculum* – of the world, of the worldly – as opposed to the sixth and seventh spiritual ages should eventually be used in the exegesis of the five materials of the statue in Daniel. Philip of Harveng joins the interpretations of St Jerome and St Augustine. First he gives a long disquisition on the parts of the figure in which he identifies the five materials as the Augustinian first five ages; then he elaborates on Jerome's exegesis while recounting the statue's end in the sixth age: 'Therefore in the sixth age a stone was cut away from the mountain without hands, that is, Christ was born of the Virgin Mary without the touch of man, Christ, who smote the statue and smashed it, that is, he showed how vile and contemptible is the glory of this age.' The rock strikes the feet of clay and iron, toppling the colossus: 'Thus it is well said that the stone smote the statue in its feet of iron and clay since Christ, who is the corner-stone, by the preaching of spiritual poverty brought to nought the vile and filthy glory of this age and destroyed it. After these things truly the stone grew into a large mountain, and filled the whole earth, it was made known to all throughout the whole world that Christ is God.'[44] Dante's sources from the exegeses on the Book of Daniel demonstrate the multiform, polysemous

meanings which the statue had long before the Poet used it for his own
mysterious and complex image in the *Commedia*. The Veglio represents not
only *original* sin in Adam but the sins of the *saeculum*, the pride and
vainglory of the *present* world.

After St Augustine, it became traditional to unite the events of the sixth
day of Creation, the sixth day of the Passion, and the sixth age of man to the
sacrament of baptism. Doctrine held axiomatically that the sixth age
brought Christ's Incarnation just as the sixth day of Holy Week brought
his Crucifixion, death, and burial. As God created Adam and Eve on the sixth
day of Creation, so in the sixth age he caused to form Ecclesia from the
wound of the dying Saviour: 'On the sixth day man is formed after the image
of God, in the sixth period of the world there is a clear discovery of our
transformation in the renewing of our mind ... as a wife was made for
Adam from his side while he slept, Ecclesia becomes the property of her
dying Saviour by the sacrament of the blood which flowed from His side after
His death.'[45] Six, the perfect number (absent in the Veglio), was thus the
number of the first Creation and the New, and, most important, *the number
of Baptism*.[46] In his *Sermon* 259 delivered at Eastertime, Augustine joins these
notions even more clearly: 'The sixth day, therefore, begins with the coming of the Lord, and we are living in that sixth day. Hence, just as in Genesis
(1:27) [we read that] man was fashioned in the image of God on the sixth day,
so in our time, as if on the sixth day of the entire era, we are born again in
baptism so that we may receive the image of our Creator.'[47] The tradition
continued through the centuries. Hugh of St Victor echoes the union of
these hexaemeric concepts in his chapter on baptism in the *De Sacramentis*:
the beginning of original sin in Eden and the washing away of original sin
in baptism are types one of the other, each taking place at the occurrence of the
number six: 'Finally in the sixth age, Christ was born of a Virgin, just as on
the sixth day the first man [Adam] was moulded from virgin earth. He Himself, therefore, as if to consummate all things, when He had come to the age
of manhood, in the thirtieth year of His age was baptized by John, not of
necessity but by dispensation, that He might sanctify the laver for those
who are to be cleansed.'[48] In the sixth age, the age of redemption, and
re-creation through baptism, the outward man perishes and the body of sin in
the present life is destroyed and buried.[49]

Elsewhere, in his *Enarratio in Psalmum* VI, 2, St Augustine allies his first
four ages to the body, and particularly to the *vetus homo*: 'Now it is clear
that the number four has a relation to the body. ... *These numbers then of the
body ... have relation to the old man and the Old Testament*.'[50] The Veglio,
as critics agree, a *vetus homo*, is cleft precisely in the four lower materials of
its body; the golden head, intact, clearly symbolized the Age of Gold, the age

of original justice and innocence which once held sway upon the earth in the northern hemisphere where the figure is located. The statue described in *Inferno* xiv, thus, through its allusive imagery and its numerology (the four-part body as *vetus homo*; its imperfect, secular five pointing towards the perfection of a six, as in the dream in Daniel), heralds not only the destruction of the impious eschatologically, but also figures, historically and anagogically, Christ's regeneration and judgment of man through his two Comings.

These concepts can help further to explain the Veglio's continuing significance for the present age and how the statue endures as the source of Hell's rivers. Though the prophets had predicted that God would, at the end of time, 'create a new heaven and a new earth,' and Isaias 51:9 had announced a new Flood at time's end, Christianity, in 2 Peter 3:3–10, saw this Flood and this re-Creation as fulfilled not in the future but in the *present* through the initiation of the individual Christian.[51] That is, Christ and the catechumen's acceptance of him in baptism were the 'last times' predicted.[52] The primal waters of the first creation were analogous to and a prefiguration of the waters of the sacrament of the Faith. As Tertullian, the earliest writer on the subject, reasoned: 'Water was the first to produce that which had life, that it might be no wonder in baptism if waters know how to give life.'[53] According to doctrine, the sacrament of baptism precludes the last Judgment, for those prepared by the water, by the faith, and by the wood of the Cross, and who repent of their sins shall escape the Judgment of God to come.[54] Augustine's fifth age actually exists in the ungodly, and the sixth in the godly contemporaneously, just as the two cities, that of the earth and that of God, exist together in temporality, only later to be divided. All men spring from condemned stock[55] and, like Adam, are only cured of original sin and made sound and spiritual by rebirth in Christ. The blessed alone, though born citizens of this world, of the *saeculum*, of the fifth age, become alien to it by finding their true home in the City of God. Passage from the fifth to the sixth age comes about not by the renewal or regeneration of *all* mankind (John 3:5) but by the *individual's* own personal passage from wickedness to goodness.[56] Thus, the sixth age, though it has begun for some, is still emerging, for the new creation is inaugurated through the believer's emergence from the baptismal font.[57] Though the Veglio represents *in malo* the 'body of sin,' still *in bono* it inversely reflects by its burial 'sotto una montagna' (103) the 'burial' of baptism in imitation of Christ (Romans 6:3–12).[58] In short, the fire, the bloody river, the entombed bleeding figure, all point to the same sacramental truth. In this canto of violent rejection of worship and belief, the poetry, satisfyingly, ironically, and fittingly, reflects the typologies and numerologies of initiation into the Faith.

6 THE IDOLATERS

While the importance of the underlying baptismal imagery has been established, other fundamentally important questions in *Inferno* xiv still remain to be answered. We may now ask again why the Cretan statue is described specifically in the canto of the 'blasphemers.' What sense and unity do the classical images hold? Why are the sodomites punished on the same plain? And, finally, perhaps, what relation does blasphemy bear to baptism? The answers lie both in the particular form of blasphemy punished here, and in the medieval interpretations of the classical *loci* alluded to in the canto.

To state that Dante's Veglio is based on a *contaminatio* of biblical and classical sources is a critical commonplace. Scholars have long identified Dante's manifold inspiration for the various metallic and ceramic sections of the statue. Besides the Book of Daniel, they have compared the episode to many passages in pagan authors: Virgil's *Aeneid* III, 104–5, VII, 324–5, and VIII, 326; his *Bucolics* IV, 6; Juvenal's *Satire* VI, 1–2, and XIII, 28–30; and Ovid's *Metamorphoses* I, 89ff.[1] Dante probably accepted the testimony of Pliny in the *Natural History* XVI, 73, as cited in St Augustine, that a gigantic body sixty-nine feet in height had been found erect on Crete, exposed from its burial place by an earthquake.[2]

Critics discussing the Veglio, however, have neglected medieval commentaries on the classical sources and allusions of the canto and have thus missed much of the Poet's meaning. Let us first turn to the tradition of the weeping statue, for we remember that tears and blood play no part in the Old-Testament story of Nebuchadnezzar's dream. Silverstein, for example, noted the inspiration of the weeping statue of Niobe,[3] but he did not consult the medieval mythographers on Ovid's weeping statue and thus did not realize how closely their interpretations coincided with the main themes of Dante's episode.

Even Ovid's original tale of Niobe has much in common with the tale of

Nebuchadnezzar and, consequently, with *Inferno* XIV. Niobe and Nebuchadnezzar, both proud monarchs, blasphemously deny their deity due worship, and idolatrously divert the devotion of their subjects to themselves.[4]
Nebuchadnezzar, forgetful of his dream of the five-part colossus, unmindful of
his advancement of Daniel and his own recognition of Jahweh's power
(Daniel 2:47, cited in the *Epistola* to Can Grande, para. 28), turns to idolatry
by setting up a golden statue of himself for adoration on the Plain of Dura,
near where the tower of Babel had been erected.[5] St Jerome in his *Commentariorum in Danielem Liber* III, cap. 1, observes:

> 'King Nebuchadnezzar made a gold statue sixty cubits in height, six
> cubits in width.' Swift is the forgetfulness of truth, so that he who a
> little while ago worshipped the servant of God just as he had worshipped
> God, now orders a statue to be made for himself, *so that he himself
> might be worshipped in the statue.*[6]

As we will have occasion to note later, Rupert of Deutz states flatly 'Nimirum
haec est idololatria bruta / Without doubt this is brutish idolatry.'[7]

Niobe, who invidiously compares herself and her fourteen offspring to
Latona and to the goddess's two children, Apollo and Diana, cheats Latona
of due worship and commands her subjects to worship herself. Even in Ovid's
original tale, Niobe is the embodiment of *superbia*. She cries,

> quaerite nunc, habeat quam nostra superbia causam.

> Ask now what cause I have for pride.
> > > > > > > > > > > > > > (*Metamorphoses* VI, 184)[8]

Latona and her divine children wreak a ghastly revenge upon the stupid
queen; they slaughter all of Niobe's offspring; she herself, though turned to
stone, continues to weep forever:

> et lacrimas etiam nunc marmora manant.

> And even to this day tears trickle from the marble.
> > > > > > > > > > > > > > (*Metamorphoses* VI, 312)[9]

Like Nebuchadnezzar in the Church Fathers, Niobe is interpreted unani-
mously in Ovid's medieval commentators as a figure of pride and idolatry;
Dante himself uses her as such in *Purgatorio* XII, 37–9. Arnulphus of Orleans,
who in all likelihood was known to Dante, interprets Niobe's children as parts

of a human body through which the sins deriving from pride may be
expressed. Latona, insulted by Niobe, Arnulphus continues, is religion;
Latona's two children are Apollo and Diana, wisdom and chastity respectively,
through whom Niobe, the errant, blaspheming Christian, is brought back
to religious devotion.[10]

Later moralizations merely echo this interpretation: Dante's contemporary,
the allegorizer of the *Ovide moralisé*, gives the following account, making
Niobe a blasphemer:

> ... ses orguelz la mist a honte.
>   Elle avoit sept filles par conte
>   Et sept filz, dont tant se prisoit
>   *Que lies damediex despisoit,*
>   Si l'en avint perte e damage
>   A lui et a tout son lignage.

> ...her pride brought shame upon her. She had seven daughters by count
> and seven sons, about whom she piqued herself so that she despised
> the gods; thus from this there occurred loss and harm to her and all
> her lineage.
>
> (vi, 1003–8)[11]

Later he explains her away as worldly pride: 'Nyobe c'est l'orgueil dou
monde' (1388). Chastity and wisdom punish and convert Niobe by killing her
offspring; her metamorphosis into a statue signifies both humility and her
devotion to the contemplative life. Then, 'autrement,' from an allegory of
pride, the moralizer twists the tale into an allegory of cupidity or greed
(1442–54),[12] for, especially, 'the covetous person hates religion': 'Convoiteus
het religion' (1476).

Later than Dante, but important for the tradition which he inherited, Bersuire (d. 1362), in his *Ovidius moralizatus*, allegorizes Niobe as the new
convert who falls into sin by waxing proud over the Gifts of the Holy Spirit
and attributes to herself that which was attributable to God alone. Apollo,
Christ, the Sun of Justice, and Diana, the blessed Virgin, take away the Gifts
and leave her 'to her own power.' Niobe's transformation into marble
readily lends itself to an allegorization of the religious progress of the individual and of mankind in general. Bersuire makes the tale parallel to the
Christian history of mankind: the story of the Fall and its effects, after which
God abstracted himself from the world and left man to his own devices,
homo sibi relictus: Niobe thus holds the same significance as Dante's Veglio:
sinful humanity abandoned by God:

[Christ and Diana] *themselves take away their gifts and power and leave her to her own devices,* and then she becomes a stone, that is, hard and insensible and undevout. Such are they, then, who do not attribute their own virtues to God. By the just judgment of God they are permitted to sin and they deserve to lose their righteous fruitfulness and to rush into the weeping of desperation. [13]

In Christian dogma, blasphemy derives from pride and reflects the original sin of Adam and Eve who desired to be 'sicut dii.' [14] Contrary to the traditional critical view of the *Commedia*, we are here, in *Inferno* xiv, surely dealing with something more than simple blasphemy. *All* souls at the Acheron 'bestemmiavano Dio e lor parenti, / l'umana spezie e'l luogo e'l tempo e'l seme / di lor semenza e di lor nascimenti / They blasphemed God, their parents, the human race, the place, the time, the seed of their begetting and of their birth' (*Inferno* iii, 103–5). The lustful in *Inferno* v, 36, 'bestemmian quivi la virtù divina / Here they blaspheme the divine power.' *Inferno* xiv deals with sinners of a more specific kind – those who *prevent* the worship of God. In the words of St Thomas, '*Idolatry includes a grievous blasphemy* inasmuch as it deprives God of the singleness of His dominion and denies faith by deeds.' [15] Indeed, the idolatrous prevention of the veneration of the deity is the worst form of blasphemy; it is in fact, theologically, the 'perfection' of that sin: 'He that speaks against God, with the intention of reviling Him, disparages the Divine goodness, not only in respect of the falsehood in his intellect, but also by reason of the wickedness of his will, *whereby he detests and strives to hinder the honour due to God, and this is perfect blasphemy.*' [16] In his poetry Dante presents, bound together in one sin, Capaneus and the two figures who form the 'sunken' metaphors of the canto, Nebuchadnezzar and Niobe, in whom, indeed, the sin of blasphemy is theologically 'perfect.' [17]

Having found evidence of the intimate connection of the weeping statue with the main theme of the canto, I would like to turn to the other major images of *Inferno* xiv which have often been considered by critics as digressions, or mere 'struttura' or 'letteratura.' First, Alexander of Macedon:

> Quali Alessandro in quelle parti calde
> d'Indïa vide sopra'l süo stuolo
> fiamme cadere infino a terra salde,
>
> ...
>
> tale scendeva l'etternale ardore ...

As the flames which Alexander, in those hot regions of India, saw fall

upon his army, entire to the ground ... so did the eternal burning
descend there ...

(31–7)

The image of the fiery flakes derives from a misinterpretation in Albertus
Magnus' *De Meteoris* I, iv, 8.[18] Critics have not noticed, however, that the
reference to Alexander the Great in the very context of fire as punishment
for blasphemy is also fundamentally important for Dante's theme. As readers
of the *Commedia*, we must reasonably inquire into the cause why Alexander and his army should suffer the same punishment on earth as do the
blasphemers in Hell. Since Alexander's tribulations apply to the damned,
does it not follow that their sin (both *culpa* and *poena*, guilt and punishment),
justly apply to him? In fact, the Church Fathers made Alexander yet another
type of the arrogant idolater – merely the first among the Graeco-Romans to
learn and to use for his own advantage the truth about the origin of the
pagan gods, an ancient secret divulged to him by the Egyptian priest of
Ammon-Zeus.[19] In the version given in St Cyprian's influential treatise
Quod idola dii non sint, 3, of the latter part of the third century, the saint
scorns the pagan gods, stating, on the authority of Alexander's letter to his
mother Olympias, that they were simply kings who had been deified.[20] St
Augustine cites the same letter three times in the *City of God*, for example:

> We may regard Numa somewhat more charitably, since in this same
> class of writings belongs a letter of Alexander of Macedon to his mother
> reporting what a certain Egyptian high priest called Leo divulged to
> him. In it, apart from Picus, Faunus, Aeneas and Romulus, or, for that
> matter, Hercules, Aesculapius, Liber the son of Semele, the twin sons
> of Tyndareus and any other mortals who have been deified, even the
> gods of higher lineage, to whom Cicero in his *Tusculans* [I, 13, 29]
> seems to allude without mentioning their names, Jupiter, Juno, Saturn,
> Vulcan, Vesta and many others, whom Varro attempts to interpret
> figuratively as the parts or elements of the universe, are exposed as
> having been men.[21]

According to Strabo, Alexander, having marched to the Libyan oracle of the
Egyptian Ammon-Zeus in 332–1 BC, announced that he had been recognized
as a son of the deity. Historians agree that Alexander commanded the
Greek cities to worship him as a god after 324 BC,[22] thus earning for himself
the condemnation of the Stoics, Peripatetics, and consequently, of the early
Christian theologians. Alexander's cult continued far into Christian times. In
387 AD St John Chrysostomos complained of the blasphemy of those who,

ignoring Christ and the Cross, still wore the coins of Alexander as amulets:
'What would you say of those who use incantations and amulets and of
those who tie bronze coins of Alexander of Macedon around their heads and
feet? Tell me, are these the things in which we place our hopes? After our
Master died for us on the Cross, will we put hope for salvation in the image of
a Greek king?'[23] Plainly, even in his seemingly incidental reference to
Alexander, Dante is intentionally calling to his reader's mind the main theme
of perfect and idolatrous blasphemy.

Close attention to the inner meaning of the canto reveals that the reference
to Alexander restrospectively elucidates the earlier reference to Cato (based
on Lucan's *Pharsalia*):

> Lo spazzo era una rena e spessa,
> non d'altra foggia fatta che colei
> che fu da' piè di Caton già soppressa.

> The ground was a dry, deep sand, not different in its fashion from that
> which once was trodden by the feet of Cato.

> (13–15)

In Dante's verses Alexander's men (the same Alexander who visited the shrine
of the ram-headed Jove-Ammon in Libya) tread out the flakes of fire on the
sands of India as Cato treads the sands of the Libyan desert, *also on his way to
visit the same Libyan shrine of 'Jovis cornigerus'* (*Pharsalia* IX, 545).[24] In
Lucan's epic, after the arduous journey, Cato and his men arrive at the humble
temple of Zeus (IX, 511–20); the hero's companions urge him to make trial
of the oracle (IX, 546–50), but, unlike Alexander who consulted the shrine
only to use the knowledge to deify himself, Cato affirms God's omnipresence, rails against sacrilege, and piously refuses divination and the testing or
tempting of the Deity in verses which Dante cites in the *Epistola* to Can
Grande (para. 22) and which most probably inspired the poet to place Cato in
Purgatorio (*Pharsalia* IX, 564–86; compare Deuteronomy 6:10 and 2 Paralipomenon 20:12).[25] Dante's artistic intent now becomes clear. The Poet will
again unite Cato and idolatry in a later episode in which he describes the
great leader precisely as a 'veglio' (*Purgatorio* I, 31–3):

> vidi presso di me un veglio solo,
> degno di tanta reverenza in vista,
> che più non dee a padre alcun figliuolo.

> I saw close to me an old man alone, worthy in his looks of so great
> reverence that no son owes more to his father.

Cato appears again as the 'veglio onesto' in *Purgatorio* II, 116–23 to chide the souls and the Wayfarer who stand idolatrously intent upon Casella's song:[26]

> Noi eravam tutti fissi e attenti
>   a le sue note; ed ecco, il veglio onesto
>   gridando: 'Che è ciò, spiriti lenti?
> qual negligenza, quale stare è questo?'

> We were all rapt and attentive to his notes, when, lo, the venerable old man, crying, 'What is this you laggard spirits? What negligence, what delay is this?'

As critics have noted, Cato's admonishment must be interpreted as a warning against the idolatrous resting in earthly things. The repetition of the term *veglio* shows that *Purgatorio* II, a repetition of Cato's abhorrence of blasphemy, must serve as a gloss on *Inferno* XIV.[27]

I would now like to return to the first major division of *Inferno* XIV, to the description of the rain of fire and its justness as a punishment upon the idolaters and blasphemers, particularly Capaneus, and to its pertinence to other classes of sinners upon the burning *landa*. Several passages of the canto challenge the reader to contemplate the *contrapasso*, the sufficient reason of God's vengeance:

> Indi venimmo al fine ove si parte
>   lo secondo giron dal terzo, e dove
>   *si vede di giustizia orribil arte.*

> Thence we came to the confine, where the second ring is divided from the third and where *a horrible mode of justice is seen.*
>
> (4–6)

> O *vendetta di Dio,* quanto tu dei
>   esser temuta de ciascun che legge
>   ciò che fu manifesto alli occhi miei!

> O *vengeance of God,* how much should you be feared by all who read what was revealed to my eyes!
>
> (16–18)[28]

Christian writings traditionally linked fire, baptism, and idolatry. Fire often appears in Apocryphal texts as a punishment for that sin. In the Apocalypse of Peter, for example, the angel 'Ezrael' prepares a place of 'much fire' to

melt idols of gold and silver and to chastise those who made them. That the
Last Judgment is to be a *baptism of fire* is recorded in the *Sibylline Oracles*; at
the last, Elias will descend to earth 'and then shall a great river of flaming
fire flow from heaven and consume all places ... the ungodly shall perish
therein ... and all that were ... sorely insolent, lawless, idolaters: and all
that forsook the great immortal God and became blasphemers and harmers of
the godly. ...'[29] Most particularly, early Church writers found a prefiguration of the sacrament of baptism in the Old Testament sacrifice of Elijah
(Elias), by which the Jewish people were delivered from the *idolatrous* cult
of Baal: 'Then *the fire of the Lord fell,* and consumed the holocaust and the
wood, and the stones and the dust and licked up the water' (3 [1] Kings 18:38).
In a text perhaps unknown to Dante, but part of the vast tradition, St Gregory
of Nyssa glosses the verses as a heralding of baptism and explains the mystical
functions of fire and water as both purifying and destructive agents: 'By that
wondrous sacrifice, Elias clearly proclaimed to us the sacramental rite of baptism that should afterwards be instituted. For the fire was kindled by water
thrice poured upon it, so that it is clearly shown that *where the mystic water
is, there is the kindling, warm and fiery Spirit, that burns up the ungodly*, and
illuminates the faithful.'[30] A further element of Dante's inspiration for the
fiery punishment of the blasphemers may have come also from St Thomas
Aquinas' disquisition on 'Whether the Damned Blaspheme,' where the saint
states that fire is the fitting punishment for the sin: ' "The men were scorched
with great heat, and they blasphemed the name of God, who hath power over
these plagues" and the gloss on these words says that they who are deservedly
punished, will nevertheless complain that God is so powerful as to torture
them thus. Now this would be blasphemy in their present state: and consequently it will also be in their future state.'[31]

A major part of the punishment of Hell, especially in evidence here,
consists in the pertinacity of the sin itself. Theologically, all the damned will
retain the iniquity of the will which turned them away from God's justice.
Perfect blasphemy in particular, however, is a sin never forgiven. According to
Matthew 12:32: 'He that shall speak against the Holy Ghost, it shall not be
forgiven him neither in this world, nor in the world to come.' On this point, St
Thomas cites St Augustine's *De Sermone in Monte* 1–22: 'So great is the
downfall of this sin that it cannot submit to the humiliation of asking for
pardon.'[32] Dante applies this theological doctrine directly to Capaneus
himself:

> 'O Capaneo, in ciò che non s'ammorza
> la tua superbia, se' tu più punito;

nullo martiro, fuor che la tua rabbia,
sarebbe al tuo furor dolor compito.'

'O Capaneus! in that your pride remains unquenched you are punished the more: no torment save your own raging would be paid to
match your fury.'

(63–6)

The punishment in the *Inferno* is thus self-inflicted through pride.

In addition, the aptness of the blasphemous Capaneus' position *prone*
upon the burning sand beneath the falling flames strikes us all the more when
we recall the classical *locus* in the *Thebaid* XI, 1–17 where, after being
struck by Jove's thunderbolt, Capaneus lies dead upon the plain 'which gasps
with the heavenly sulphur' (16–18) before Thebes:

sic gravat iniectus terras hostiliaque urit
arva et anhelantem caelesti sulpure campum.

So burdens he the earth, flung prostrate, and scars the hostile fields and
the plain that gasps with the heavenly sulphur.[33]

In Dante's Poem it is as the giant was in *death*, that he is in *second death*. The
Poet's erudite sarcasm is here most biting as he inversely mocks Capaneus'
words, 'Qual fui *vivo*, tal son *morto*' (51). The giant's posturing is a lie, as
readers familiar with Statius' epic will perceive. In the various texts which
offered *figurae* for the *contrapasso*, the Poet obviously enjoyed the remarkable
consonance of pagan history and Judeo-Christian theological sources.

Reading further into the next canto, *Inferno* XV, there can be little doubt
of the 'punishment's fitting the crime': the rain of fire upon the sodomites
most manifestly fulfils in Hell the rain of fire upon the Cities of the Plain
(Genesis 19). But why should they suffer the same punishment as that afflict-
ing the idolaters? The joining is also biblical. In Romans 1:23–7, St Paul
himself links the sin of idolatry to sodomy, and makes the latter the divine
punishment of the former: '*And they changed the glory of the incorrupti-
ble God into the likeness of the image of a corruptible man* and of birds, and of
fourfooted beasts and of creeping things. Wherefore, God gave them up to
the desires of their heart, unto uncleanness: to dishonour their own bodies
among themselves ... the men ... leaving the natural use of the women,
have burned in their lusts, one towards another.'[34] In a gloss on the passage in
the *Summa Theologica*, St Thomas Aquinas deals with the appropriateness
of linking the two sins: 'The sin against nature is less grievous than the sin of
idolatry. But since it is more manifest, it is assigned as a fitting punishment

of the sin of idolatry in order that, as by idolatry man abuses the order of divine honour, so by the sin against nature he may suffer confusion from the abuse of his own nature.'[35]

Taking idolatry as the key to the episode, we can also begin to understand some of the allegorical reasons for the 'geographical' location of the statue of sinful humanity. The Veglio's feet stand planted in Crete, the island identified by the pseudo-Bernardus Silvestris in his commentary on the *Aeneid* as 'the flesh': 'Per Cretam enim intelligimus naturam corpoream.'[36] In this medieval interpretation, familiar to Dante, Aeneas is an allegory of the soul of man which seeks its good mistakenly in 'Creta'; that is, in the 'clay' of the corporeal. Thus, in Dante's time, Crete symbolized the 'flesh' in the Poets just as the 'vetus homo' symbolized the 'flesh' in the Bible and in the Church Fathers.[37] Dante thus aptly transfers the biblical image of man's earthly nature to a pagan setting which in itself symbolizes man's tendency to fall into the idolatry of resting in earthly things.

There are still further ramifications to the association of this Mediterranean island with the theme of idolatry. Virgil first introduces the Veglio to the Wayfarer's notice by drawing his attention to the river of boiling blood (88–9). He then proceeds, somewhat bewilderingly, with the tale of Jove's birth on Crete in the Golden Age. The pagan terrestrial paradise is now a wasteland, a thing 'outworn':

> 'In mezzo mar siede un paese guasto,'
> diss'elli allora, 'che s'appella Creta,
> sotto 'l cui rege fu già 'l mondo casto.
> Una montagna v'è che già fu lieta
> d'acqua e di fronde, che si chiamò Ida;
> or è diserta come cosa vieta.
> Rëa la scelse già per cuna fida
> del suo figliuolo, e per celarlo meglio,
> quando piangea, ve facea far le grida.

> 'In the middle of the sea there lies a wasted country,' he then said, 'which is named Crete, under whose king the world once was chaste. A mountain is there, called Ida, which once was glad with waters and with foliage; now it is deserted like a thing outworn. Rhea chose it of old for the faithful cradle of her son and, the better to conceal him when he cried, made them raise shouts there.'   (94–102)

Without break or transition, in the next verse Virgil launches into the description of a buried statue which stands beneath the mountain:

> Dentro dal monte sta dritto un gran veglio
>
> Within the mountain stands a huge Old Man
>
> (103)

The lines which had dealt with the birth and childhood of Zeus now deal with a death and burial. Dantisti have so far not realized that these two tales are actually *one*. Verses 94–120 recount together a legend which is the foundation of the Poet's meaning here: that is, the tradition surrounding the life and death of Zeus Cretagenes, or Jove born on Crete.

Let us first turn to the classical legend as it occurs *outside* of the Poem, and then examine how Dante learned of it. Mount Ida was renowned in the ancient world as being sacred to the worship of Jove. Not only was Jupiter born on Crete and raised on Mount Ida but, as the Cretans claimed, he was *buried* there as well.[38] In this claim, as we will see, rests much of the meaning of Dante's statue under Ida. On Crete the Olympian majesty venerated in other parts of the Graeco-Roman world was fused with a local fertility deity.[39] Each year this native Zeus was eaten ritually as a live bull and each year he rose again from the dead in a cave.[40] Among the many extant accounts about the birth-cave of Zeus on Mount Ida and the legends surrounding the deity, one of the oddest (and surely unknown to Dante) is that of Antoninus Liberalis, who cites Boios' *Ornithogony*:

> They say that in Crete there is a cave. ... Tradition has it that in this cave Rhea gave birth to Zeus, and neither god nor man may enter it. Every year at a definite time there is seen a great glare of fire from the cavern. This happens, so the story goes, when the blood from the birth of Zeus boils out.[41]

Callimachus' tale in his Homeric *Hymn* I, in praise of Jove, includes the creation of several rivers in which Jove's mother, Rhea, cleanses herself after her delivery labours. She 'loosens her girdle' and addresses the Earth; and, exhorting the orb to give birth in turn, the goddess strikes a mountain with her staff in the manner of the biblical tale of Moses, and the torrents flow forth (30–3). In this version, the nymphs, Styx, Neda, and Philyra, after whom the rivers so created are named, care for the child-god; the Kouretes meanwhile make a din to drown out the baby's cries (51–3).

The Cretans' pretensions about a Jove who died and was buried were scandalous and abhorrent to the pagan world. A modern classical historian who had Dante far from his thoughts puts it thus: 'That Zeus should have been born in Crete was not thought to be an impiety, but that he should have been dead and buried, that was blasphemy, blasphemy of the first water.'[42]

In a lost text, Epimenides, a Cretan himself, supposedly anathematized the legend and coined the saying that 'the Cretans always lied,' thus beginning a proverb repeated in countless texts. The saying also appears in Callimachus' *Hymn* I, cited above.

> O Zeus, some say that thou wert born on the hills of Ida; others O Zeus, say in Arcadia; did these or those, O Father, lie? 'Cretans are ever liars.' Yea a tomb, O Lord, for thee the Cretans builded but thou didst not die, for thou art forever.[43]

The reader will be immediately aware that some form of this legend is the mysterious source for the birth and burial of Jove in *Inferno* XIV and perhaps also for many other aspects of Dante's canto as well. Such tantalizing parallels and eerie similarities may be specious, however, and it still remains to be seen how and in what form Dante came to know and interpret the tale.[44]

For this we may first turn to the Bible itself. The 'scandal' to the Greeks is referred to in St Paul's Epistle to Titus, the Bishop of Crete, in which the Apostle urges the Bishop to chastise and improve his flock: 'One of them a prophet of their own, said: "The Cretians are always liars, evil beasts, slothful bellies"' (Titus 1:12). Through St Paul the curious legend of Zeus Cretagenes came to the attention of Church writers as well. Dante probably knew several commentaries on the biblical passage, among them that of St Jerome:

> There are those who think this verse was taken from Callimachus the Cyrenaean poet, and in one respect they are not wrong. For if he himself, accustomed to write in praise of Jove against the Cretans, who boast that they display his tomb, said: 'Cretans are always liars; it is they who have impiously fabricated his tomb.' However, as we said above, the verse was taken entire by the Apostle from Epimenides the poet; and it is his exordium that Callimachus used in his own poem. Or if it is a vulgar proverb, by which the Cretans were called liars, he brought it back into his verse without stealing from another's work. Some think the Apostle ought to be blamed because he erred imprudently and, while he accused the false doctors, he approved this little verse at the same time, on account of which the *Cretans were called liars because they constructed an empty tomb of Jupiter*. For if, they say, Epimenides or Callimachus for this reason blamed the Cretans as liars and evil beasts and lazy bellies since they do not know divine things and *they portray Jove, who reigns in heaven, as buried on their island*, and the saying of the Apostle proves that which they say to be true, it follows that Jove is not dead but alive.[45]

Fittingly, in the *Commedia* the burial of Jove, which even the pagans themselves had considered blasphemy and sacrilege, appears in the circle of perfect blasphemy as the source of all the rivers of Hell!

John Chrysostomos (347–407) also commented on the lines in his *Homily II on Titus* (1:12–14), but this saint perspicaciously turned the mystery of Zeus' death and resurrection to excellent account, emphasizing and diverting to pious Christian use the striking similarities of Zeus Cretagenes with the life of Jesus:

> It was Epimenides who said this, himself a Cretan, and whence he was moved to say it, it is necessary to mention. It is this. The Cretans have a tomb of Jupiter, with this inscription: 'Here lieth Zan, whom they call Jove.' On account of this inscription, then, the poet ridiculing the Cretans as liars, as he proceeds, introduces, to increase the ridicule, this passage:
>
> > For even a tomb, O King, of thee
> > They made, who never diest, but aye shalt be.
>
> If then this testimony is true, observe what a difficulty! ... How shall we solve this? ... *How then does Paul wrest what is said of Jupiter to the God of the universe? He has not transferred to God what belongs to Jupiter. But what is applicable to God, and was neither justly nor properly applied to Jupiter, this he restores to God*, since the name of God belongs to Him alone, and is not lawfully bestowed on idols.[46]

The passage from St Paul's Epistle was thus traditionally interpreted as saying that the Apostle had meant to refer to the blasphemous lie about the birth and death of Zeus, and that he had transferred the unjust ascription of resurrection from the pagan god to Christ. This very transference of the legend from Jove to the True God in the Church Fathers may have inspired Dante to equate the deities ironically in *Inferno* xiv. Specifically, it is *Jove* who is blasphemed by Capaneus and to whom Capaneus credits his eternal punishment.[47]

Naturally the legend of Zeus Cretagenes provided grist for the mill of early Christian euhemerism. Most important for us is Lactantius' *Divine Institutes*, where the tale occurs with appropriate allusions to its pagan source, the *Sacred History* of Ennius (fragment 12), and to the Christian *Sibylline Oracles* (8:47, 48):

> When his age was completely spent in Crete, he exchanged this life, and passed to the gods. The Curetes, his sons, took care of him and hon-

oured him. His sepulchre is in Crete, in the town of Cnossos (Vesta is said to have founded this city) and on his sepulchre is inscribed in ancient Greek characters, ZAN KPONOY; in Latin, Jupiter son of Saturn. This indeed, the poets do not hand down, but the ancient chroniclers. And these things are so true that they are confirmed by the Sibylline verses ... Cicero, in *The Nature of the Gods*, after mentioning that 'three Jupiters' have been enumerated by theologians, says the third was the Cretan son of Saturn and that his tomb is shown on that island. How can he have a temple here and a sepulchre there?[48]

Lactantius interprets Jove not as a god, but merely as a proud, covetous blasphemer who (we may say, like Niobe, Alexander, and Nebuchadnezzar!) arrogated to himself the worship due to the True God. The Church writer exploits the traditions of Ovid and Juvenal in his argument: in the beginning came the Age of Gold during which God was worshipped; the world was just, fair, and pious under the governance of Cronos-Saturn.[49] Jove was the human ruler through whom sin and injustice came into the world, destroying the Golden Age of Saturn and the monotheism natural to man. Original justice and innocence were banished.[50] Human society broke down completely as various forces and factions fought among themselves for earthly glory; from the rupture of society, thus began the flow of human blood.[51] As Lactantius unified injustice and perfect blasphemy in his account of the loss of the Age of Gold, so Dante links the concept of injustice to perfect blasphemy in *Inferno* xiv (6, 16, 96). Zeus-Jove committed idolatry in preventing the worship of God and instituting the worship of himself:

> In this condition did that king constitute human life, who, after his sire had been defeated and put to flight, seized not a kingdom but an impious tyranny of force of armed men. He took away that golden and just age and forced men to become evil and wicked from this very fact, *that he turned them from God to adoring himself*, which terror of most overweening power had wrung out from them.[52]

Lactantius, in fact, attributed the change of the Golden Age to the age of injustice solely to the 'desertion of divine religion' and the world's conversion to idolatry. He thus performed the useful task of changing a lying legend into truthful history: the results of paganism and perfect blasphemy are one with the results of the Fall in Christianity, the loss of original justice and the coming of death. The buried statue beneath Ida points to the same meaning as do the other historical, classical allusions of *Inferno* xiv. In Dante's lines, the body of Jove buried on Crete is fused with the statue from the Book of Daniel: both tales are exempla of idolatry.

Having noted above that Dante's *statue* of idolatry stood in the *place* of the 'flesh' and idolatry, let us now turn briefly to the object of the Veglio's gaze, the mirror: 'Roma guarda come süo speglio' (105). The Neoplatonists commonly described the world of the senses with the image of the mirror. Plotinus compared matter to a glass which, though empty, reflected everything.[53] Thus, traditionally, the mirror took on a dual significance: one derogatory, in that the deceptive world of the senses was but a reflection of the forms, or ideas, above: the other, positive, in so far as the world of matter was an emanation of forms in the real world. In the Platonic traditions of Christian theology, the divine part of man is also the mirror of God, since God made man in his image. The soul must reject the lesser goods of the earth, turn within itself and thus, in the words of Gregory of Nyssa, 'look towards the archetype because of its own beauty as if looking into a mirror and image.'[54] Only by thus becoming pure can the soul cleanse itself of rust, offering, in Gregory of Nyssa's metaphors, a mirror of the purity of God.[55] Western Christian writers naturally reinterpreted the metaphor: *in bono* the 'speculum' represents the faith, the invisible things of God which man sees 'per speculum et in aenigmate' (1 Corinthians 13:2);[56] however, *in malo* it signifies the 'favores saecularium,' those things which man rests in idolatrously, which God will destroy.[57] In *Inferno* XIV the impure, cleft, temporal simulacrum of the human soul is defrauded by false images – Narcissus-like, it sees only its sinful, idolatrous self.[58]

The 'mirror' stands for Rome. In the first centuries of Christianity this city, with its 'false and lying gods,' was the butt of the whole euhemeristic tradition, the theme of such treatises as *Quod idola dii non sint, De idololatria, De errore profanarum religionum, Divinae institutiones*, and the *De civitate Dei*, among countless other works. For the Apostle Peter, Rome had been the idolatrous 'other Babylon' (1 Peter 5:13), a theme expanded in St Augustine (*The City of God* I, 18) and the other Fathers.[59] But perhaps most important, Rupert of Deutz' far later exegesis on Nebuchadnezzar's dream echoes the early tradition, seeing the sin of the Babylonian king fulfilled in the idolatry of the Romans:

> King Nebuchadnezzar made a golden statue. ... Surely this is stupid idolatry, that which the Babylonian king raised; Nero, the most depraved king, [was a] source of shame to the Roman Empire, which – that is, Rome – was a second Babylon, as Peter the Apostle bears witness when he says 'The church that is in Babylon, elected together with you, saluteth you' (1 Peter 5:13).[60]

Rome indeed is the 'mirror' of Babylon. The Poet's invocation of the eternal city's name has more than historical relevance; Dante also implies a current criticism of contemporary Rome and of the temporal corruption of the Roman Church in the ironic object of the Veglio's gaze. The city is the perversion of the spiritual Rome of Paradise which Beatrice will term later in *Purgatorio* XXXII, 102: 'Quella Roma onde Cristo è romano / That Rome wherefore Christ is Roman.'[61] It is particularly fitting that the statue's stance and position fulfil textually both biblical and pagan *figurae* of the same sin. Described like the colossus of Nebuchadnezzar, yet standing on the heathen soil of an island famed for the idolatry of 'Jove,' and gazing on Rome, the touchstone of the same sin, the Veglio mocks in a sinful inversion the Platonist-Christian theme of the soul as mirror of God. The statue stares upon a glass which reflects back its own perverse nature.[62] Thus all of Dante's images are centripetal to the theme of 'perfect blasphemy.'

That the Veglio's *fessura* is the wound of original sin, the defect of nature, is a fact accepted by most critics, but how is this relevant to the other images of the episode? The Fathers of the Church consider the pride of Lucifer and Adam in coveting God's likeness inordinately to be intimately related to the sins of blasphemy and idolatry. Several points may be adduced. First, these sins differ not essentially but in degree. St Thomas Aquinas cites St Augustine (*De Genesi ad litteram* XI, 30): 'Both [Lucifer and Adam] coveted somewhat to be equal with God, in so far as each wished to rely on himself in contempt of the order of Divine rule.'[63] Blasphemy is more serious: 'Though pride, of its genus, has a certain pre-eminence over other sins, yet the pride whereby one denies or blasphemes God is greater than the pride whereby one covets God's likeness inordinately.'[64] In another passage, St Thomas makes the connection between the effects of the Fall, the *vulneratio naturae* and idolatry, a unity of cause and effect: '*The dispositive cause of idolatry was on the part of man, a defect of nature*, either through ignorance in his intellect or disorder in his affections ... and this pertains to guilt.'[65] St Thomas continues the same paragraph giving us a clear doctrinal reason why Dante's idolatrous statue is the fitting source of the rivers of Hell: '*Again, idolatry is stated to be the cause, beginning and end of all sin because there is no kind of sin that idolatry does not produce at some time*, either through leading expressly to that sin by causing it or through being an occasion thereof, either as a beginning or as an end.'[66] Here again the results of original sin at the Fall (and in pagan history, the end of the Golden Age) and the results of idolatry are one. Dante's use of the indefinite article, 'sta dritto *un* gran veglio,' emerges in its full import. The Veglio represents the single 'body of sin,' the body of all men in Adam: 'Through *one* man sin entered into the world' (Romans 5:12–17; Luke 4:58; 1 Corinthians 15:21–2).[67] Yet the statue of the Old Man in Adam finds identification with a blasphemous idol of Jove who in turn represents the cause from whom, mythically and euhemeristically, man's woes sprang, and because of whom man's blood first flowed. Biblical and pagan histories converge into one God-ordained linear, spiritual progression.

The evocation of baptismal typologies and numerologies in *Inferno* xiv which we examined in chapter 5 is both apt and ironic because, from the beginning of Christianity, the sacrament as prefigured in the Exodus signified precisely *the abandonment of idolatry*. (Origen, for example, addresses the newly baptized in his *Homily on Joshua* iv, 1: 'You who, having just now abandoned the darkness of idolatry, desire to come near to hear the divine Law, you begin by abandoning Egypt.')[68] Further, *through the sacrament of the Faith man may be 'as God' without sacrilege or blasphemy in a configuration with Christ*. The tradition, arising from St Paul's words in Romans 6:4 and Galatians 3:27–8, can be represented by St Cyril, who states unequivocally: 'Baptized in Christ, and having put on Christ, you have become conformed to the Son of God. ... Become participants in Christ, *you are rightly called Christ. But you were made Christs* when you received the sacrament of the Holy Spirit.'[69] The pseudo-Dionysius echoes the same concept as he identifies the sacrament as an imitation of God: 'He who receives the Sacrament of Baptism and is plunged three times into the water, learns to imitate mysteriously this triarchic death that was the burial of Jesus for three days and three nights, *in the measure, at least that it is permitted to man to imitate God.'*[70] In his *Sermo* xiii *De Tempore* (quoted by St Thomas in the *Summa Theologica*), St Augustine puts it most succinctly: 'God was made man, that man might be made God.'[71]

Those, therefore, who, after Silverstein, have seen in the statue a reflection of Christ, and who, after Pascoli and Busnelli, have identified the *fessura* with the wound of nature on different grounds, are justified in their views by these previously unnoted classical and theological bases. The facts that we have adduced force a re-evaluation of the episode. Clearly it is not mere blasphemy but *perfect* blasphemy, the prevention and diverting of the due worship of the Deity, that is, *idolatry*, which is justly punished here. Far from being fragmented or inconsistent, the episode has an organic unity which is at once historical, theoretical, and poetic; all images conform to a single ideological schema. The statue symbolizes *both* blasphemous idolatry and the effects of the Fall, for they are *one*. The unifying theme, the sin punished in the episode, is also theologically, like its twins, pride and covetousness, the source of all other sin. Thus we can grasp why the idol of Crete is the fitting physical, moral, and poetic source of all the rivers of Hell's punishing divisions, and why Dante describes the figure precisely in *Inferno* xiv.

7 ULYSSES

In the case of Ulysses the romantic-positivistic interpretation has been slower to cede the field than in the case of other episodes; however, in the last three decades one can observe a steadily growing disinclination on the part of critics to view Ulysses as a character apart from Hell, and as a noble, tragic hero morally superior to the 'evil pouches' to which he is sentenced in second death. Since so much has been said about the canto,[1] I shall try in this chapter only to examine the *contrapasso* and to state what has not been said before in any complete and satisfying way.

The opening lines of the episode (*Inferno* xxvi, 25–30), with their attractive peacefulness, immediately act as a kind of *captatio benevolentiae* for Ulysses and Diomedes before their appearance – at least this is how Dante makes the description work on the literal level. The bucolic scene with its evening insects almost inspires the heart to rest in the beauty of the visual spectacle:

> Quante 'l villan ch'al poggio si riposa,
>   nel tempo che colui che'l mondo schiara
>   la faccia sua a noi tien meno ascosa,
> come la mosca cede a la zanzara,
>   vede lucciole giù per la vallea,
>   forse colà dov'e' vendemmia e ara ...

As many as the fireflies which the peasant, resting on the hill – in the season when he that lights the world least hides his face from us, and at the hour when the fly yields to the gnat – sees down along the valley, there perhaps where he harvests grapes and tills. ...

(25–30)

However, the underlying implications of the imagery led even the first readers to a degree of suspicion. Among the earliest commentators, Guido da Pisa, citing Ovid and Isidore of Seville, informs us that the insects mentioned are generated from rotting water, wine, and carrion.[2] Particularly, the firefly is 'generated from rotting ears of corn' and the gnat ('zanzara,' or Latin, 'culex'), 'from the resolution of putrid vapour.' In its biblical locus (a New-Testament *hapax*), the gnat appears in the midst of Christ's invective against the dissembling and hypocrisy of scribes and Pharisees, where the Redeemer warns his disciples against emulating their ambition, for they are 'blind guides, who strain out a gnat and swallow a camel' (Matt. 23:24). The Church Fathers identified the metaphorical gnat so 'strained out' as the seditious thief Barabbas freed by the Jews.[3] The interpretation and its biblical resonances along with many consonant images which Dante employs in the canto, such as the thieves of Florence (4), the flames which 'steal away' the sinners (42), and the theft of the Palladium (63), immediately give a negative font of meaning for Dante's episode, invoking as they do theft and hypocrisy.

The image of the peasant and the gnat also has, of course, an important classical locus. Dante's bucolic description is calqued in great part on the pseudo-Virgilian poem 'Culex,' 'The Gnat.'[4] In this mock-heroic work, a shepherd tending his sheep on the mountainside falls asleep on a summer's eve and only avoids the fatal bite of a serpent through the kind offices of a gnat who 'warns him by its sting to avoid death' (184). The shepherd merely swats his saviour. Later when the shepherd falls asleep again, he is visited by the shade of the gnat who recounts his experiences in the underworld. Upon awakening the shepherd plants a memorial garden in a valley to show gratitude to his benefactor. The various classical figures and places seen and recounted by the insect of course also appear in Dante's Poem: Lethe, Charon, Tisiphone, Cerberus,[5] the Erinys, Phlegethon, Dis, and so on. Most important, however, the gnat meets Penelope, 'the Ithacan's wife. ... deemed the glory of womankind,' and tells at length of the Trojan War, its victims and heroes; particularly he blames the overthrow of Troy on the 'Ithacan's wiles,' 'dolis Ithaci' (326). Thus there was available to Dante not only an erudite body of lore linking the gnat to the theme of theft, fraud, and dissembling, but also, significantly, a *mock-heroic* context directly tying the insect to the guile and deceptions of Ithaca's king, Ulysses. Taken by itself, the image of *Inferno* xxvi, 28 might have little importance, but when we join it to those which follow we can grasp that Dante is working out a consistently scornful and negative symbolism in the canto.

In fact, throughout the episode, Dante points to the tropological or moral message of his text by sowing it with signs that there was 'something wrong' with Ulysses' quest. The Greek and his companions are 'old and slow' when they set out on a voyage demanding the stamina of young men (as we noted in the previous chapters, old age was in itself a medieval metaphor of the taint of sin). Ulysses sails west, not east to his home in Ithaca, not towards the east of Olympus, Crete, or Jerusalem. He sails 'sempre acquistando dal lato mancino / always gaining on the left' toward the 'sinister' direction rather than the righteous one. The very number symbolism of the fivefold waxing and waning of the moon during his voyage points to a purely earthly and sinful interest: five was, after all, the number of the senses, and the number of the *saeculum*, the world.[6] Even Ulysses' 'orazion picciola' is self-contradictory in essence and structure. The first exhortation urges his crew to the full experience of what remains of the life of the senses and echoes his own burning desire to experience, not a contemplative ideal beyond, but the world down here ('l'ardore ... a divenire del mondo esperto'):

> a questa tanto picciola vigilia
> d'i nostri sensi ch'è del rimanente
>   non vogliate negar l'esperïenza ...
>   ... del mondo sanza gente.

To this so brief vigil of our senses that remains to us, choose not to deny experience ... of the world which has no people.

(114–17)

While these lines reveal his real aim, those which follow substitute an imprecise, glossy ideal of something he calls 'virtù,' something which is calculated to appeal to the worldly vanity of his crew:[7]

> Considerate la vostra semenza:
>   fatti non foste a viver come bruti,
>   ma per seguir virtute e canoscenza.

Consider your origin: you were not made to live as brutes but to pursue virtue and knowledge.

(118–20)

While it is a critical commonplace that Ulysses' search for the knowledge of good and evil repeats the Fall, it seems not to have been noticed before that when Ulysses urges experience of a 'world which has no people,' then the knowledge of 'vizi umani,' 'human vices,' which he had mentioned to Virgil, can *only* be of those sins committed by himself and his crew! Since he puts vice and worth on the same plane, undifferentiated according to any universal hierarchy or eschatological end, he thereby denies the necessity of moral choice between the two; even on the literal level, Ulysses simply urges his crew to sin, playing the tempting serpent to his men's Adam and Eve. Dante hides nothing.[7]

In approaching the episode of Ulysses, we cannot forget that the Poet's dissemblers in Malebolge must be viewed in the light of the monstrous figure who introduced this circle of Hell, Geryon, the 'sozza imagine di froda' (the 'foul image of fraud') whose 'just' face is belied by his bestial spots and scorpion's tail. It is likewise impossible to square a noble Ulysses with Virgil's description of the inhabitants of all these *bolge* as 'simile lordura.'[8]

Despite the work of centuries of Dante scholarship, three major cruxes remain unanswered in *Inferno* xxvi. First, what made Dante think that Ulysses' oration and ambition had anything to do with the sin of false counsel? Secondly, how, to Dante's medieval mind, are Ulysses' abandonment of family and his undertaking of a long voyage connected to the sins of deception and fraud? Lastly, and most important, how does Dante make Ulysses exemplify 'consiglio frodolente'? In the following pages I explore these questions and put forward what I believe can be satisfying solutions to these interpretive puzzles.

A major stumbling block to an understanding of the true unity of the Ulysses episode has been the critics' tendency to ignore ecclesiastical concepts of the generation and interrelation of sins, and to consider the one here punished in a dogmatic vacuum. The perplexity sometimes expressed by critics over Ulysses' various crimes mentioned in *Inferno* xxvi is actually a false problem. The most serious sin, naturally, determines the soul's location in Hell, but lesser sins are evoked, as usual, to show the path of wickedness followed by the sinner. The modern critical confusion that one sin alone condemns the souls to these lower circles violates church doctrine: the damned represent a *habitus*, an habitual, mortal sin arrived at by degrees. Pride, as we know, is the beginning of all sin; cupidity is its root; the daughters of pride and avarice, the seven mortal sins, in turn, give rise to others.[9] Recently some critics have observed that Ulysses is punished not for one incident of fraudulent counsel but for his whole sinful career; and although they have not documented it, doctrine supports their view.[10] Sin engenders sin.[11] We can, in fact, see Ulysses' descent into hypocrisy as parallel to the steps which St Thomas Aquinas outlined in describing the familiar 'daughters of covetousness.' *Cupiditas* (or *Avaritia*) leads step by step through the vices of mercilessness, restlessness, violent rapine or theft, falsehood, perjury, and fraud.[12] From insensibility to family, friends, and allies, to burning desire for worldly experience, through the theft of the Palladium, the fraud and falsehood of the Trojan horse, the perjury to Deidamia and the fraudulence of his final speech urging the last voyage, Ulysses' sins are a paradigm of the road to damnation and a reversal of the path of salvation.

The appearance of Ulysses before the two poets seems also to invert, in order, the seven steps toward divine wisdom in the Christian tradition; that is, the Seven Gifts of the Holy Ghost. First, Ulysses is introduced to us as 'lo maggior corno,' 'the greater horn' (we should also note the repetition of the noun in the following canto, *Inferno* XXVII, 132). In *Inferno* XXXI, 12, Dante's use of the word may reflect such glosses as that in the *Allegoriae in Sacram Scripturam* which gives as its primary reading *in malo*, the familiar 'cornu, superbia,'[13] that is, 'pride,' the reverse of the first spiritual gift, fear (a subject which I have discussed at length elsewhere).[14] Secondly, Dante introduces *pietas* – by its absence: 'né la pieta del vecchio padre' (94). The phrase (97–8) 'l'ardore ... a divenir del mondo esperto' inverts the third gift, knowledge. In his discussion of the seven gifts in *De doctrina Christiana* II, 7, St Augustine explains this gift and its attainment with the warning: 'The student first will discover that he has been enmeshed in the love of this world, or of temporal things, a love far remote from the kind of love of God and of our neighbor which Scripture itself prescribes.'[15] Patristically, knowledge is submission to sacred authority, and Ulysses' deliberate passing of the pillars forbidden by the deified Hercules represents precisely a violation of a pagan godly authority. Fortitude, the fourth gift, inverted as a solitary, unaided, and god-challenging foolhardiness, appears next in the lines, 'sol con un legno e con quella compagna picciola / with one vessel only, and with that small company' (101–2). (Note, in passing, Dante's ironic use of liturgical vocabulary; this *legno* is not the *lignum*, or the wood of the Cross; the small company is not the Twelve!) Most important and most obvious is the reversal in the *orazion picciola* (112 ff.) of divine counsel, the *fifth* gift, a matter to which we will return. Purity of heart, the sixth, appears speciously in Ulysses' words, 'fatti non foste a viver come bruti, ma per seguir virtute' (119–20). The last word of the line and, ironically, the last of his speech, *canoscenza*, the striving for worldly knowledge, inverts the final step in the Holy Spirit's seven gifts to man, wisdom, the peace of Heaven.

There is further irony in the fact that Ulysses sees God's mountain as 'bruna per la distanza' – darkly – and then rejoices. The last few traditional steps of the Christian way to wisdom strengthen the spiritual sight; the closer one comes to the triune Godhead the clearer vision becomes. Again we can cite St Augustine from the same passage in which he discusses the Gifts: 'When, in so far as [man] is able, he has seen this Trinity *glowing in the distance*, and has discovered that because of his weakness he cannot sustain the sight of that light. ... When he arrives at the ... sixth step ... he cleanses that eye through which God may be seen, in so far as He can be seen by those who die to the world as much as they are able. For they are able to see only in so far as they are dead to this world; in so far as they live in it, they do not see. And now although the light of the Trinity begins to appear more certainly, and not only more tolerably but also more *joyfully, it is still said to appear "through a glass in a dark manner [in aenigmate]."* ' The final 'turbo / whirlwind' and shipwreck also contrast with the final, seventh, step where 'peace and tranquility' are attained in true Wisdom.[16]

Without insisting too much on numerology, we must note that the number five, the number of the *saeculum*, the world, stressed in *Inferno* XXVI, links Ulysses' desire to experience the life of the five senses to the main sin punished. False counsel reverses divine counsel, the fifth step towards true wisdom, the very gift parodied by the punishment within tongues of fire; the punishment is a reversal of the Pentecost, itself a five times ten.[17] The 'counsel' of the *orazion picciola* is thus intimately linked to the *contrapasso* in ways hitherto unnoticed.

Dante's didactic aim is also made clear by the similes with which he introduces Ulysses and Diomedes within their double flame. The images provide an informing metaphoric structure. Let us first examine the funeral pyre of Eteocles and Polynices:

> chi è'n quel foco che vien sì diviso
> di sopra, che par surger de la pira
> dov'Eteòcle col fratel fu miso?

> Who is in that fire which comes so divided at its top that it seems to rise
> from the pyre where Eteocles was laid with his brother?

(52–3)

The image provides another major clue to the speciousness of Ulysses and his companion, for it gives the lie to Ulysses' arrogation of virtue. The simile occurs to Dante Wayfarer as the observer of the episode; he is struck only by the surface resemblance of the two divided flames, one historically past, the other literally present. The Poet, however, chose a most damning comparison. From Statius' *Thebaid*, and from commentaries of the mythographer Fulgentius on that epic, Dante learned that the brothers were foul figures of sin: 'Out of this incestuous union [of Oedipus and Jocasta] are produced ... other creatures ... *having the appearance of virtue, but not virtue itself*, namely, the two sons, one of them called *Eteocles is the destruction of morals*, that is greed [*cupiditas*], whereby morals are destroyed, for it is the origin and root of all evils ... Polynices conquering many in this world, is lust, to which many yield.'[18] The allusion, then, should further alert us to the deceptiveness of Ulysses' 'virtù.'

Even more significant is the earlier simile (34 to 39) concerning the translation of Elijah [Elias]:

E qual colui che si vengiò con li orsi
   vide 'l carro d'Elia al dipartire,
   quando i cavalli al cielo erti levorsi,
che nol potea sì con li occhi seguire.
   che'l vedesse altro che la fiamma sola,
   sì come nuvoletta, in su salire:
tal si move ciascuna per la gola
   del fosso ...

And as he who was avenged by the bears saw Elijah's chariot at its
departure, when the horses rose erect to heaven – for he could not so
follow it with his eyes as to see aught save the flame alone, like a little
cloud ascending: so each flame moves along the gullet of the ditch ...

(34–41)

The typology here goes beyond simply that of the journey motif (ascent to
Heaven versus descent to Hell). Dante intends to present Ulysses as a
corresponding pagan negative to the positive figural pattern in biblical history.[19] The image serves two functions: it gives a key to the aptness of the
contrapasso, and it undermines the view which Ulysses will create for himself
on the literal level.

The Jewish prophet, whose very spirit meant 'the doing of virtuous works,'
bore within him 'the holy smouldering of righteous zeal,'[20] and, at the end
of time, he will come again with Enoch as a witness 'in whose mouth will stand
the word of God.'[21] As Ulysses, the false counsellor, is imprisoned in a
physical flame which speaks like a tongue, so, in life, the true prophet Elijah,
enclosed in a spiritual flame, was also a metaphorical 'flaming mouth.'[22]
Rupert of Deutz echoes and glosses this biblical epithet for the Prophet in the
De Victoria Verbi Dei: 'It was said of him truly, "He was as fire: and his
word burnt like a torch" [Ecclesiasticus (Sirach) 48:1].'[23] Other parallels to
Elijah underline the contrast between the biblical type of the truthful, continent,
and abstemious contemplative and the classical type of the excessive, fraudulent trickster. In contrast with Ulysses and his 'folle volo' for knowledge of the
saeculum, Elijah was the *figura* of flight *from* the world (*fuga saeculi*), the
one who reached heaven by his virtue. Unlike the Greek whose foray exceeded
the bounds of human knowledge by his own efforts, the prophet did not
attempt such an ascent by his own power but was rapt by God's chariot 'so that
it might openly show how a pure man stands in need of help outside himself.'[24] St Ambrose describes the Prophet's holiness: '[Elijah] fled from the
world in such a way that he did not even seek out food for his body. ... He
endured a weariness of this life, not a desire for it, but *he was fleeing worldly
enticement and the contagion of filthy conduct and the impious acts of an*

unholy and sinful generation.'[25] The evocation of the Prophet clearly puts into perspective the 'mad flight' of Ulysses, who, though old and tired, bears hardships to experience 'il mondo' and the filth of his own 'vizi.'

Elijah who rejected the senses and attained heaven while in this life, is indeed the antithesis of Ulysses, the pursuer of the life of the senses. As Elijah fled from the unchaste Jezebel, 'the outpouring of vanity,' Ulysses stayed with Circe who delayed him 'more than a year.'[26] Just as the 'ardor of the Lord' burned in the heart of the Prophet and allowed him to perform eight miracles by his virtues (as Rupert of Deutz says, the 'zeal of divine love stirred him up with burning ardor'),[27] so there burned in the heart of the Greek the 'ardor of the world,' the seed of his own destruction. As Elijah united families by raising the dead (the widow's son, 3 [1] Kings 17:17–24),[28] so Ulysses broke the bond of family, both those of Achilles (who never returned alive to Deidamia), and those of his own.

Yet another way in which Ulysses can be seen as the typological antithesis of Elijah lies in his punishment in a *double* flame:

quel foco che vien sì diviso

that fire which comes so divided

(52)

la fiamma cornuta

the hornèd flame

(68)

O voi che siete due dentro ad un foco ...

O you who are two within one fire

(79)

Even before we meet the twofold flame of the spirits of Diomedes and Ulysses and the metaphor of Eteocles and Polynices, the poet, by allegorical inference, introduces the 'double flame' of Elijah. We recall that before Elijah was assumed into the heaven of air, Elisha begged him for a double gift of holy power so that his own acts might be efficacious: '*Spiritus tuus duplex, obsecro in me requiescat* / I beseech thee that in me may be thy double spirit' (4 [2] Kings 2:9–11).[29] Elisha then received this 'double spirit' from the elder Prophet *precisely as the younger prophet watched Elijah's ascent in the fiery chariot* (4 [2] Kings 2:11) – the very moment alluded to in *Inferno* xxvi, 34–9. As critics have realized, the motif of the 'turbo' in Dante must obviously be seen in the same context: Elijah was assumed into the heavens; Ulysses is absorbed into the abyss of Hell. The whirlwind of the Holy Spirit which rapt Elijah heavenward and gave the Gift of Cloven Tongues to the Apostles is the same tool of destruction which brings damnation to the Greek hero (137); the historical pattern of God's plan in pagan and Christian history reflected here in both the literal and allegorical levels of Dante's Poem is neat and plain.

Other biblical passages can help us to understand not only the sufficient reason for the wily Ulysses' death in a whirlwind, but also the sinner's power to deceive us. In Job 36:13–14, for example, 'Dissemblers and crafty men prove the wrath of God ... their soul shall die in a storm.' St Gregory's comments on this passage, although somewhat less known, are particularly illuminating. In his gloss, the saint cites Jesus' words in Matthew 23:27–8 concerning the specious appearance of dissemblers (the very passage where the 'gnat' image comes in the Bible): 'Woe to you, scribes and Pharisees, hypocrites; because you are like to whitèd sepulchres, which outwardly appear to men beautiful but within are full of dead men's bones and of all filthiness. So you also outwardly indeed appear to men as just: but inwardly you are full of hypocrisy and iniquity.'[30] St Gregory continues in a passage which may provide a doctrinal reason for the dissembling Ulysses' seeming disregard of the *bolgia* and its horror. His gloss on the succeeding verse in Job dealing with dissemblers ('Neither shall they cry out, when they are bound') parallels both Ulysses' earthly state (bound to the mast) and his behaviour in Hell; Gregory's metaphors compare the change in the opinion of men from calm to turbulence with a sudden disturbance in the atmosphere; the outward blasts are a sign of inward suffering and divine punishment upon dissimulators: 'For they were seeming to live as if in calm, when they were taking care to rejoice in the credit of holiness. But their soul which used to rejoice in the fatal tranquility of human praise, dies by a sudden tempest. For most commonly an unexpected tempest suddenly produces a change in all the calm blandishment of the air, and danger cannot be avoided, inasmuch as it could not be foreseen. *Whence dissemblers*, who neglect to watch over their conduct, *are said to die in a tempest. For the sudden whirlwind of an inward shock casts them forth hence*, whom the pride of outward applause exalts on high.'[31] We can easily hear the echo of Gregory's words in Dante's verses:

> Noi ci allegrammo, e tosto tornò in pianto;
>   ché de la nova terra un turbo nacque. ...

> We rejoiced, but soon our joy was turned to grief, for from the new land a whirlwind arose. ...

> (136–7)

Elijah, viewed nor merely as simile but as historical archetype, and, textually, as structuring metaphor, can also help us understand that Ulysses' abandonment of his family for the sake of sensory knowledge could only lead directly to his death in accordance with Scripture. Ulysses also fulfils the last prophecy concerning the abstemious prophet 'filled with the law,' as Elijah appears in Malachias 4:5-6: 'Behold I will send you Elias the prophet before the coming of the great and dreadful day of the Lord. And he shall turn the heart of the fathers to the children and the heart of the children to their fathers: *lest I come and strike* [Vulgate: '*percutiam*'] *the earth with anathema.*' Not even the most sacred familial ties could quench Ulysses' ardour for earthly experience:

> né dolcezza di figlio, né la pieta
>   del vecchio padre. ...

> Neither fondness for my son, nor filial piety toward my agèd father.
> ...

(94-5)

Biblically, the abandonment of such basic natural duties earns the just punishment of God (1 Timothy 5:8), and Dante reflects the prophecy of Malachias in his choice of vocabulary:

> ... un *turbo* nacque
> e *percosse* del legno il primo canto

> A whirlwind arose and struck the forepart of the ship.

(137-8)

The images of Elijah and of cloven tongues of flame[32] central to Dante's episode are naturally bound up in patristic commentaries on the Pentecost and with them are included the further recurring image of *wings* also present in the Ulysses episode ('Fiorenza ... batti l'ali / O Florence ... you beat your wings,' 1-2, and 'de' remi facemmo ali / we made of our oars wings,' 125). For the Church Fathers, Elijah prefigures the Gift of Tongues to the Apostles, as, for example, in St Ambrose's gloss on Acts 2:2, 3: ' "The Holy Spirit also came down and filled the whole house, where very many were sitting, and there appeared *cloven tongues* as of fire." Good are the *wings of love*, the *true wings that flew about through the mouths of the Apostles*, and the *wings of fire* that spoke the pure word (Psalm 11 [12]:7) ... *on these wings Elias flew* when he was transported by the fiery chariot and the fiery horses to the

regions above.'³³ As is traditional, the saint urges his reader to flee this
world and to 'take up these wings, since like flames they aim for the higher
regions.'³⁴ The Truth, the Word of God, both born by Elijah, fulfilled in the
New Testament and figured again in the infernal punishment, contrasts sharp-
ly and ironically with the fraudulent word of Ulysses.

Although recently critics have noted that the images of 'ali' and 'remi' have
significances and unite the episode in ways I feel no need to deal with again
here,³⁵ we also need to consider the metaphor, common in the Church Fathers,
of the 'wings of fraud.' Only in this context can we see the connection
between the greedy, hypocritical, and thievish wings of Florence (2–4) and the
'wings' of Ulysses' oars. St Gregory, for example, compares the behaviour
of dissemblers to the wings of the ostrich, the symbol of fraud (Job 39:13): 'it
raises its wings, in appearance as if to fly, but yet never raises itself from
the earth in flying. Thus doubtless are all dissemblers, who, while they simu-
late conduct of the good, possess a resemblance of holy appearance, but
have no reality of holy conduct. They have, in truth, wings for flight, in
appearance, but in their doing they creep along the ground, because they
spread their wings, by the semblance of sanctity, but overwhelmed by the
weight of secular cares, they are not raised from the earth.'³⁶ The meaning
of 'alae' as symbolizing *in malo*, the purposes of dissemblers (cogitationes
hypocritae') and the greed of the avaricious ('cupiditas rapacium'), set forth
again, for example, in the *Allegoriae in Sacram Scripturam*,³⁷ must be added
to the other images which point directly to the negativity of Ulysses' counsel and quest. The 'wing' metaphors point directly to the true nature of the sin
punished in this *bolgia*: they are the 'wings of fraud,' particularly the
wings of ambition and fraudulent counsel.

As Dante probably knew, Richard of St Victor used this image in his
treatment of the paradigms of the very sin of fraudulence in the *De eruditione
hominis interioris*. Far from being a 'fluid notion,' as some critics have
believed,³⁸ *fraudulentia* was strictly defined and had specific characteristics in
its purpose and operation; I might add that it was also defined in a manner
somewhat different from that which the twentieth-century mind might con-
ceive. The Victorine's treatise, like so many other treatises concerning the
descent into sin, deals with the various grades of corruption sinking by steps
into fraud. Indeed, Richard's description of fraud might almost be a sce-
nario for Dante's Ulysses. In his *De eruditione*, part III, he asks: 'Do you still
want to know more fully *what sort of wings fraudulence has*? So therefore
I will briefly express what I feel: let one be said to be of simulation, the second
of dissimulation, the third that of ostentation, the fourth of excuse.'³⁹ The
left wings of fraud he identifies as simulation and dissembling because 'we
correctly understand those things to be more secret which are done by the

left hand.' He continues in a passage which finds other strong parallels in Ulysses' actions: '*The fraudulence of dissemblers pursues in everything that it does, the promotion of its honour. For everything it does, or intends to do, serves ambition.* Moreover, ambition is nothing other than a striving [*affectatio*] for honour. Moreover, the first kind of this evil is a striving after liberty; the second is a striving after dignity; the third is a striving after authority; the fourth is a striving after power.'[40] Fraudulence, then, is born of 'ambition,' the pursuit of worldly honour.

Richard next defines the 'four heads' of fraudulence in a way which can help us to understand Ulysses' violation of the prohibition of Hercules, as well as his eloquent advice and his power over his men in the arduous undertaking: '*Behold how ambition divides itself into four heads to which, as it were, every action of dissemblers is a slave.* [First] there is the striving after liberty when now *one escapes being ruled by others.* [Second] the striving after dignity is the pursuit of greater things step by step through constant toil. [Third] *the striving for authority is when now someone tries to appear to all men to be a man of great counsel and judgment.* [Fourth] the striving after power is when now he tries to be in charge of others. ...'[41] The crafty Greek's sin lies in his ambition to pose as a man of great and honourable counsel. Dante's warning to himself at the outset of the episode can only be understood clearly when we bear in mind such statements as those of Richard of St Victor. The Poet's self-admonishment provides the reader with his first clue to the interpretation of the episode to come and of the true character of Ulysses:

> Allor mi dolsi, e ora mi ridoglio
>   quando drizzo la mente a ciò ch'io vidi,
>   e più lo'ngegno affreno ch'i' non soglio
> perché non corra che virtù nol guidi ...

> I sorrowed then, and sorrow now again, when I turn my mind to what I saw; and I curb my genius more than I am wont, lest it run where virtue does not guide it. ...

>   (19–22)

Realizing the intimate bond which connects ambition and pretence to counsel with fraudulence, the Poet, who by the grace of God has learned his lesson concerning the mere appearance of virtue and the danger it poses, invokes that lesson here even before he sets about describing the encounter with the Greeks.[42]

The main point of Dante's episode is that all of the actions attributed to Ulysses are doctrinally and generically typical of dissemblers. The Church Fathers note, in fact, that such sinners are known to sacrifice familial and divine interests to an ardent pursuit of worldly purpose and honour.[43] As St Gregory the Great writes, earthly striving so hardens their hearts that they do not even acknowledge the sons they beget; in fact *they typically abandon their offspring to undertake arduous voyages.* The saint's images more than coincidentally parallel Dante's own: 'Dissimulators, therefore, because they collect not the thoughts of their mind ... are dead to heavenly things for which they ought to burn; and *burn anxiously for earthly objects,* to which they would laudably have been dead. *For thou mayest often* [!] *behold them, having put aside the care of their children, preparing themselves for dangers of immense labour, crossing seas.'*[44] Dante's words 'né dolcezza di figlio,' with all that follows, finally come into perspective. Ulysses, far from being the exceptional paragon imagined by romantic-minded critics, was chosen by the Poet as the exemplary ambitious, dissembling pretender to noble counsel, one whose aims and posturing advice were as deceptive as the rest of the 'lordura' held in this ditch of Malebolge. Doctrinal precedent establishes that Dante's tale is calculated as a negative exemplum for the benefit of his readers' souls. All the allusions and images contribute morally, theologically, and artistically to a unified whole, teaching the reader that Ulysses' own siren song must be resisted.

As Dante has it, God's own counsel speaks symbolically in the punishing flame of Ulysses' *contrapasso.*

8 SATAN

We come to the final lines of the *Inferno*: Dante and Virgil at last see the stars of heaven as they come forth from Hell through a narrow passage carved by the waters which descend from Mount Purgatory to the lowest depths. It is Easter morning, and the arising of the two Poets from the prison and grave of the damned repeats the Resurrection of Christ after his *descensus ad inferos*. The initial verbs of the following canticle, 'salire,' 'risurga,' 'surga,' enhance the parallel. The vocabulary of 'arising' concludes the first stage of the traditional pattern which informs the structure of the *Commedia*, that of descent to humility before ascent to grace; allegorically, in the Wayfarer's journey, made in imitation of Christ, the exit from Hell marks the completion of the first stage.[1] Dante unites in metaphor the crowded 'tomba' of the damned with the empty tomb of Christ, completing, with this final term of the equation, the parodic picture of 'Belzebù,' the Lord of the Flies, whom he depicts in *Inferno* xxxiv as being in everything the inverse of the Three Persons of the Trinity.[2]

Left behind at the centre deep within, the 'King of Hell' stands in his 'tristo buco' ('dismal hole'), in all ways the negation of the Godhead. His materiality reverses Divine Substance; his imprisonment in locality mocks his desire for infinity. His hideous heads reflect absurdly the Three Persons bound in One, the Triune God; his impotence inverts the power of God the Father. As a reversal of the Son, the Logos, Truth becomes ignorance; as the Word Made Flesh, his cruciform figure dripping tears and bloody drool apes the Passion. Like the sinners encountered earlier in the *Inferno*, who imitate and herald his satanic stance (Farinata seen 'from the waist up,' the Giants 'from the navel down'), Satan looms in his 'pozzo' or pit protruding 'from mid-breast' (29).[3] In this way the immersed sinners throughout Hell 'prefigure' the Arch-Fiend below; in the progress of the narrative, the shades of his minions act as his 'adumbrations' or 'typologies,' thus parodying in this

Old-Testament realm Christ's prefigurations in Old-Testament history. Satan's hulking form half-submerged in the ice, like the other immersed figures, is yet another, and more detailed, image of baptism, the sacrament whose doctrines and typologies are so often both perverted and fulfilled in this canticle. We noted earlier that in Hell the sacrament appears only in its initial aspect as death and burial (following Luke 12:15 and Romans 6:4), and that through Old-Testament typologies 'immersion' or descent into the baptismal pool imitated Christ's *descensus ad inferos* and signified the death of the 'old man,' that is, the end of the former life and sinful acts of the catechumen (Romans 6:3–4), while 'emersion' or emergence signified rebirth in the 'new man,' Jesus Christ.[4] It is clear, however, that no matter how they are punished, all the sinners of Dante's *Inferno* are forever fixed in immersion in Hell, that is, in baptism's aspect as the wrath and judgment of God.[5]

More particularly, Satan's stance in the impure waters of Cocytus surrounded by the suspended souls of the damned also imitates conventional artistic depictions of Christ at his baptism immersed in the waters of the river Jordan along with the submerged spirit or spirits of the river.

> Già era, e con paura il metto in metro,
>   là dove l'ombre tutte eran coperte,
>   e trasparien come festuca in vetro.
> Altre sono a giacere; altre stanno erte,
>   quella col capo e quella con le piante;
>   altra, com'arco, il volto a' piè rinverte.

> I was now (and with fear I do put it into verse!) where the shades were wholly covered, showing through like straw in glass. Some are lying, some are erect, this with the head, that with the soles uppermost; another, like a bow, bends his face to his feet.

> (*Inferno* XXXIV, 11–15)

In some pictorial and sculptural renderings of the Jordan as the 'waters of death,' Christ's descent into the river becomes a figure of his descent into Hell and of his victory over Satan's hosts; Christ is shown surrounded by the souls or forms of the damned.[6] A very striking example is the Byzantine fresco in the Church of Perebleptos (plate 28), in which the attitude of several souls beneath the waves closely parallels Dante's description of the shades in Cocytus (plate 29).[7] Among the scores of other examples which one could cite are the depiction of the Baptism in the Baptistry and in the Pala d'Oro of St Mark's in Venice, and the tympanal stone relief (1221) above the portal of

Sta Maria della Pieve in Arezzo which shows Christ in the waters similarly attended by a submerged heathen spirit of the river (plate 30).[8] Dante's image of Lucifer immersed in Cocytus is a complete inversion of the incono-graphy of the Baptism of the Redeemer.

Charles Singleton's profound observation that the first verse of the canto and the freezing blasts emitted by Satan parody the 'spiration' and 'proces-sion' of the Holy Spirit (*Inferno* xxxiv, 4) deserves expansion.[9] The Prince of Darkness spirates forth in local movement the icy wind of hate in precisely the manner of 'spiration' and 'procession' which St Thomas Aquinas denies of the true Godhead; Satan's is not an 'intelligible emanation' which remains in the intelligent agent but a *physical* 'cause proceeding forth to its exterior effect' just as 'heat proceeds from the agent to the thing made hot.'[10] His mindless triple winds are, in fact, a double reversal: they are physical not intelligible and, unlike the Sprit of God which warms the righteous, they freeze the waters and souls of Cocytus:

> ... quelle [penne] svolazzava,
> sì che tre venti si movean da ello:
> quindi Cocito tutto s'aggelava.

> ... he was flapping them [his wings], so that three winds went forth from him, whereby Cocytus was all congealed.

(50–2)

The congealed water is the very antithesis of the tradition which had it that the fiery dove of the Holy Ghost descended upon the Jordan at Jesus' baptism.[11] Here again Dante reverses baptismal *epiclesis*, and in the profoundest theological and sacramental sense.

In the earliest liturgies for the blessing of the baptismal waters (*De benedictione aquae baptismalis*) the priest breathed three times over the water following the pattern of the Spirit of God floating on the face of the waters at Creation (Genesis 1:2).[12] Satan's very presence in Cocytus parodies the liturgical exorcism of the Enemy from the font; this, together with his three icy spirations (4), completely reverses the consecration ceremony by which the waters gain efficacy for initiating catechumens into the faith.[13] Far from being washed clean, the traitors in Cocytus merely pollute it as debris or unwanted impurities ('straws in glass,' 12) and parody physically the liturgical 'arcane admixture of Divine Power' with the holy water of baptism. They lie with their satanic master 'Belzebù,' in total contrast to Christ who was baptized 'not to be cleansed but to cleanse the waters.'[14]

Dante evokes still other typologies of the Redeemer in the depiction of the depths of the *Inferno*. The Old-Testament tale of Joseph placed in an ancient pit and betrayed by his brothers was, in the Church Fathers, an important antitype. St Ambrose in his *De Joseph patriarcha* discourses at length on the parallel.[15] Citing Psalm 87:7 [88:6], he allies Joseph's pit to the grave of Christ: 'The Lord says of Himself: "They have laid me in the lower pit: in the dark places, and in the shadow of death." '[16] This typology was also very popular in Christian art: Joseph depicted standing waist-up or being placed in a round well or pit figures Christ's death, *descensus*, and Resurrection, as well as mankind's deliverance through baptism. In figurative representations, Joseph's well is often indistinguishable from the font. One can compare, for example, the thirteenth-century mosaic of St Matthew baptizing in the nave of St Mark's in Venice (plate 31) with its contemporary, the Joseph cycle in a cupola in the north atrium of that basilica (plate 32). The well and font of the two mosaics are, in turn, almost identical to the well in the Joseph panel of Maximinian's chair in the Episcopal Museum in Ravenna (plate 33). There is, therefore, something immensely satisfying in Satan's *contrapasso* for treachery: he who seeks man's damnation is punished not only as the betrayed Christ the Saviour at his baptism, but also as Christ in the salvific sacrament as it is adumbrated by the betrayed Joseph.

The figure of Satan as a mill fixed in ice, the pain of the three sinners in his jaws, and the connection of these retributions with that of the souls frozen 'as straw' below can all be understood more clearly when we consult earlier Christian traditions. As we might expect, all the major words and images of the Satan episode point to the doctrines of temptation and damnation. First, the condition of being 'devoured by Satan's mouth' itself meant to fall into temptation. St Gregory in his treatise on trial and temptation, the *Moralia in Job*, describes Adam's sin in the same metaphor; Adam, believing Satan, and 'from incautiously remaining external to the meaning of [Satan's] words, utterly exposed himself to be devoured by his mouth.'[17] Similarly, the sinful, both before and after Christ, suffer the same penalty; temptation, 'devouring,' is followed by damnation, 'swallowing': Satan swallowed nearly all men before Christ's coming and, since the Coming, not a few. Belief in Christ's sacrifice was, of course, traditionally said to save us from falling into Satan's jaws.[18]

The justness of the punishment of the three traitors (Judas, Brutus, Cassius) in the monster's mouths also lies in the fact that their condition after death literalizes in the extreme the metaphorical-moral condition of trial and temptation in this life. Those sinners who followed Adam in sin and who allowed themselves to be devoured and swallowed contrast with those such as David and St Peter whom God suffered to be tempted in order to test and strengthen them. The latter two are said to have 'fallen through the holes of his jaws,'[19] that is, to have escaped damnation through penitence. Judas who betrayed Jesus for money contrasts with Peter who *almost* betrayed Christ through denial.

Further, the winds – here issuing from Satan's wings ('tre venti,' 51) – might, as we learn from the *Allegoriae in Sacram Scripturam*, signify 'inner temptation,' and 'the wickedness of the mind.'[20] Dante surely had kept in mind Gregory the Great's typical rhetorical question in the *Morals*, 'And what is a great wind but a strong temptation?'[21] The chill of the wind which freezes the Wayfarer ('io divenni alor gelato,' 22) is also a figure of moral test and a literalization of the same idea. St Gregory, discussing the 'growing cold' or 'freezing' of hearts through Satan's enticements, uses the very metaphors which appear again structurally in Dante's last canto of the *Inferno*: those who wax proud in their lofty virtues are deceived by the tempter and 'grow cold through the pride.'[22] Gregory's exegesis at this point is of considerable importance since he is discussing Job 38:30, the locus where Dante found biblical authority for the freezing of Hell: 'The waters are hardened like a stone: and the surface of the deep is congealed.' Satan himself is 'frost and ice,' and further, his effect on sinners is to extend that coldness: 'When he fell, he bound as frost the hearts of his followers in the coldness of sin. ... "The waters therefore were hardened after the likeness of stone" when he came on earth, because men, imitating his wickedness, lost the soft bowels of charity. And because his crafty designs cannot be detected by men who have been led astray, it is rightly subjoined: "And the surface of the deep is congealed."'[23] We can now appreciate even more how, for Dante, the collocation of the traitors encased in ice around the Arch-Traitor is poetically and morally apt.

The image of hay or straw ('festuca,' 12), as we would expect, has the same function as those preceding. Obliquely in Dante and expressly in St Gregory, Satan's trial of mankind fulfils the metaphor of Isaias 11:7, 'The lion shall eat straw like the ox / Leo sicut bos comedet paleas.' Gregory invokes the passage to explain Job 40:10, which he cites as 'He [Satan] shall eat hay as an ox.' '[Satan] therefore seeks to eat hay as an ox, because he seeks to wound with the fang of his suggestion the pure life of the spiritual.' Through temptation, he 'devours the sinner's life'; those who succumb are his fodder.[24]

Pervading the canto is an insistent metaphor of a perverse and broken Eucharist. Gradually we come to see that all the images cluster around concepts dealing with winnowing (wind, straw) and milling (mill, grinding). Not surprisingly, the image of winnowing-as-temptation is common in the writings of the Church Fathers, who had in turn taken it from various biblical passages such as Amos 9:9 and from Christ's warning to Peter in Luke

22:31. Let us compare St Ambrose, for example, as he discusses *The Prayer of Job and David*:

> There generally comes a turning point in events, when sorrows come from heaven's wrath and indignation, so that the wicked are winnowed as chaff in the wind [Job 21:18]. The unjust are winnowed as chaff; the just as wheat. Therefore, heed the Lord as He says to Peter: 'Behold Satan has desired to winnow you as wheat, but I have prayed for you, that your faith may not fail [Luke 22:31–32]. Those who are winnowed as chaff fail, but that man does not fail who is like the seed that fell and sprang up, augmented and increased by very many fruits [Luke 8:8]. And so the prophet says, 'Woe is me! For I am become as one who gathers the stubble in the harvest.' [Micheas 7:1] Thus wickedness is compared to the stubble which is quickly burned, and the dust. And so, Job said subsequently, 'They will be like chaff driven by the wind' [Job 21:18].[25]

For St Gregory also, the straw left in the field is the very metaphor of fallen man.[26]

In their discussions on the 'winnowing of souls' the Church Fathers naturally included the image of the grist-mill. For Dante, invoking the tradition, the major initial simile of his Satan episode is that of a mill turned by the wind: 'un molin che il vento gira' (6).

The Poet uses the term 'molino' twice in the *Inferno* (XXIII, 47; XXIV, 6) – the diminutive is morally disparaging. In the *Paradiso* he uses 'mola' twice as well (XXI, 3; XXI, 81) and in both of these instances, the word describes the perfect circular dance of the saints, their movements representing perfect concord.[27] As in the Bible (Jeremias 25:10 and Revelation 18:22), where the silence of the mill signified desolation and its joyful sound the peace of Jerusalem, so in the last canticle of the *Commedia* the 'mola' symbolizes the Peace of Heaven. In the last canto of *Inferno* we are left not with the sound of a real mill, but with a chimera, the product of confusion – only the blast of Satan's hate, the punishing grinding of his bestial molars upon the chaff of the world.[28]

The intricate polysemous interpretations which Dante uses were already present in ecclesiastical exegesis. The parable of the two women grinding at the mill (Matthew 24:41; Luke 13:35) was the most important biblical source for the image. Exegetes progressed through a series of developing interpretations: the woman 'taken' was the Church, the one 'left' at the mill (with damp grain, as the Fathers insisted), the Synagogue; later the former became the

Christian soul contrasted with the unpleasing heathen soul; and, finally and
more universally, she became an image of the sinless soul taken to glory while
the sinful soul lay damned.[29] The mill, then, performed the function of
showing the true 'inner kernel,' that is, the truth of man's guilt or innocence.
It was an easy step to see the mill eschatalogically as an image of the Last
Judgment.[30]

St Ambrose had seen the 'mill of this world' as the place of temptation
where men were tried and tested:

> The mill is the world. ... Therefore in this mill ... the soul which is
> servile to crimes and the grain which is wet in the milling and corrupted
> by heavy moisture cannot separate its inside from its outside, and for
> this reason it is left since its flour is displeasing. But the Holy Church, or
> rather the soul stained by no infections of wickedness, the soul which
> grinds such wheat as can be baked by the heat of the eternal sun ... offers
> good flour from the inner man to God, commending the offerings of
> its own sacrifice.[31]

St Ambrose interpreted the two women as the two proclivities of the soul: one
by which the intellect obeys the law of God and abjures sin; the other by
which the mind is bound by sin, and becomes 'flesh' itself as it sins.[32] The
baser instincts cause the mind to become flesh when they cause it to give
itself wholly over to the flesh and its delights: 'And so when it is overcome,
the mind is flesh, not having error from its nature, but from the flesh which
is weak, even as the vanquished follows the name and characteristics of the
victor.'[33] The doctrinal tradition reflected in the saint's imagery is surely not
least important for the flesh-and-blood materiality of Dante's sinners in this
lowest part of Hell.

Interestingly, St Ambrose allies his discussion of the women at the mill
with the metaphor of blood-as-sin as he reinterprets Leviticus 17:14. The
woman left behind, who loses her crop through damp and mildew, is termed
'bloody'; she is the sinful soul who indulges in the fleshly, 'bloody' pleasures of the body. Ignoring the spiritual food of the flesh of Christ, the soul
indulges in the sinful 'food of blood' violating, via a typical patristic interpretation, the Jewish law against eating blood.[34]

The three traitors chewed by a mechanical, oxlike Satan are the negative,
eschatological fulfilment of these Old- and New-Testament concepts in the
Poem. Continuing the image of a grinding mill, Satan literally chews their
fleshly souls in blood:

> ... per tre menti
> gocciava 'l pianto e sanguinosa bava.
> Da ogne bocca dirompea co' denti
> un peccatore, a guisa di maciulla ...

> ... over three chins there dripped tears and bloody slobber. In each
> mouth he ground a sinner with his teeth, like a heckle ...

(53–5)

Unlike the tormented Christ on the Cross, Satan drips blood which is not his own but that of those whom he tortures: he bodies forth the 'blood' guilt of the three traitors in his mouths who, chewed and tortured, are forced, in turn, to parody physically Christ's mystical presence in the Eucharist. The literalized mode of temptation and salvation becomes the eternal mode of second death, damnation.[35]

The prevalence of inverted baptismal and eucharistic imagery takes on new significance in the light of the metaphors and doctrines of temptation: for through these sacraments is loosed the bond of Satan. As baptism removes original and mortal sin by which men are made the Devil's playthings, so the eucharist blots out venial sins, removes punishment, and bestows grace.[36]

The theme of *avoiding* temptation and *escaping* damnation is also mirrored in the narrative line and its allegorical significance. The Wayfarer journeys on, past the dividing hulk of Satan, using his shaggy fur as a ladder. As we noted above, unrepentant sinners are metaphorically swallowed like Adam at the Fall, while those repentant in this life are said to fall from Satan's mouth, 'through the holes in his jaws,' as Gregory would have it.[37] Here again the metaphor is literalized in the Poem: Dante escapes hellmouth through a trinity of real holes, through a 'foro' (85), a 'buca' (131), and a 'pertugio' (139). Unlike the fixed mill of the tempter and the damned, immobile like straws within the ice, the Wayfarer goes forth to the realm of justification, Purgatory, separating himself from them physically and spiritually. From now on his journey prefigures his future salvation.

In another related patristic tradition, the grist-mill held a similar dividing function, since it also figured the Pauline exegetical 'mill' or method whereby the wheat of the Old Testament was converted into the fine flour of the New.[38] This concord of the two Testaments figured, for example, in the Abbot Suger's stained-glass windows at St Denis made about 1140 (unfortunately no longer extant). As Suger himself tells us, one of them represented the Apostle Paul, turning the mill as the prophets brought sacks of grain. It bore the following legend: 'Paul, by working the mill you raise meal from the chaff; you make known the inner secrets of Mosaic Law. True Bread without chaff is made from so many grains, our everlasting and angelic food.'[39] An extant pilaster capital in Vézelay depicts what appears to be Moses pouring the grain of the Old Testament while St Paul cranks a mill and receives the refined flour in a sack (plate 34).[40] The 'mill' image thus sat at the dividing line between the Old and New Law, the very position held by Satan in the Poem. Perversely reflecting in spatial terms Christ's own temporal dividing position in Christian history, Satan also separates the realm of Old-Testament eye-for-an-eye justice from the purgatorial realm of Grace and Justification. St Eucherius, among others, interprets the mill as 'the conversion of this life,'[41] an interpretation which can also help shed light on the Wayfarer's progress, literally, from the state of souls in second death to the state of those headed for everlasting life, and, tropologically, his movement from the realm of sin to the path of future blessedness. Later, in *Purgatorio* II, Dante the Pilgrim himself expresses an intimation of having come to a 'New Law' as he asks Casella to sing a song of consolation:

> E io: 'Se *nuova legge* non ti toglie
> memoria o uso a l'amoroso canto
> che mi solea quetar tutte mie voglie ...'

And I, 'If *a new law* does not take from you memory or practice of the songs of love which used to quiet in me all my longings ...'

(106–8)

Dante Wayfarer's hesitant intuition is then rudely confirmed by Cato's scolding of the souls for their negligent distraction by such earthly, poetic delights which do nothing to purify them for the sight of God.[42] The Pilgrim has indeed reached the place where the New Law *does* obtain and, ironically, to which Satan himself has formed the passage-way. As readers, we issue forth now with Dante Wayfarer to see the stars of Justice.

1 Angel on suspended lid: women at the sepulchre

2 Farinata   3 Farinata

4 Man of Sorrows

5 Man of Sorrows and Mater Dolorosa

6 Man of Sorrows

7 Man of Sorrows with Arma Christi

8 Man of Sorrows

10 Man of Sorrows (*right*)

9 Man of Sorrows (*below*)

11 Noah in the ark

12 Noah in the ark with three Hebrews in furnace

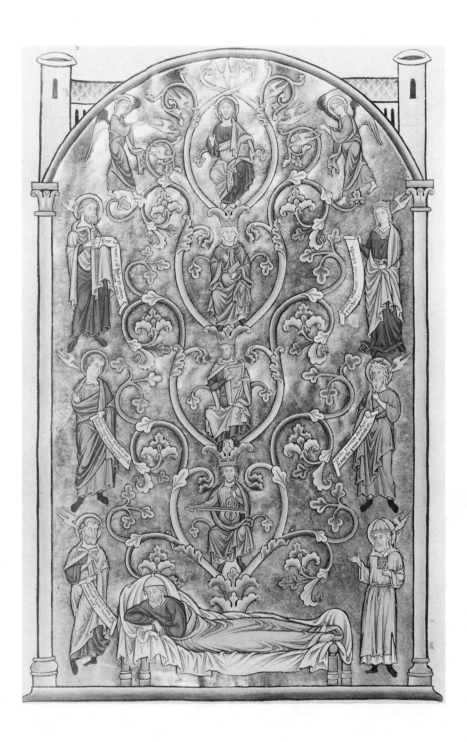

13 Tree of Jesse (*left*)

14 Tree of Jesse and the Tree of the Cross

15 Death of Judas

16 Death of Judas

17 Death of Judas

BELOW

18 Death of Judas (*left*)

19 Death of Judas (*right*)

20 Death of Judas

21 Death of Judas

22 Death of Judas

alchuna vista dilui xe alchu-
na vestigia di quel o arte xe
della sua vebla rimane anchor

sul passo darno xe sopra el ponte pe

23 Pier della Vigna's body
impaled on a tree (*top*)

24 Pier della Vigna's body
hanging from a tree

Achitofel
consiliari⁹
Absalon
postqm uidit ab
salonē sic ee mor
tuū t depūisse su
um gsilium: pre
dolore laqueo se
suspendit.

Achitofel
figurat iu
dam tra
ditorem q propt
magnitudinē p
cati in desperatio
nem cecidit t p
dolore laqueo se
suspendit.

25 Judas and Ahithophel

26 Judas and Ahithophel (*right*)

27 Death of Judas (*left*)

28 Baptism of Christ (*opposite*)

29 Satan submerged in Cocytus (*below*)

30 Baptism of Christ (*opposite*)

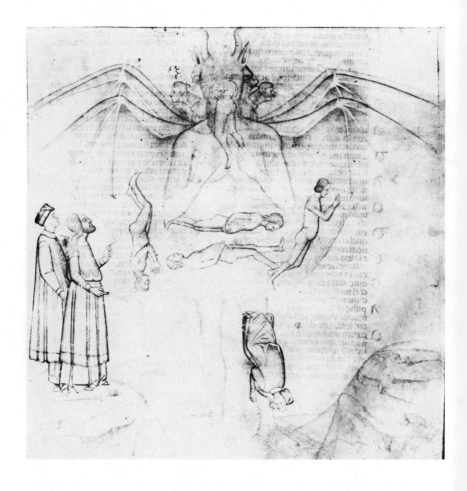

31 St Matthew baptizing

32 Joseph's brothers placing him in the well

33 Joseph's brothers placing him in the well

34 St Paul and Moses at the mill

List of Plates

Notes

CHAPTER ONE: JUSTICE AND THE *CONTRAPASSO*

1 A useful and convenient gathering of texts and commentary on the *contrapasso* is given by Charles S. Singleton in *Inferno: Commentary*, pp. 522–4. He cites especially St Thomas, *In decem libros Ethicorum ad Nicomachum expositio*, ed. Raimondo M. Spiazzi, OP, 3rd ed. (Turin: Marietti 1964), 266, and Francesco D'Ovidio, 'Così s'osserva in me lo contrapasso,' part v of 'Sette chiose alla *Commedia*,' *Studi danteschi*, 7 (1923), 27–34, esp. p. 29. Silvio Pasquazi's essay and bibliography on 'Contrapasso' in the *Enciclopedia dantesca, sub voce*, is most helpful. See also: W.H.V. Reade, *The Moral System of Dante's Inferno* (Oxford: Clarendon Press 1909); M. Baldini, *La costruzione morale dell'Inferno di Dante* (Città di Castello: S. Lapi 1914); Antonio Santi, *L'ordinamento morale e l'allegoria della Divina Commedia* (Palermo: Biblioteca Sandron 1923); Steno Vazzana, *Il contrapasso nella Divina Commedia: Studio sull'unità del poema* (Rome: M. Ciranna 1959).

2 Singleton cites D'Ovidio (p. 29), *Inferno: Commentary*, p. 524.

3 Following Aristotle's *Ethics* v, 2, St Thomas Aquinas distinguishes between distributive justice (for example, the just social distribution of wealth in a whole society) from commutative justice, which, he explains, concerns equalizing matters between individuals, and, ultimately, between man and God: 'Distributive justice directs distributions, while commutative justice directs commutations that can take place between two persons' (*ST* II–II, qu. 61, art. 3). Later Thomas makes the point clearer by discussing injuries to person, reputation, and chattel: 'In all cases [of injury], however, repayment must be made on a basis of equality according to the requirements of commutative justice, namely *that the recompense of suffering be equal to the action*. Now these would not always be equality if suffering were in the same species as the action. Because, in the first place, when a person injures the person of one who is greater, the action surpasses any suffering of the same species that he might undergo, wherefore he that strikes a prince, is

not only struck back, but is much more severely punished' (*ST* II–II, qu. 61, art. 4).
St Thomas directly allies retaliation and commutative justice with God's judgment: 'This form of the divine judgment [retaliation] is in accordance with the
conditions of commutative justice, in so far as rewards are apportioned to merits, and punishments to sins' (*ST* II–II, qu. 61, art. 4, reply to obj. 1).

4 Theologically, *poena* is not in itself an evil since it is administered by God;
St Thomas cites the pseudo-Dionysius, 'Punishment is not an evil, but to *deserve*
punishment is' (*ST* I–II, qu. 87, art. 1, reply obj. 2). The evil is of human cause,
not of God's.

5 There abides in Dante the supposition of thirteen hundred years of Christian
thought that human metaphor can itself be a metaphor of God's unfathomable
ways: to be a poet and a realist in these terms is to take the metaphor as the only
reality, the only literality. Although critics have adduced various medieval dream
visions of the other world as sources, only in Dante do we observe an appeal to
doctrinal aptness through poetic metaphor instead of whim. It is my thesis, contrary to the usual *indagini* into the 'ordinamento morale dell'*Inferno*,' that the
paradigmatic ordering will only be seen when we consider the guilt of man rather
than the mysterious will of Dante's Deity. Compare St Augustine's view of the
comprehension of the degrees of perdition: 'The diversity of punishments is as
great as the diversity of sin. And Divine Wisdom judges more deeply the nature
of this diversity than human conjecture can explore or express.' (*In Joannis
Evangelium*, Tractatus LXXXIX, 4; *PL* 35, col. 1858; *Homily* LXXXIX, 4 on John
15:22–3 in *Homilies on the Gospel According to St. John and his First Epistle*,
in A Library of Fathers of the Holy Catholic Church Anterior to the Division of
East and West [Oxford: John Henry Parker 1849], II, 864.

6 *Epistola* XIII (in older editions, *Epistola* X), pp. 438–40; see also the text and
translation in *Dantis Alaghieri Epistolae: The Letters of Dante*, ed. Paget Toynbee,
2nd ed. with bibliographical appendix by Colin G. Hardie (Oxford: Clarendon
Press 1966), 174–7, 200–1. In paragraph 16 of the *Epistola*, the writer insists that
the branch of philosophy to which the *Commedia* belongs is that of morals and
ethics. The Poem as a whole is conceived with a practical object, that is, the doctrinal goal of teaching right action (p. 438; Toynbee ed., pp. 178–9, 202).

On the authenticity of the *Epistola* see the seminal studies of Francesco D'Ovidio
in *Studii sulla Divina Commedia* (Milan and Palermo: Sandron 1901), 448–85,
and Edward Moore in *Studies in Dante*, 3rd series (Oxford: Clarendon Press 1903),
284–369. A.C. Charity gives a helpful discussion and bibliography in *Events
and Their Afterlife: The Dialectics of Christian Typology in the Bible and Dante*
(Cambridge: Cambridge Univ. Press 1966), 170–1; 199–207 et passim. See also
the useful bibliography in Colin Hardie's edition of Toynbee's *Epistolae*, pp.
256–7, and that of Robert Hollander in *Allegory in Dante's Commedia* (Princeton,
NJ: Princeton Univ. Press 1969), 321–5.

7 *Epistola* XIII, p. 440; Toynbee ed., pp. 178, 202.

8 *Epistola* XIII, p. 438; Toynbee ed., pp. 173–4, 199.

9 St Bonaventure's works were also fundamental, especially his *Breviloquium*, Prol.
IV, 'De profunditate Sacrae Scripturae' (S. Bonaventurae, *Opuscula Varia Theo-logica* in *Opera Omnia*, vol. V [Quaracchi: Typographia Collegii S. Bonaventurae
1891], 205–6). For the threefold manner of allegory see Hugh of St Victor, *De
Sacramentis*, Prol. IV (*PL* 176, cols. 184–5); *On the Sacraments*, trans. Roy J.
Deferrari (Cambridge, Mass.: Mediaeval Academy of America 1951), 5. See also
Hugh's *Didascalicon* VI, 3–12 (*PL* 176, cols. 799–809); Hugonis de Sancto Victore,
Didascalicon de studio legendi, ed. Charles Henry Buttimer, The Catholic Univer-sity of America Studies in Medieval and Renaissance Latin, X (Washington, DC:
Catholic Univ. Press 1939), 113–30. St Thomas Aquinas, *Quaestiones quodlibe-tales* VII, vi, 15–16 (ed. R.P. Mandonnet [Paris: Lethielleux 1926], 279–80.

The epitome of the system is usually given in the distich attributed to Nicholas
of Lyra or Augustine of Dacia: 'Littera gesta docet, quid credas allegoria, / moralis
quid agas, quo tendas anagogia. / The literal level teaches the deeds; the allegory
what to believe; the moral how to act; the eschatological toward what you should
strive.'

To be brief, past, present, and future were represented by the various levels of
meaning. The literal level involved the historical events of the Old Testament;
the 'quid credas,' or allegory proper, dealt with the life of Christ and life in Christ;
it included the tradition of the Christian past. The moral, or tropological, level
involved prescription for present action; and the anagogical, or teleological, con-cerned the future 'last things' of the soul in the glory of heaven – or, as in the
present study, the state of souls in damnation.

Since the subject has been treated so often and so thoroughly, there is no
reason to give more than a short bibliographical outline here. The most important
study for biblical allegory is the monumental work by Henri de Lubac, *Exégèse
médiévale: les quatre sens de l'Ecriture*, 2 vols. in 2 parts (Paris: Aubier 1959–64)
(for the distich, vol. I, pt. 1, p. 23; see also Charity, *Events*, p. 174; Hollander,
Allegory, pp. 27–8). Also indispensable is C. Spicq's *Esquisse d'une histoire de
l'exégèse latine au Moyen Age*, Bibliothèque Thomiste, XXVI (Paris: Vrin 1944).
See also de Lubac's *Histoire et Esprit* (Paris: Aubier 1950), and Jean Daniélou,
Sacramentum futuri: Etudes sur les origines de la typologie biblique (Paris:
Aubier 1950).

Fundamental for the allegorical senses of the *Commedia* are Charles S. Single-ton's *Elements* (his chapter on 'Allegory,' pp. 1–17; 'Symbolism,' pp. 18–44; 'Two
Kinds of Allegory,' pp. 84–98). Useful also are the essay 'Sopra i quattro sensi
delle scritture' by G. Busnelli and G. Vandelli in their Appendix to the edition of
the *Convivio*, I, 240–2; Rocco Montano, *Storia della Poesia di Dante*, vol. I
(Naples: Quaderni di Delta 1962); Gian Roberto Sarolli, 'Autoesegesi dantesca e

tradizione esegetica medievale,' in *Prolegomena alla Divina Commedia*, Biblioteca dell'*Archivum Romanicum*, 112 (Florence: Olschki 1971), 1–39; Charity, *Events* (see his Bibliography, pp. 262–72); Hollander, *Allegory* (Hollander's Bibliography is definitive to 1969, pp. 321–35). For more recent studies, see Maria Picchio Simonelli, 'Allegoria e simbolo dal *Convivio* alla *Commedia* nello sfondo della cultura bolognese,' in *Dante e Bologna nei tempi di Dante* (Bologna: Commissione per i Testi di Lingua 1967), 207–26, her 'Vernacular Poetic Sources for Dante's Use of Allegory,' *Dante Studies*, 93 (1975), 131–42, and Robert Hollander's *Studies in Dante* (Ravenna: Longo 1980).

10 *ST*, I, qu. 1, art. 10; *Quaestiones quodlibetales* VII, vi, 16.

11 *Epistola* XIII, pp. 438–9; Toynbee ed., pp. 174, 199–200: 'His visis, manifestum est quod duplex oportet esse subiectum, circa quod currant alterni sensus. Et ideo videndum est de subiecto huius operis, prout ad literam accipitur; deinde de subiecto, prout allegorice sententiatur. Est ergo subiectum totius operis, literaliter tantum accepti, status animarum post mortem simpliciter sumptus. Nam de illo et circa illum totius operis versatur processus. Si vero accipiatur opus allegorice, subiectum est homo prout merendo et demerendo per arbitrii libertatem iustitiae praemiandi et puniendi obnoxius est.'

12 All commentators on allegory mention these facts. See D.W. Robertson, 'Some Medieval Literary Terminology,' *Studies in Philology*, 48 (1951), 687. See also Hollander's *Allegory*: 'Not all of Scripture (nor all of the *Divine Comedy*) is written in the historical, [literal] mode.' Further, 'if parable is excluded from containing fourfold senses, so are certain non-further-signifying historical passages' (pp. 22–3, 264 n. 38, p. 265). Singleton had warned in *Elements*: 'The historical sense, keeping its full force as such, can and does yield another sense. It *may* do this, indeed *will* do it *intermittently*' (p. 15; my italics).

13 Singleton, *Elements*, pp. 1–17, esp. p. 2.

14 'After death the souls will have a will unchangeable in evil.' St Thomas Aquinas, *Summa contra gentiles* IV, cap. 93; *On the Truth of the Catholic Faith: Summa contra gentiles: Book Four: Salvation*, trans. Charles J. O'Neil, Image Books (Garden City, NY: Doubleday 1957), 341–2.

15 These theories were propounded and thoroughly discussed by Erich Auerbach in 'Figura,' trans. Ralph Manheim in *Scenes from the Drama of European Literature: Six Essays by Erich Auerbach* (New York: Meridian Books 1959), 11–76, and in 'Figurative Texts Illustrating Certain Passages of Dante's *Commedia*,' *Speculum*, 21 (1946), 474–89; by Charles S. Singleton in *Elements* and *Journey*; and by Robert Hollander in *Allegory* and in his 'Dante *theologus-poeta*,' *Dante Studies*, 94 (1976), 91–136, reprint in his *Studies in Dante*, pp. 39–89.

16 *Epistola* XIII, p. 438; Toynbee ed., pp. 173–4, 199.

17 Charles S. Singleton, 'The Book of Memory,' in *An Essay on the Vita Nuova* (Cambridge, Mass.: Harvard Univ. Press 1958), 25–54. Gian Roberto Sarolli,

'Dante "scriba Dei," ' *Convivium*, 31 (1963), 385–422; 513–44; 641–71.

18 This was forcefully argued by Singleton, *Elements*, pp. 84–98. I use the term 'four levels' of meaning rather than 'four senses,' because Dante's text demands not only a linear, horizontal appreciation (of the story, the adventure) but also a vertical contemplation. The addresses to the reader tell us to pause and raise our minds. The point is made clear in *Purgatorio* II, 104–23 where attention to a poetic text 'as if nothing else touched our minds' is an act censured by the poet through Cato. The extra-textual (and intertextual) considerations are a primary imperative in Christian medieval literature. In this conception, the vertical contemplation which leads the mind to the Trinity avoids the confusion of *uti* and *frui*, the distinction which St Augustine explains in *De doctrina christiana* I, 3, 4, and 5.

19 Richard of St Victor, *De eruditione hominis interioris* II, cap. 1 (*PL* 196, col. 1347).

20 A failure to recognize the pattern of deiform images in the *Inferno* vitiated Allen H. Gilbert's study on Dante's *Conception of Justice* (Durham, NC: Duke Univ. Press 1925). His explanations of the punishments, like those of many critics, are for the most part mere guesswork.

See Paul Priest's interesting and useful study, 'Looking Back from the Vision: Trinitarian Structure and Poetry in the *Commedia*,' *Dante Studies*, 91 (1973), 113–30. Gian Roberto Sarolli reminds us that 'la *clavis lecturae* della *Divina Commedia* non rimane soltanto *cristocentrico* ma diventa *trinitariocentrico*.' *Prolegomena alla Divina Commedia*, p. 8.

21 This was the traditional exegesis on Numbers 21:9 and John 3:14; cf. St Cyril of Jerusalem, *Catechesis* XIII, 20 (*PG*, 33, cols. 797–8), and Rabanus Maurus, *Enarrationes in Librum Numerorum*, Lib. III, cap. ii (*PL*, 108, col. 713).

22 For an example of the thirsting Christ as a lyre, see *De vitis mystica* VIII, 31; *PL*, 184, col. 655. Rupert of Deutz uses the same tradition in his commentary *In Matthaeum*, 4 (*PL* 168, col. 1389); here Christ is 'the glorious lyre, sweet and sonorous, in which the music of the Father is inserted.' See also Glyn P. Norton, ' "Contrapasso" and Archetypal Metamorphoses in the Seventh Bolgia of Dante's *Inferno*,' *Symposium*, 25 (1971), 162–70; Norton misses the important biblical typologies.

The limner of ms. XIII. c. 4 in the Biblioteca Nazionale of Naples depicted Mastro Adamo literally as a lute; see the illustration, Tav. XXIII, in Mario Rotili, *I Codici danteschi miniati a Napoli* (Naples: Libreria Scientifica 1972). Some of the naivety of that illustrator may fade when we consider that Dante's artistic process in the depiction of the sins of Hell is also, precisely, the reduction of traditional metaphor to its 'dead letter' – to 'scritta morta.'

23 *Epistola* XIII, p. 443; Toynbee ed., pp. 185, 206. Cf. St Augustine, *Confessions* I, ii.

24 I agree entirely with Paul Priest's short summary: 'Bertrand made discord in Christian society, which is the Church, the body of Christ its Head. Therefore Bertrand and his head are disunited forever. But the language here is like "three

in one and one in three." Having divided a father and a son, Bertrand has symbolically blasphemed the chief bond of the Trinity itself. The words of the clearest doctrinal allusion are also those of the greatest poetic intensity' ('Trinitarian Structure,' p. 114).

25 The useful term was coined and expounded by Robert Hollander in his homonymous chapter (3) in *Allegory*, pp. 104–35. Throughout my study I have used some of the principles which Hollander there expresses. I have also consulted Johan Chydenius' *The Typological Problem in Dante*, Societas Scientiarum Fennica Commentationes Humanarum Litterarum, xxv (Helsinki 1958), 1–159, and his *Theory of Medieval Symbolism*, in the same series, vol. xxvii (1960), 1–42.

26 See Olin H. Moore, 'The Young King: Henry Plantagenet 1155–1183' in *History, Literature and Tradition* (Columbus: Ohio State Univ. Press 1925), esp. p. 10, where Moore cites William of Newburgh's reporting that Henry ii himself had called Prince Henry 'Absalom.' See also Teodolinda Barolini's careful and informative essay, 'Bertran de Born and Sordello: The Poetry of Politics in Dante's *Comedy*,' *PMLA*, 94 (1979), 395–405, esp. p. 405 n. 15.

27 Particularly, as I shall note in chapter 4, pp. 50–1, the exegesis of Psalm 108 was most influential. David's imprecations on Absalom were interpreted as being those of the Saviour upon Judas. Cf. St Jerome, *Breviarium in Psalmos, Psalm. CVIII* (*PL* 26, col. 1155). In medieval art Absalom was shown swinging by the hair of his head in accordance with 2 Kings (2 Samuel) 18:9, just as Bertran's head swings from his hand: 'e'l capo tronco tenea per le chiome' (*Inf.* xxviii, 121). See chapter 4, n. 37, below.

For other useful studies on Bertran de Born, see: Michele Scherillo, 'Bertram dal Bornio e il Re Giovane,' *Nuova antologia*, 154 (1897), 452–78; Hayden Boyers, 'Cleavage in Bertran de Born and Dante,' *Modern Philology*, 24 (1926–7), 1–3; Mario Fubini, 'Il canto xxviii dell' *Inferno*,' *Lectura dantis scaligera* (Florence: Le Monnier 1967), 999–1021; Marianne Shapiro, 'The Fictionalization of Bertran de Born,' *Dante Studies*, 92 (1974), 107–16; William D. Paden, Jr, 'Bertran de Born in Italy,' in *Italian Literature: Roots and Branches: Essays in Honor of Thomas Goddard Bergin*, ed. Giosè Rimanelli and Kenneth John Atchity (New Haven: Yale Univ. Press 1976), 39–66; Antonio Viscardi, 'Bertram dal Bornio,' *Enciclopedia dantesca, sub voce*.

28 The problem, which many other critics have seen, is that the literal level of Dante's Poem – omitting the Prologue scene – is also an eschatological one. Thus, often, the fourfold allegory of the Bible and the quadruple typology of the *Comedy* bear a relationship which might be patterned as follows:

Biblical exegesis	*Comedy*
literal or historical (past)	*Eschatological*, in that it deals with the hereafter, but now (in the fiction) it is a *past*, 'historical,' experience for Dante,
Old Testament	*scriba*, the Poet. The past sins of the damned, like the good works of the saved, are depicted in their state.

allegorical (past)	*Allegorical* (the *quid credas*) in that it reflects the life of Christ and *in* Christ in the events of the Journey.
New Testament	*Symbolical*, in that it reflects the Trinity in the New Testament, the sacraments, liturgy, art, liturgical drama, etc.
moral or tropological (present)	The past acts of the sinners and the blessed, which are now the cause of their eternal, ever-present state, act as *exempla* for our present life here. The moral sense is especially given through the *contrapasso*.
anagogical (future)	1 / The past journey to the hereafter which awaits us in the future.
	2 / The predicted perfection of the souls' punishments in Hell; the perfection of heavenly reward for the blessed in regaining their glorified bodies.
	3 / The predictions of Dante's own salvation in the Poem.
	4 / The ultimate effect on the reader who chooses the path to salvation.

What I have called, for simplicity, the 'static' quality of the punishments in Hell applies to the eternity of their state; there is, as I mention in section 2 above, the additional prophetic, teleological perfection of their *poena*: the heresiarchs' tombs will be closed on Judgment Day; the suicides' bodies will be hanged on their thorn bushes; the last simonist will thrust his predecessor deeper into his fiery font, and so on. The essence of the punishments, however, will abide forever.

29 John Freccero, 'Bestial Sign and Bread of Angels (*Inferno* 32–33),' *Yale Italian Studies*, 1 (1977), 53–66.

30 'In Exitu Israel de Aegypto,' *Seventy-eighth Annual Report of the Dante Society*, 78 (1960), 1–24, now in *Dante: A Collection of Critical Essays*, ed. John Freccero, Twentieth-Century Views (Englewood Cliffs, NJ: Prentice-Hall 1965), 102–21. Dunstan J. Tucker, OSB, 'In exitu Israel de Aegypto: The *Divine Comedy* in the Light of the Easter Liturgy,' *The American Benedictine Review*, 11 (1960), 43–61.

31 Per Lundberg, *La Typologie baptismale dans l'ancienne Eglise*, Acta Seminarii Neotestamentici Upsaliensis, x (Uppsala: Almquist and Wiksell 1942); Jean Daniélou, *The Bible and the Liturgy*, ed. Michael A. Mathis, Liturgical Studies (Notre Dame, Indiana: Univ. of Notre Dame Press 1956), esp. pp. 70–113. See also John Freccero, 'The River of Death: *Inferno* II, 108,' in *The World of Dante: Six Studies in Language and Thought*, ed. S. Bernard Chandler and Julius A. Molinaro (Toronto: Published for the Dante Society [of Toronto] by University of Toronto Press 1966), 25–42, and John F. Vickrey, ' "Exodus" and the Battle in the Sea,' *Traditio*, 27 (1972), 119–40.

32 Dante's description of the movement of the 'messo' or angel over the swamp of Styx also repeats Christ's method of *descensus ad inferos*; St Thomas informs us that 'Christ's soul descended into Hell not by the same kind of motion as that

whereby bodies are moved, *but by that kind whereby angels are moved*' (*ST* III, qu. 52, art. 1).

33 See Ronald B. Herzman and William A. Stephany, ' "O miseri seguaci": Sacramental Inversion in *Inferno* XIX,' *Dante Studies*, 96 (1978), 39–65; and Reginald French, 'Simony and Pentecost,' *Annual Report of the Dante Society*, 82 (1964), 3–17.

34 Carl-Martin Edsman, *Le Baptême de feu*, Acta Seminarii Neotestamentici Upsaliensis, IX (Leipzig: Alfred Lorentz, Uppsala: A.-B. Lundequist; Almquist and Wiksell 1940). Compare also St Thomas, *ST* III, qu. 39, art. 5, reply to obj. 2.

35 Matthew 3:15. On the question of the journey to justice see Charles S. Singleton, *Journey*.

36 See Singleton's discussion in *Elements*, pp. 24–9.

37 Singleton, *Elements*, pp. 18–44; John Freccero, 'Casella's Song (*Purg.* II, 112),' *Dante Studies*, 91 (1973), 73–80.

38 On the difference in the structure of vision in the three realms, see especially Francis X. Newman's 'St. Augustine's Three Visions and the Structure of the *Commedia*,' *Modern Language Notes*, 82 (1967), 56–78, and Marguerite Mills Chiarenza, 'The Imageless Vision and Dante's *Paradiso*,' *Dante Studies*, 90 (1972), 77–92.

39 Even if we were to ignore the *Epistola* to Can Grande, Cacciaguida's urging Dante to write of his otherworld experiences (*Paradiso* XVII, 124–32) gives the same didactic aim:

... 'Coscienza fusca
  o de la propria o de l'altrui vergogna
  pur sentirà la tua parola brusca.
Ma nondimen, rimossa ogne menzogna,
  tutta tua visïon fa manifesta;
  e lascia pur grattar dov'è la rogna.
Ché se la voce tua sarà molesta
  nel primo gusto, vital nodrimento
  lascerà poi, quando sarà digesta ...'

A conscience dark, either with its own or with another's shame, will indeed feel your speech to be harsh. But none the less, all falsehood set aside, make manifest all that you have seen; and then let them scratch where the itch is. For if at first taste your voice be grievous, yet shall it leave thereafter vital nourishment when digested.

By these lines, A.C. Charity insists that 'Dante consciously intends to alter his reader through the poem, to offend in order to edify' (*Events*, p. 221 n. 2). Later Charity reiterates: 'The poem does aim, and persistently, to provoke the reader into implicit self-criticism.' To demonstrate how this may be so, however, the critic uses only the example of Francesca (pp. 212–26).

CHAPTER TWO: FARINATA

1 Among the most important items on Farinata, I recommend to the reader's attention: Francesco de Sanctis, 'Il Farinata di Dante,' in *Nuovi Saggi Critici*, 27th edition (Naples: Morano 1914), 21–50; Erich Auerbach, 'Farinata and Cavalcante,' in *Mimesis*, trans. Willard Trask (Princeton, NJ: Princeton Univ. Press 1953; reprint Garden City, NY: Doubleday Anchor Books 1957), 151–77; Antonio Pagliaro, 'Il disdegno di Guido,' *Saggi di critica semantica*, Biblioteca di cultura contemporanea, 40 (Messina: G. D'Anna 1961), 359–80; see also his *Ulisse: ricerche semantiche sulla Divina Commedia* (Messina: G. D'Anna 1967), II, 185–224; Mario Lucidi, 'Ancora sul "disdegno" di Guido,' *Cultura Neolatina*, 14 (1954), 203–16; Rocco Montano, 'Mio figlio ov'è? Perché non è ei teco?' *Delta*, n.s. 2–3, nos. 11–12 (1957), 17–32; J.A. Mazzeo, 'Dante and Epicurus,' *Comparative Literature*, 10 (1958), 106–20; Giorgio Padoan, 'Il canto degli Epicurei,' *Convivium*, anno XXVII, 1 (1959), 12–39; Giorgio Padoan, 'Il Canto X dell'*Inferno*,' *Letture Classensi*, 5 (1975), 81–99; Giorgio Padoan and Rocco Montano, 'Per l'interpretazione del Canto degli Epicurei,' *Convivium*, anno XXVIII, 6 (1960), 707–28; Charles S. Singleton, '*Inferno* X: Guido's Disdain,' *Modern Language Notes*, 77 (1962), 49–65; John A. Scott, 'Inferno X: Farinata as "magnanimo,"' *Romance Philology*, 15 (1962), 395–411. Robert M. Durling has independently identified some of the iconographical and sacramental imagery in the canto: see his important 'Farinata and the Body of Christ, *Stanford Italian Review*, 2 (Spring, 1981), 5–35. As his title suggests, Durling concentrates more on the eucharistic imagery and thus complements this chapter on the baptismal implications.

2 Padoan, 'Canto X,' pp. 23–5.

3 To assert and increase their standing over other men, heresiarchs appealed to the *secret*, occult qualities of the knowledge supposedly vouchsafed them, according to the Fathers of the Church. Cf: St Gregory the Great, *Moralia in Job* V, 45; V, 49; XX, 18; XX, 23 (the caves of the earth are the 'hidden preachings' of heretics), *PL* 75, 76; *Morals* I, 275, 277; II, 461, 466. St Bernard, in *Sermo* LXV, 2, *Super Cantica Canticorum* in Sancti Bernardi *Opera*, ed. J. Leclerq et al. (Rome: Editiones Cistercienses 1958), II, 173, echoes St Gregory in referring to the *secret* meeting places of heretics. Guido da Pisa glosses Dante's line thus: 'Quia mos est omnium hereticorum suos errores et fallacias occultare.' *Expositiones et Glose super Comediam Dantis or Commentary on Dante's Inferno*, ed. Vincenzo Cioffari (Albany, NY: State Univ. of New York Press 1974), 194.

4 *DCD* XV, iv (vol. 4, pp. 424–5); XIX, v (vol. 6, pp. 138–43). Herbert A. Deane's *The Political and Social Ideas of St Augustine* (New York and London: Columbia Univ. Press 1963) is most useful on this subject, esp. pp. 78–115; Etienne Gilson, *Introduction à l'étude de Saint Augustin*, 2nd ed. (Paris: J. Vrin 1943), has a select bibliography, pp. 338–40. Gilson points out: 'La cité terrestre n'est pas

l'Etat. En effet, tous les membres de cette cité sont prédestinés à la damnation finale' (p. 237). This 'città' or 'terra' symbolizes the city of Florence only in so far as we deal with its sinful, damned members. For a clarification of the term 'city of God,' consult F. Edward Cranz, 'De Civitate Dei, xv, 2, and Augustine's Idea of the Christian Society,' Speculum, 25 (1950), 215–25; reprinted in Augustine, A Collection of Critical Essays, ed. Robert A. Markus (Garden City, NY: Double-day Anchor Books 1972), 404–21. See Joan M. Ferrante, 'Florence and Rome: The Two Cities of Man in the Divine Comedy,' in The Early Renaissance (Acta 5), ed. Aldo S. Bernardo (Binghamton: Center for Medieval and Early Renaissance Studies, State University of New York, 1978), 1–19. I should also add that, in their illustrations, both Botticelli and Domenico di Michelino use Florence's gates with their merlatura guelfa as the gate of Hell.

5 DCD v, xiv, xv (vol. 2, pp. 211–15). Epistula cxviii, ed. A. Goldbacher, CSEL (1895), xxxiv, pt. 2, p. 285: 'Unless humility precedes, accompanies, and follows every good action ... pride wrests wholly from our hand any good work [aliquo bono facto] on which we are congratulating ourselves.' Cf. Inf. vi, 88.

6 DCD v, xiii (vol. 2, pp. 208–9): 'Minus turpes sunt.'

7 DCD xix, xii (vol. 6, pp. 170–1).

8 DCD xix, xv (vol. 6, pp. 186–7).

9 DCD xvi, ii (vol. 6, pp. 6–7). The chapter deals with the 'calida inquietudo' of heretics. In Contra litteras Petiliani Donatistae cortensis episcopi ii, 219, St Augustine writes: 'Dissensio quippe vos et divisio facit haereticos: pax vero et unitas facit catholicos' (PL 43, col. 333).

10 Brunetto Latini, Livres dou Trésor, ed. Francis J. Carmody, Univ. of California Publications in Modern Philology, 22 (Berkeley 1948), 313.

11 Garnier de Rochefort (attributed to Rabanus Maurus), Allegoriae in Sacram Scripturam (PL 112, col. 895); Guido da Pisa, p. 197; Alanus de Insulis, Liber in distinctionibus dictionum theologicum, PL 210, cols. 746 (collum), 737 (cervix); Summa de Arte Praedicatoria, PL 210, col. 132 ('Contra Superbiam'); St Augustine, DCD xix, iv (vol. 6, pp. 132–3). Heretics are 'tauri cervicosi' in St Bruno, Expositio in Psalmos (Ps. lxvii), PL 152, cols. 965–6. See St Gregory, Moralia xxxv, 14, on the heretics' 'neck of pride' (PL 76, col. 757; Morals iii, pt. 2, p. 671).

12 Allegoriae in Sacram Scripturam (PL 112, cols. 1023–4).

13 DCD xiv, xxviii (vol. 4, pp. 404–5).

14 St Gregory, Moralia, Praef., cap. vi (15), PL 75, col. 525; Morals i, 27. St Thomas Aquinas, ST ii–ii, qu. 162, art. 2; art. 6.

15 Padoan, 'Canto x,' p. 28. St Augustine, Enarratio in Psalmum cxxiv, 5 (PL 37, col. 1652). Pride apes fortitude and daring (St Thomas, ST ii–ii, qu. 162, art. 6).

16 DCD v, xv, xx (vol. 2, pp. 214–17, 244–5); v, xix (vol. 2, pp. 242–3): 'There is no true virtue where virtue is subordinated to human glory.'

17 Moralia xvii, 5; PL 76, col. 12; Morals ii, 281–2.

18 *Moralia* III, 45; *PL* 75, col. 622; *Morals* I, 161–2.
19 Giorgio Petrocchi, 'Tre Postille in margine a Farinata,' *Studi danteschi*, 42 (1965), esp. pp. 275–80.
20 *Moralia* III, 43; *PL* 75, col. 621; *Morals* I, 160.
21 Francesco de Sanctis, *Nuovi saggi critici*, p. 38; Michele Barbi, 'Il Canto di Farinata,' *Studi danteschi*, 8 (1924), 105. Compare Rocco Montano, 'Mio figlio,' p. 19: 'Farinata non è l'amore della patria o la passione politica, è l'epicureo, l'uomo che ha fatto della patria terrena il vero fine, il fascista cieco e superbo.'
22 St Thomas Aquinas, *ST* II–II, qu. 11, art. 2. Cf. Padoan, 'Canto degli Epicurei,' p. 722, and Montano, 'Mio filio,' p. 19.
    In his well-researched essay, 'Farinata and the Body of Christ,' Robert Durling makes a suggestion which at first blush seems most attractive: he identifies Farinata as a Stoic and Cavalcante as an Epicurean. The personalities are indeed drawn as being quite distinct within the poem, and, in the Acts of the Apostles, Boethius, St Augustine, and other Fathers, the Stoics and the Epicureans are lumped together for vituperation. I cannot, however, ultimately agree with this interpretation for a number of intra- and extratextual reasons.
    First, Dante does not here name the Stoics at all:
        Suo cimitero da questa parte hanno
            con Epicuro tutti suoi seguaci
            che l'anima col corpo morta fanno.

                                                                    (13–15)
Most serious against the argument is the fact that *the Stoa did not deny the immortality of the soul*, but rather, believed firmly in its transmigration, a fact known from classical times to the fourteenth century from countless sources but especially through such writers as Lactantius and St Augustine. In the *Divine Institutes* III, 18, Lactantius tells us: 'Others ... hold ... that *souls do remain after death*. These are chiefly Pythagoreans and Stoics. ... For because *they feared that argument* from which it might be gathered *that it is necessary that souls die with the bodies*, since they are born with them, they said that souls are not born but rather are put into bodies and migrate from one to another.' *PL* 6, cols. 405–6; Lactantius, *The Divine Institutes*, trans. Sister Mary Francis McDonald, Fathers of the Church, 49 (Washington: Catholic Univ. of America 1964), 213. Dante himself in *Convivio* II, viii cites the Stoics' belief in the soul's immortality: 'Se noi rivolgiamo tutte le scritture ... tutti concordano in questo, che in noi sia parte alcuna perpetuale ... questo par volere massimamente ciascuno Stoïco.'
    My main argument, and one which Durling supports, is that the very iconography of Farinata and the diction in which his posturing is described evokes with harsh negative irony the Christian immortality of the soul and the Resurrection of the Flesh. Any intrusion of a pagan idea of the survival of the soul, therefore, would spoil Dante's poetic conception.
    In Dante's own time the term 'Ghibelline' was confused and equated with the

term 'Epicurean' (see n. 23, below); Farinata was the Ghibelline leader. Lastly, following St Augustine, Dante says that sinners are buried with their co-sectarians (*Inf.* IX, 130); thus, according to the text itself, both Cavalcante and Farinata are followers of Epicurus. The Stoic, Cato, is placed by Dante in the *Purgatorio*. (See also *Divine Institutes* III, 17, 19, and 27; VII, 8–12 for Cato, the Stoics, and transmigration; on the question in Augustine, see *DCD* I, 23–4; see also Hippolytus, *Refutation of all Heresies* I, 18–19 in the Ante-Nicene Fathers, vol. 5, trans. Alexander Roberts and James Donaldson [Grand Rapids, Michigan: Eerdmans 1971], 20–1).

23 'Il termine 'epicurii'è poi usato costantemente dal Villani per indicare insieme e i ghibellini e i patarini, secondo la consueta confusione guelfo-popolare.' Padoan, 'Canto X', p. 21. See Gioacchino Volpe, 'Ghibellinismo, Impero ed eresia,' *Movimenti religiosi e sette ereticali nella società medievale italiana, secoli XI–XIV* (Florence: Sansoni 1961), 127–34.

24 St Augustine, *In Epistolam Johannis ad Parthos* IX, 5; *PL* 35, col. 2049. See also *Ad Parthos* IX, 2, 3, 4, and 6.

25 *Moralia* V, 29; *PL* 75, cols. 694–5; *Morals* I, 263.

26 Hugh of St Victor (in 'De qualitate tormentorum gehennalium,' *De Sacramentis* II, xvi, 5; *PL* 176, cols. 587–90) cites pertinent passages from St Augustine's *DCD* and from St Gregory's *Moralia* on this question (pp. 441–4).

27 Fire recurs as a symbol of unbelief in the *Inferno*. The 'foco' of Limbo (*Inf.* IV, 68), though it indicates a lack of true Faith, seems to represent more a regretful reminder of the limitation of human intellect than a punishment. For this reason I omit its discussion here. Cf. *Purg.* VII, 7–8: 'Io son Virgilio; e per null'altro rio / lo ciel perdei che per non aver fé.'

28 Titulus, I, B: 'De hereticis et paterenis,' *Historia diplomatica Friderici Secundi,* ed. J.-L.-A. Huillard-Bréholles (Paris: Plon 1854; reprint Turin: Bottega D'Erasmo 1963), tom. IV. pars I, p. 7.

29 Henry Charles Lea, *A History of the Inquisition in the Middle Ages* (New York: Russell and Russell 1955), I, 221. For a recent bibliography on heresy in Florence in the thirteenth century, see John N. Stephens, 'Heresy in Medieval and Renaissance Florence,' *Past and Present*, 54 (1972), esp. pp. 25–34. See also Felice Tocco, *Quel che non c'è nella Divina Commedia o Dante e l'eresia*, Biblioteca storico-critico della letteratura dantesca, VI (Bologna: Zanichelli 1899); Alfonso Ricolfi, 'La setta dei Catari a Firenze e la "Mandetta" di Guido Cavalcanti,' *Nuova rivista storica*, 14 (1930), 560–71; Alfonso De Salvio, *Dante and Heresy* (Boston: Dumas Bookshop 1936); and Maria Picchio Simonelli's excellent essay 'L'Inquisizione e Dante: alcune osservazioni,' in *Dante Studies*, 97 (1979), 129–49.

30 The phrase appears in St Bernard, *Sermo* LXVI, 12 (*Opera* II, 186); *Cantica Canticorum*, trans. and ed. Samuel J. Eales (London: Elliot Stock 1895), 406.

31 Stefano Orlandi, '*Necrologio*' *di S. Maria Novella* (Florence: Olschki 1955), I,

230 (see also p. 10, et passim); Lea, I, 327. The great Aldobrandino later became prior of Santa Maria Novella, Bishop of Orvieto, and, in Rome, Vicar of the Pope; he died in 1279 (*Necrologio*, pp. 230–5).

32 Niccolò Ottokar, 'Intorno a Farinata e alla sua famiglia,' *Archivio storico italiano* (1919), II, 126–63 (esp. pp. 159–63), reprinted in *Studi comunali e fiorentini* (Florence: La Nuovo Italia 1948), 118. Ottokar publishes the original order of posthumous cremation. According to this document, the bones of Farinata and his wife were to be exhumed 'if they could be told from those of the faithful' ('si a fidelium hossibus discerni poterunt'); it is possible that the manner of gathering and placing these bones on the flames in public display influenced the strong visual and olfactory images of *Inf.* IX and X. (Cf. *Purg.* XXVII, 17–18, 'imaginando forte / umani corpi già veduti accesi.')

33 *Moralia* III, 45; *PL* 75, col. 622; *Morals* I, 161.

34 *Moralia* XX, 23; *PL* 76, col. 151; *Morals* II, 465.

35 *Sermo* LXVI, 12 (*Opera* II, 186); *Cantica Canticorum*, p. 406.

36 *Moralia* XVIII, 42; *PL* 76, col. 59; *Morals* II, 345–6 (italics added).

37 *De Cathechizandis rudibus* XIX, 31; *PL* 40, col. 333; *The First Catechetical Instruction*, trans. Joseph P. Christopher (Westminster, Md.: Newman Bookshop 1946), 61 (italics added). The theme is common in the Church Fathers. Compare St Gregory, *Moralia* IX, 98 (*PL* 75, col. 913; *Morals* I, 568); St Augustine, *Ad Fratres in eremo Sermo* LXVIII (*PL* 40, col. 1355).

38 Joannes Abricensis [John of Avranches], *Liber de Officiis Ecclesiasticis*, 'Ordo Paschae' (*PL* 147, cols. 53–8).

   Compare also the *Allegoriae in Sacram Scripturam* (*PL* 112, col. 864): 'Arca, Ecclesia, ut in Psalmis [131:8]: "Surge, Domine, in requiem tuam," id est, surge a mortuis, surgat et Ecclesia, quam dignatus es sanctificare.' I believe the passage in the Psalm to be the basis of the 'Imago pietatis' or 'Man of Sorrows' depictions discussed below. Dante's inversion is evident.

39 Cited by Carla Gottlieb, 'The Living Host,' *Konsthistorisk Tidskrift* (Stockholm), 38 (1969), 30–46, esp. p. 31; my thanks to Allen Stuart Weller for this reference. *Eclogae de Officio Missae* (*PL* 105, col. 1326). One might add that not only was the altar a tomb but that the manger of the Christ Child was also depicted as both a tomb and altar in art.

40 *Historia francorum* x, xv (*PL* 71, col. 544). Compare also the *Allegoriae in Sacram Scripturam* (*PL* 112, col. 864): 'Arca est corpus Christi.'

41 Karl Young, *The Drama of the Medieval Church* (Oxford: Clarendon Press 1933; reprint 1962), I, 240–410. Neil C. Brooks, *The Sepulchre of Christ in Art and Liturgy with Special Reference to Liturgical Drama*, Univ. of Illinois Studies in Language and Literature, VII (Urbana: Univ. of Illinois Press 1921), 46–9, 58. *Liber de Officiis* (*PL* 147, col. 54): 'Post tertium responsorium officium sepulcri celebretur. ...'

42 Though it may be argued that such a tradition is due to lack of perspective, such an argument cannot hold in the cases where the lid upon which the angel sits is depicted alone, without the tomb, and clearly on a higher plane than the ground upon which the Marys stand. The lid moves as angels move. See plate 1. See also Brooks, *The Sepulchre*, p. 24.

43 See the illustrations from the eleventh, twelfth, and thirteenth centuries in Gertrud Schiller's so far un-Englished volume, *Ikonographie der christlichen Kunst*, Bd. III (Gütersloh: Gerd Mohn 1971), plates 187, 188, 190, 191, 192, and 193. These illustrations do not show Christ actually stepping forth from the tomb and are thus parallel to the posture of Farinata.

44 On this question see: J.A. Endres, 'Die Darstellung des Gregorsmesse im Mittelalter,' *Zeitschrift für christliche Kunst*, 30 (1917), 146–56; Georg Swarzenski, 'Insinuationes divinae pietatis,' *Festschrift für Adolph Goldschmidt, zum 60. Geburtstag* (Leipzig: E.A. Seemann 1923), 65–74; Romuald Bauerreiss, OSB, 'Der gregorianische Schmerzensmann und das "Sacramentum Sancti Gregorii" in Andechs, *Studien und Mitteilungen zur Geschichte des Benediktinerordens und seiner Zweige* (Salzburg), 44, n.s. 13 (1926), 55–79; Romuald Bauerreiss, OSB, *Pie Jesu (Das Schmerzensmannbild)* (Munich: K. Widmann 1931); Erwin Panofsky, ' "Imago pietatis": Ein Beitrag zur Typengeschichte des "Schmerzensmannes" und der "Maria Mediatrix," ' *Festschrift für Max J. Friedländer zum 60. Geburtstage* (Leipzig: E.A. Seemann 1927), 261–308; Hubert Schrade, 'Beiträge zur Erklärung des Schmerzensmannbildes,' *Deutschkundliches, Friedrich Panzer zum 60. Geburtstag, Beiträge zur neueren Literaturgeschichte*, XVI (Heidelberg: Carl Winter 1930), 164–82; Gert von der Osten, 'Der Schmerzensmann: Typengeschichte eines deutschen Andachtsbildwerkes von 1300 bis 1600,' *Forschungen zur deutschen Kunstgeschichte*, 7 (Berlin: Deutscher Verein für Kunstwissenschaft 1935); Wiltrud Mersmann, *Der Schmerzensmann* (Düsseldorf: L. Schwann 1952); Gertrud Schiller, *Iconography of Christian Art*, vol. II, *The Passion of Jesus Christ*, trans. Janet Seligman (Greenwich, Conn.: New York Graphic Society 1972), 184–230.

45 Emile Mâle, *L'Art religieux de la fin du Moyen Age: étude sur l'iconographie du moyen âge en France et ses sources d'inspiration* (Paris: A. Colin 1908), 91ff; Gabriel Millet, *Recherches sur l'iconographie de l'évangile aux XIVe, XVe et XVIe siècles d'après les monuments de Mistra, de la Macédoine et du Mont-Athos*, Bibliothèque des Ecoles Françaises d'Athènes et de Rome (Paris: Fontemoing 1916), 483–8.

For a résumé of the literature on the subject see Romuald Bauerreiss, OSB, 'Ο ΒΑΣΙΛΕΥΣ ΤΗΣ ΔΟ≡ΗΣ: Ein frühes eucharistisches Bild und seine Auswirkung,' *Pro mundi vita, Festschrift zum Eucharistischen Weltkongress, 1960* (Munich: M. Hueber 1960), 49–67. Bauerreiss states that the original Man of

Sorrows was in the Chapel of John VII in Old Saint Peter's together with the Veil of Veronica. See also Schiller, *Iconography* II, 199.

46 Carlo Bertelli, 'The Image of Pity in Santa Croce in Gerusalemme,' *Essays in the History of Art Presented to Rudolf Wittkower*, vol. II, ed. Douglas Fraser et al. (London: Phaidon 1967), 40–55.

47 Panofsky, 'Imago pietatis,' p. 261; Mersmann, p. xxxiii; Schiller, *Iconography* II, 208–11.

48 Schiller, *Iconography* II, plate 684.

49 Mersmann, p. xxxiii, plate 8.

50 This fresco most probably dates after Dante's death and certainly after his exile; it is noted to indicate the prevalence of the Man of Sorrows figure.

51 See Rudolf Berliner, 'Arma Christi,' *Münchner Jahrbuch der bildenden Kunst*, 6 (1955), 35–152. Schiller, 'The "Arma Christi" and Man of Sorrows,' *Iconography* II, 184–230.

52 In such illustrations, St Mary represented the New Law after Christ, while St John the Divine was made to represent the Old Law before his coming. St John's identification was due to his having arrived first at the Holy Sepulchre before St Peter, but having failed to enter it; Dante refers to the episode in *Par.* XXIV, 124–6). In a curious infernal parody, Dante and Virgil 'flanking' Farinata's tomb mirror such an 'AD' and 'BC' presence.

Concerning the verses in John 20:3–8, see *De Mon.* III, ix, 16 and *Par.* XXIV, 124–6.

53 Gertrud Schiller, however, follows Gert von der Osten's erroneous assertion that 'Sculptural rendering of the Man of Sorrows was unknown in Italy in the Middle Ages' (*Iconography* II, 204 n. 30). I have been able to collect scores of examples in northern Italy and in the precise areas of Dante's exile.

54 On Can Grande's tomb see Erwin Panofsky, in *Tomb Sculpture*, ed. H.W. Janson (New York: Harry N. Abrams n.d.), 75, 84; plates 385–7. Unfortunately, the Panofsky volume does not reproduce a detail of the important Man of Sorrows figure. For many reproductions of the *Schmerzensmann*, see Schiller, *Iconography* II, plates 681–761.

Since Christ's stepping from his tomb was not specifically described in the Gospels, one finds few artistic depictions of the act before the thirteenth century; but it gained an immense popularity thereafter. The event of the Resurrection was previously most commonly celebrated by the scene of the women and the angel at the sepulchre. Emile Mâle, *The Gothic Image: Religious Art in France in the Thirteenth Century*, trans. Dora Nussey (New York: Harper and Row 1958), 194 n. 1; Brooks, *The Sepulchre*, pp. 7, 13. The death of Christ and his burial, however, *was* so described and, as we point out, the figure of 'Cristo morto' was a common funerary motif. Dante appears to have the two latter scenes uppermost

in his mind in *Inf.* IX and X. Medieval Christian liturgical ceremonies were celebrated at a *sepulcrum* as altar to symbolize the tomb of Christ. On Good Friday
came the *depositio* in which the cross, crucifix, and or the Host was placed within
the tomb or 'arca'; on Easter morning at the *elevatio* the 'buried' symbols were
raised to represent the Resurrection (Brooks, pp. 7, 37–58). Karl Young, *The
Dramatic Associations of the Easter Sepulchre*, Univ. of Wisconsin Studies in
Language and Literature, X (Madison 1920). Reprinted in his *Drama of the Medieval Church* I, ch. 4.

   See the illustrations in Schiller's *Ikonographie*, Bd. III, *Die Auferstehung und
Erhöhung Christi*, the Resurrection, pp. 328–9, 379–409; the Women at the
Tomb, pp. 310–26; the Harrowing, pp. 348–79.

55 Josef Fink's *Noe der Gerechte in der frühchristlichen Kunst*, Beihefte zum Archiv
   für Kulturgeschichte, 4 (Münster and Cologne: Böhlau-Verlag 1955) presents sixty
   pages with representations of the theme from both wall paintings and sculpture.
   See also Friedrich W. Deichmann, *Repertorium der christlich-antiken Sarkophage*
   (Wiesbaden: F. Steiner 1967); Josef Wilpert, *I sarcofagi cristiani antichi* (Rome:
   Istituto Pontificio di Archeologia Cristiana 1929–36), 3 vols.; see esp. vol. I,
   Tavole, IV, 3; LVII; vol. II, *Tavole*, CLXX; CLXXIV, 10; CLXXV, 6, 8; CLXXVII, 2, 3, 5;
   CCXXVIII, 1; CLXXXI, 2, 3, 4, 5; CCXXIV, 7; and CCLV, 7.

   Compare the illustrations in Peter Brieger, Millard Meiss, and Charles S.
   Singleton, *Illuminated Manuscripts of the Divine Comedy*, Bollingen Series 81
   (Princeton Univ. Press 1969), II, 135–49.

   Noah was merely one of several Old Testament sarcophagal themes of deliverance foreshadowing Christ's redemption. Among others were the Fall itself,
   Elijah's chariot, Abraham and Isaac, the Three Hebrew Children in the fiery furnace, Daniel in the lion's den, Susannah and the Elders, Jonah and the whale,
   and Joseph in the well. (Joseph in his stone structure, like Noah opening the Ark
   and Jonah coming forth from the whale, was shown from the waist up.) Most of
   these events also figure in the *Commendatio animarum* or Office of the Dead.

   The heretics' tombs also resemble other related themes of resurrection in art:
   the biblical raising of Lazarus and other such resuscitation miracles from the Apocrypha; the Harrowing of Hell and the Descent to Limbo based on the Gospel of
   Nicodemus or the Acts of Pilate (in which the Patriarchs are often shown arising
   from open tombs as Christ removes them from Hell); and the opening of the
   graves at the Last Judgment. This last is vividly portrayed in the mosaics in the
   Baptistry of Florence created during Dante's lifetime.

56 *In Genesin*, Cap. VII, 1 (*PL* 83, col. 229).

57 *Glossa ordinaria, Lib. Gen.* VI (*PL* 113, col. 105).

   For Noah as the type of Christ see St Augustine, *De doctrina cristiana* IV, xxi, 45
   (*On Christian Doctrine*, trans. D.W. Robertson, Library of Liberal Arts [Indian-
   apolis and New York: Bobbs-Merrill 1958], 153). For Noah as the 'vir justus' see

R.E. Kaske, 'Sì si conserva il seme d'ogne giusto (*Purg.* XXXII, 48),' *Dante Studies*, 89 (1971), 49–54.

58 *De cat.* XXVII, 53; *PL* 40, col. 346; *First Cat.*, p. 84. *DCD* XV, xxvi (vol. 4, pp. 564–7): 'We doubtless have here [in the Ark] a symbolic representation of the City of God sojourning as an alien in this world; that is, of the church which wins salvation by virtue of the wood on which the mediator between God and men, the man Christ Jesus, was suspended.' *DCD* XVI, vii (vol. 5, pp. 40–1): 'It appears much more obvious that all species were in the ark not so much for the sake of renewing animal life as to typify the different races of mankind [quam figurandarum variarum gentium] in order to symbolize the Church.' Origen, *In Genesim Homilia* II, 65; *PG* 12, col. 171 (Noah is Christ; the ark is the Church). Hugh of St Victor, *De Arca Noe* I, iv, 'De arca Ecclesiae, seu Ecclesia' (*PL* 176, cols. 629–30). Similarly, Hugh of St Victor describes the three 'mansiones' of the Ark which are defined by three states of the present life; the second or central one is of interest here: 'secundus status est illorum hominum, qui vocantur animales, de quibus dicit rursum: "Animalis autem homo non percepit ea quae sunt Spiritus Dei" (1 Cor. 2:14).' The middle son of Noah is Ham, the heretic. The images are parallel to the medieval reputation of Epicurus 'of the herd of swine.'

59 *De cat.* XIX, 32; *PL* 40, col. 334; *First Cat.*, p. 62.

60 St Jerome, *Liber de nominibus hebraicis*, *PL* 23, col. 777: *DCD* XVI, ii (vol. 5, pp. 6–7, italics added). Rabanus Maurus quotes sections of St Augustine's passage verbatim (*Commentaria in Genesim* II, ix [*PL* 107, col. 526]). See also St Ambrose, *De Noe et Arca*, cap. XXXII, *PL* 14, col. 414; Rupert of Deutz, *De Trinitate et operibus eius*, lib. IV, cap. xxxviii, *PL* 167, cols. 362–3; Hugh of St Victor, *De arca Noe* I, cap. iv, 'De arca Ecclesiae, seu Ecclesia' (*PL* 176, cols. 629–30).

61 Wilpert, vol. II, *Tavole*, CLXXIV, 10; CLXXV, 7; CLXXXI, 3; CLXXXI, 5.

62 *PL* 176, cols. 653–7; 697–8.

63 *PL* 176, cols. 653–7; 697–8. For comparison I refer for convenience to Migne's edition which is, at this point, adequate: *Glossa ordinaria, Lib. Gen.* VI, 16–18, (*PL* 113, col. 106).

64 *PL* 176, col. 698.

65 On the importance of the souls' foresight and lack of present knowledge, see Antonio Gramsci, *Letteratura e vita nazionale* (Turin: Einaudi 1950; reprint 1954), VI, 34–45; *Lettere dal carcere* (Turin: Einaudi 1947; reprint 1955), 138.

66 Even if such an absolute determination will not be accepted by all critics, we can at least assert the fittingness that the explanation should *occur* here among the Epicureans and nowhere else.

67 See Charles S. Singleton, *Inferno: Commentary*, p. 157 n. 99.

68 See the illustration in Singleton, *Inferno: Commentary*, 142–3.

69 *On the Soul and Resurrection* in *Ascetical Works*, trans. Virginia Woods Callahan, The Fathers of the Church (Washington, DC: Catholic Univ. of America Press

1967), 202; *PG* 46, cols. 22–3. I cannot ascertain at this time whether or not Dante knew this work. We should recall also the retort that Boccaccio assigns to Guido Cavalcanti in the *Decameron* VI, ix: Guido calls the sarcophagi (*arche*) around the Florentine Baptistry the '*houses*' of his insulters: 'Signori, voi mi potete dire *a casa vostra* ciò che vi piace! E posta la mano sopra una di quelle *arche*, che grandi erano, sì como colui legerissimo era, prese un salto, e fussi gittato dall'altra parte. ...'

70 *Moralia* IX, 103; *PL* 75, col. 916; *Morals* I, 571–2 (trans. slightly adapted; italics added). The similarity of the punishment of the simonists in *Inferno* XIX is due to their being considered 'heretics in deed'; the sin is 'simoniac heresy.' Hugh of St Victor, *De Sacramentis* II, 10; *On the Sacraments*, trans. Roy J. Deferrari (Cambridge, Mass.: Mediaeval Academy of America 1951), 322–4).

71 *Moralia* XVIII, 22; *PL* 76, col. 49; *Morals* II, 332 (translation adapted; italics added). Compare the biblical expression 'sepultus ... in inferno' meaning 'damned in Hell' (cf. Luke 16: 22).

72 'Avvertimento, ammonimento,' Niccolò Tommaseo and Bernardo Bellini, *Dizionario della Lingua Italiana* (Turin: Unione tipografico-editrice 1861–79), III, *sub voce*.

73 St Thomas, *ST* II–II, qu. 11, art. 3. St Gregory had noted particularly the futile strivings of the heretics, that the more they exerted their proud intellects the more they were overtaken by the night of ignorance: 'Therefore heretics, because in proportion as they aim to be more completely filled by sublime perception, so much the more entirely they become empty.' Most certainly the 'mala luce' of the poem reflects this concept (*Moralia* XX, 18; *PL* 76, col. 147; *Morals* II, 462).

74 St Augustine, *Contra Faustum Manichaeum* XII, 24 (*PL* 42, col. 267); *Reply to Faustus the Manichaean*, trans. R. Stothert, A Select Library of the Nicene and Post Nicene Fathers (New York: Charles Scribner's Sons 1901), IV, 191.

CHAPTER THREE: PIER DELLA VIGNA

1 Leo Spitzer concentrated brilliantly on the stylistics of the text in 'Speech and Language in *Inferno* XIII,' *Italica*, 19 (1942), 81–104; republished in *Romanische Literaturstudien 1936–1956* (Tübingen: Max Niemeyer 1959), 544–68.

Others have demonstrated or refuted that the diction of the Canto is a portrait or parody of the major figure: Francesco Novati, 'Pier della Vigna,' in *Con Dante e per Dante* (Milan: Hoepli 1898), esp. pp. 17–18, 31; Francesco D'Ovidio, 'Pier della Vigna,' in *Nuovi Studii danteschi* (Milan: Hoepli 1907), esp. pp. 229–38; C.H. Grandgent, *Companion to the Divine Comedy*, ed. Charles S. Singleton (Cambridge, Mass.: Harvard Univ. Press 1975), 60–1; Spitzer, pp. 544–5, 555–68.

Others have re-entered the worn lists of a *querelle des anciens et des modernes* to prove the superiority or inferiority of Virgil's achievement in the *Aeneid*'s

Polydorus incident in comparison with Dante's creation in the wood of the suicides: Ireneo Sanesi, 'Polidoro e Pier della Vigna,' *Studi medievali*, n.s. 5 (1932), 207–16; Giovanni Patroni, 'L'Episodio virgiliano di Polidoro ed i Dantisti,' *Rendiconti dell'Istituto Lombardo di Scienze e Lettere* (Milan), 71 (1937), 59–72. And many have argued without decision over the identity of the unnamed Florentine suicide at the end of *Inf.* xiii: D'Ovidio, pp. 325–33; Spitzer, pp. 563–8; Sebastiano Aglianò, 'Lettura del canto xiii dell'*Inferno*,' *Studi danteschi*, 33 (1955), 141–86, here, 183–5; Gino Masi, 'Fra savi e mercanti suicidi del tempo di Dante,' *Il Giornale dantesco*, 39 n.s. 9 (1938), 199–238.

Among useful articles not otherwise appearing in the notes are the following: Marcello Camilucci, 'Il Canto di Pier delle Vigne,' in *Letture dell'Inferno* a cura di Vittorio Vettori, Lectura Dantis Internazionale (Milan: Marzorati 1963), 115–39; Ettore Bonora, 'Il canto xiii dell'*Inferno*,' *Cultura e scuola*, 4 (1965), 446–54; Etienne Gilson, 'Poésie et théologie dans la Divine Comédie,' *Atti del Congresso Internazionale di Studi Danteschi* (Florence: Sansoni 1965), 197–223; Umberto Bosco, 'Il canto dei suicidi,' in *Dante vicino* (Caltanisetta and Rome: Salvatore Sciascia 1966), 255–73; Ignazio Baldelli, 'Il canto xiii dell'*Inferno*,' *Nuove letture dantesche* (Florence: Le Monnier 1968), ii, 33–45; Ettore Paratore, 'Analisi "retorica" del canto di Pier della Vigna,' in *Tradizione e struttura in Dante* (Florence: Sansoni 1968), 178–220; Georges Güntert, 'Pier delle Vigne e l'unità del canto,' *Lettere italiane*, anno xxiii, n. 4 (1971), 548–55; Daniel Rolfs, 'Dante and the Problem of Suicide,' *Michigan Academician*, 4 (1974), 367–75; David H. Higgins, 'Cicero, Aquinas, and St. Matthew in *Inferno* xiii,' *Dante Studies*, 93 (1975), 61–94. William Stephany, in 'Pier della Vigna's Self-Fulfilling Prophecies: The Eulogy of Frederick ii and *Inferno* xiii,' *Traditio*, 38 (1982, actually 1983), 193–212, presents further careful research which complements the present chapter.

2 Leonard Olschki, in 'Dante and Peter de Vinea,' *Romanic Review*, 31 (1940), 105–111, affirmed the Protonotary's historical guilt but believed that Dante invented the 'pious fable' of innocence because he identified himself with Piero: both had been charged with corruption in office. Olschki thus believed that Dante intended to 'rehabilitate' the notary 'as a fellow sufferer' (pp. 105, 110), an untenable interpretation, as we will show. Umberto D'Aquino, in 'Una chiosa su Pier della Vigna,' *Dante e l'Italia meridionale: Atti del II Congresso Nazionale di Studi Danteschi* (Florence: Olschki 1966), 105–10, insisted: 'In una parola Pietro non è un condannato e la sua, nell'inferno, è più una esaltazione che una dannazione' (p. 107). Friedrich Schneider, in 'Kaiser Friedrich ii. und Petrus von Vinea im Urteil Dantes,' *Deutsches Dante-Jahrbuch*, 27, n.f. 18 (1948), 230–50, concludes erroneously that the *Divina Commedia* is 'eine historische Quelle ersten Ranges, die Petrus von Vinea unschuldig erklärt' (p. 250).

Other major studies include: Ernst H. Kantorowicz, *Kaiser Friedrich der Zweite*, vol. I (Berlin: Georg Bondi 1927), *Ergänzungsband* (Berlin: Georg Bondi 1931) (both vols. reprinted Düsseldorf and Munich: Helmut Küpper vormals Georg Bondi 1963); the *Ergänzungsband* contains a vast bibliography. The study, without the second volume, appeared in English as *Frederick the Second, 1194–1250*, trans. E.O. Lorimer (London: Constable 1931).

Important also is the bibliography in Thomas Curtis Van Cleve, *The Emperor Frederick II of Hohenstaufen: Immutator Mundi* (Oxford: Clarendon Press 1972), 543–98, and the book by Antonio Casertano, *Un oscuro dramma politico del secolo XIII: Pietro della Vigna* (Rome: Libreria del Littorio 1928).

The most useful, penetrating, and convincing study on Piero's historical guilt is by Friedrich Baethgen, 'Dante und Petrus de Vinea: eine kritische Studie,' *Sitzungsberichte der Bayerischen Akademie der Wissenschaften, Philosophisch-historische Klasse* (1955, Heft 3), 3–49; reprint in *Medievalia* (Stuttgart: Hiersemann 1960), II, 413–41; I cite from the original printing.

3 Cf. *De Mon.* I, 8: 'De intentione Dei est ut omne causatum in tantum divinam similitudinem representet, in quantum propria natura recipere potest. Propter quod dictum est, "Faciamus hominem ad ymaginem et similitudinem nostram"; quod licet "ad ymaginem" de rebus inferioribus ab homine dici non possit, "ad similitudinem" tamen de qualibet dici potest, cum totum universum nichil aliud sit quam vestigium quoddam divine bonitatis' (361).

4 Arthur Watson, *The Early Iconography of the Tree of Jesse* (London: Oxford Univ. Press 1934), 52–4, 87; Schiller, *Iconography* II, 134–7. Robert Hollander also noted the parallel between *Inf.* XIII and the plucking and renewal of the reed in *Purg.* I; della Vigna's bough simply bleeds. Hollander sees the episodes as 'verbal figuralism' operating in the Poem, an opinion which I wish he had stated more boldly, and which I fully share. He continues briefly commenting on the figuralism of Christ and Judas behind the suicides' punishments: 'The further punishment that awaits ... the suicides upon the Day of Judgment is that they will get their bodies back, only to have them hang upon the trees that they had become. Surely they can be seen here as being forced to enact eternally a cruel and perverse imitation of the form of Christ's sacrifice or more properly, of Judas' suicide, itself a perverse prefiguration of the Crucifixion.' *Allegory in Dante's Commedia* (Princeton, NJ: Princeton Univ. Press 1969), 130.

5 For the symbolism of the Tree in the description of Satan (*Inf.* XXXIV), see John Freccero's article, 'The Sign of Satan,' *Modern Language Notes*, 80 (1965), 11–26.

One should also bear in mind that Dante is probably alluding to the legend which stems from the Second Book of Esdras 5:5, viz. that all trees bled in sympathy with the Redeemer on the Tree of the Cross: 'Blood shall drip from wood, and the stone shall utter its voice.'

6 Similarly, though death has come to the wastrels, they obstinately yearn for the

annihilation of their souls: 'Or accorri, accorri, morte!' (*Inf.* XIII, 118). By a contemporary pun, the wasting of their 'substance' was one with the destruction of the single 'substance' of body and soul. For Aristotle, in the *Nicomachaean Ethics* IV, 1, profligacy was a form of self-destruction. Ed. Martin Ostwald, Library of Liberal Arts (Indianapolis and New York: Bobbs-Merrill 1962), 83.

7 See for example the absurd tale told by Giacomo d'Acqui (ca 1334) in J.-L.-A. Huillard-Bréholles, *Vie et Correspondance de Pierre de la Vigne* (Paris: Plon 1864), 67–8. Huillard-Bréholles' study, which contains many primary sources in the section 'Pièces justificatives,' will be cited hereafter as *Pierre*.

8 See the letters published in *Pierre*, pp. 289–91.

9 Schiller, *Iconography* II, plate 442. The identification of Christ with the mystic vine affected Christian iconography so deeply that Christ is often depicted squeezed in a wine press; see the illustrations in Alois Thomas, *Die Darstellung Christi in der Kelter: eine theologische und kulturhistorische Studie*, Forschungen zur Volkskunde, 20–1 (Düsseldorf: L. Schwann 1936); Watson, 61.

10 St Augustine, *In Joannis Evangelium*, Tractatus LXXX (*PL* 35, col. 1839), my italics; St Augustine, *Homilies on the Gospel According to St. John and his First Epistle*, A Library of Fathers of the Holy Catholic Church Anterior to the Division of the East and West (Oxford: John Henry Parker 1849), II, 825; St Thomas Aquinas, *Catena aurea super quattuor Evangelistas* (Basel: Michael Wenssler 1476), Joannes XV, 1; *Catena Aurea* (Oxford and London: James Parker 1874), VI, 474.

11 'An forte quis ambigat Dei esse *plantationem* bonum hominem? Audi sanctum David de viro bono quid canat: "Erit," ait, "tamquam lignum quod *plantatum est* secus decursus aquarum, quod fructum suum dabit in tempore suo, et folium eius non defluet." Audi Ieremiam eodem spiritu concinentem, et hisdem pene verbis: "Erit tanquam lignum," inquit, "quod *plantatum est* secus decursus aquarum, quod ad humorem mittit radices suas, et non timebit cum venerit aestus." Item Propheta: "Iustus ut palma florebit, et sicut cedrus Libani multiplicabitur." Et de seipso: "Ego autem sicut oliva fructifera in domo Dei."' *Sermo 23 in Cantica Canticorum*, *Opera*, I, 141–2. Pope Innocent III writes in his *De miseria condicionis humane*, pars I, 8: 'Quid enim est homo secundum formam nisi quedam arbor eversa? Cuius radices sunt crines, truncus est capud [sic] cum collo, stipes est pectus cum alvo, rami sunt ulne cum tibiis, frondes sunt digiti cum articulis. Hoc est folium quod a vento rapitur et stipula que a sole siccatur.' Ed. Robert E. Lewis, The Chaucer Library (Athens, Ga.: Univ. of Georgia Press, 1978), 107.

12 *Catachesis XX, Mystagogica III* (*PG* 33, col. 1082–4). Cited by Jean Daniélou, *The Bible and the Liturgy*, ed. Michael A. Mathis, Liturgical Studies (Notre Dame, Ind.: Univ. of Notre Dame Press 1965), 45.

13 Mgr Palémon Glorieux, *Pour revaloriser Migne: Tables rectificatives*, Mélanges de

Science religieuse, ixme année: Cahier supplémentaire (Lille: Facultés Catholiques 1952), 72.

14 *De vitis mystica seu tractatus de passione Domini* II, 2; *PL* 184, col. 637.

15 *De vitis* III, 5–11; col. 637–44.

16 *De vitis* IV, 12; col. 644. Beyond the obvious echoes of St Peter's keys (the thorn tree *is* a 'Piero'), the parallels to Christ as vine are at least as important as the allusions to Christ's Vicar. The metaphor of 'locking and unlocking' the Emperor's heart is an unwitting revelation by Piero that he had made of his prince his only heaven. By blind application to such political matters, he damns himself, playing blasphemous vicar to Frederick's pose as deity.

17 *De vitis* IV, 14; col. 645.

18 *De vitis* VI, 28; col. 652.

19 Ibid.

20 *De vitis* VIII, 52; col. 655. 'Quanti viroris est hoc folium!' (IX, 34; col. 657). Vittorio Gelsomino, in 'Dante e la "vitis mystica,"' *Giornale italiano di filologia*, 21 (1969), 193–202, does not realize the relation with *Inf.* XIII and thus touches on none of the above points.

21 *Moralia in Job* XX, 21 (*PL* 76, col. 150).

22 *PL* 112, 'spinae,' col. 1056; 'ramus,' col. 1037.

23 Watson, *Tree of Jesse*, pp. 167–8; Schiller, *Iconography*, I, 15–22.

24 Schiller, *Iconography* II, 135, 136–7. Other examples include two panels in the Galleria dell'Accademia in Florence: the first a Tree of Jesse by Pacino di Buonaguida (cat. no. 8459) shows, instead of a dove, a red pelican feeding its young with its own blood; and second, a crucifix attributed only to the 'Scuola fiorentina' from the beginning of the fourteenth century, bears a white pelican feeding its young above the head of Christ (cat. no. 436).

25 For example, Peter Damian begins his *De exaltatione Sanctae Crucis*: 'De verga Jesse devenimus ad virgam crucis, et principium redemptionis fine concludimus' (*Sermo* XLVII, 1; *PL* 144, col. 761); Watson, *The Tree of Jesse*, pp. 52–3. See also George Ferguson, *Signs and Symbols in Christian Art*, Hesperides Books (New York: Oxford Univ. Press 1961), 39.

26 Related to the Tree of Jesse, and an offshoot of the 'daughters of avarice' doctrine to which we must return later, was the common parable of the two trees of good and evil (Gal. 5:19–23; Matt. 7:17–20). Adolf Katzenellenbogen, in *Allegories of the Virtues and Vices in Medieval Art* (New York: Norton 1964), 63–8; plates 64, 65, 66, and 67, describes several important examples, among them the following: 'The original of the *Liber floridus Lamberti*, the illustrated encyclopedia written about 1120 by the prebendary of St. Omer shows the reader the "Arbor bona" as a symbol of the "Ecclesia fidelium" ... Beside ... [it] the "Arbor mala," also named "Synagoga," gives an impression of deadness and coldness ("Haec arbor autumnalis est infructuosa, bis mortua, eradicata, cui procella tenebrarum conser-

vata est in aeternum"). *Cupiditas* is the root, and twelve vices, some of which were enumerated by St. Paul as the works of the flesh (Galat. 5:19ff.) are the evil fruits.' A copy of the Pseudo-Hugo, *De fructibus carnis et spiritus* contrasts 'the "Arbor vitiorum" and the "Arbor virtutum." Numerous inscriptions interpret in full detail the meaning of the two pictures. The growth of destruction, designated as "sinistra," is given the place befitting all depravity, the left ("Stirps, flos, fructus, odor sanctis fuga, sontibus error – Mortis ab hac stirpe vicii genus effluit omne")' (pp. 65, 66).

27 Pier della Vigna's life as based on existing documents is found in *Pierre*, pp. 1–90. For the events in the light of his fall, Kantorowicz, *Kaiser Friedrich* I, 606–9; Baethgen, pp. 3–11; Van Cleve, pp. 519–23.

28 *Pierre*, p. 11. Pier della Vigna's letters were used widely throughout Europe as models of prose. See Ernst H. Kantorowicz, 'Petrus de Vinea in England,' *Mitteilungen des österreichischen Instituts für Geschichtsforschung*, 51 (1937), 43–88.

29 *Pierre*, p. 12.

30 *Pierre*, p. 14.

31 Van Cleve, pp. 256, 323.

32 The closing sentences of the Latin text of the *Constitutiones* declare that the Emperor had commanded his Justice of the High Court to codify the laws: 'Accipite gratanter, o populi, constitutiones istas … quas per magistrum Petrum de Vineis Capuanum, magnae curiae nostrae judicem et fidelem nostrum, mandavimus compilari.' J.-L.-A. Huillard-Bréholles, *Historia diplomatica Friderici Secundi*, vol. IV, pars I (Paris: Plon 1856; reprint Turin: Bottega d'Erasmo 1963), 176; *Pierre*, p. 15.

   James M. Powell, *The Liber Augustalis or Constitutions of Melfi Promulgated by the Emperor Frederick II for the Kingdom of Sicily in 1231* (Syracuse, NY: Syracuse Univ. Press 1971).

33 The Norman Kings of Sicily had borrowed the term 'logotheta' from the Greeks to designate the minister who drew up the laws and edicts. In his *Cronica* a cura di Giuseppe Scalia, Scrittori d'Italia, no. 232–3 (Bari: Laterza 1966), II, 501, Salimbene de Adam defines it thus: '*De logothéta, quid sit*: Componitur quoque logós cum theta, quod est positio; et dicitur hic et hec logothéta, qui sermonem facit in popolo vel qui edictum imperatoris vel alicuius principis popolo nuntiat.' Huillard-Bréholles notes that his duties were in the main fiscal (*Pierre*, pp. 49–51). See also Baethgen, p. 6.

34 Francesco Pippino described the painting: Frederick, personifying 'Justitia,' was seated on a throne pointing his finger towards Pier della Vigna seated below; in the foreground kneeling subjects appealed for justice. The following legends were inscribed: [Populus:] 'Caesar amor legum, Friderice piissime regum / Causarum telas nostrasque resolve querelas.' [Fridericus:] 'Pro vestra lite censorum juris adite: / Hic est: jura dabit vel per me danda rogabit. / Vinee cognomen Petrus judex

est sibi nomen.' *Chronica*, cap. 39; in Ludovico Muratori, *Rerum italicarum scriptores*, vol. ix (Mediolani: Typographia Societatis Palatinae 1726), col. 660. Guido da Pisa also transcribes these legends in his *Commentary: Expositiones et Glose super Comediam Dantis or Commentary on Dante's Inferno*, ed. Vincenzo Cioffari (Albany, NY: State Univ. of New York Press 1974), 249. Guido's text differs only in small details.

35 Guidonis Bonati, *De Astronomia tractatus X*, pars 1ª (Basileae: s.n., 1550), col. 210. Domenico Guerri, 'Un astrologo condannato da Dante,' *Bullettino della Società Dantesca Italiana*, 22 (1915), 200–54. *Pierre*, pp. 69–70. For the Frederician gold *Augustalis*, see Van Cleve, pp. 277–8; illustrations of the coin, nos. 4 and 6.

36 'Ascendit ad tantum dignitatem, quod beatus reputabatur, qui poterat fimbriolam aliquam habere gratie ipsius; et quicquid ipse faciebat, imperator habebat ratum, ipse autem multa retractabat et infingebat de his que faciebat imperator.' Guido Bonatti, col. 210. On Bonatti, see the recent study by Cesare Vasoli, 'L'Astrologo forlivese Guido Bonatti,' *Atti del convegno internazionale di studi danteschi* a cura del Commune di Ravenna e della Società Dantesca Italiana, Ravenna, 10–12 settembre, 1971 (Ravenna: Longo 1979), 239–60.

37 *Pierre*, pp. 87–8; Kantorowicz, *Ergänzungsband*, p. 246; Antonio Casertano, *Un oscuro dramma*.

38 The physician was condemned to death (*Historia diplomatica* vi, 708; Baethgen's edition, pp. 42–4); no mention is made in the document of *two* assassins. Historians have proved that this missive does not refer to Pier della Vigna (*Pierre*, pp. 80–2; Baethgen, pp. 12–16).

39 Matthaei Parisiensis, Monachi sancti Albani, *Chronica Majora*, ed. Henry Richards Luard, pt. v, Rolls Series, vol. 57 (London: Longman et al. 1880), 68–9: '*Fretheriscus letiferam potionem evadit a Petro de Vinea paratum*' 'Petrus: "O domine mi, pluries dedit iste meus phisicus salutarem vobis potionem, quare modo formidatis?"'

40 Salimbene de Adam, *Cronica* i, 288–9; *Pierre*, pp. 38–9; Baethgen, p. 26.

41 The Emperor learned that, 'Messires Pierres de la Vigne l'avoit traï à la [sic] Pape et le sot par unes letres, qui furent trouvées en ses coffres.' *Ex historiis anonymi remensis*, ed. O. Holder-Egger, in *Monumenta Germaniae historica, Scriptorum* tom. xxvi (Hannover: Hahn 1882), 536, para. 240. See also Baethgen, p. 26.

42 'Gli era da molti baroni e grandi uomini portata fiera invidia; e stando essi continuamente attenti … avvenne, che, avendo Federigo guerra con la Chiesa, essi con lettere false e con testimoni subornati, diedero a vedere allo 'mperadore questo maestro Piero aver col papa certo occulto trattato contro allo stato dello 'mperadore e avergli ancora alcun segreto dello 'mperadore rivelato.' Giovanni Boccaccio, *Esposizioni sopra la Comedia di Dante* a cura di Giorgio Padoan, in *Tutte le opere di Giovanni Boccaccio*, vol. vi (Milan: Arnoldo Mondadori 1965), 610. Similarly Giovanni Villani (Lib. vi, cap. 22) had asserted della Vigna's

innocence and shows some unwillingness to affirm that the chancellor had actually committed suicide: 'Lo 'mperadore fece abbacinare il savio uomo maestro Piero dalle Vigne, il buono dittatore, opponendogli tradigione, ma ciò gli fu fatto per invidia di suo grande stato, per la qual cosa il detto per dolore si lasciò tosto morire in pregione, e chi disse ch'egli medesimo si tolse la vita.' *Cronica*, compilata da Francesco Gherardi Dragomanni (Florence: Sansone Coen 1844), I, 244.

43 'Tanquam pacis turbatorem cum candenti ferro fecit exoculari' (Flaminio dal Borgo, *Dissertazioni sopra l'istoria pisana* [Pisa: Giovanni Paolo Giovannelli 1761], tom. I, parte 1, Diss. IV, p. 211); *Pierre*, p. 66.

44 Pippino, 'De magistro Petro de Vineis,' *Chronica*, cap. 39: 'Sed quum in honore esset Petrus, non intellexit; nam ex proditionis nota, ut aliqui ferunt, ab Imperatore carceri trusus atque coecatus, horrendo squallore misere vitam finivit. Male enim tractasse dicitur super discordia inter Imperatorem et Papam. Aliqui ad hanc infidelitatem perductum esse ferunt, quod nudatus imperator thesauris suis ex ipsa discordia, ipsum Petrum magno thesauro privaverit. *Nonnulli referunt, quod in vitula eius arabat.*' (Italics added.) Baethgen, pp. 27–8; *Pierre*, p. 67.

45 dal Borgo, *Dissertazioni*, tom. I, parte 1, Diss. IV, p. 212; Baethgen, p. 27.

46 In 1246 the Pope rewarded conspirators who escaped prosecution by the Emperor, and cared for their families, but in 1249 the Pope deprived Piero's nephew Giovanni of the benefice of his Church of San Pietro *ad cellas* in the diocese of Teano and awarded it to one of his secretaries. Innocent IV's letters are published in *Pierre*, pp. 315–16 ('Pièces justificatives,' nos. 16 and 17). The Pope disposed of Pier della Vigna's belongings as an enemy of Church (*Pierre*, pp. 62–4, and for the pertinent papal letters, pp. 318–19).

47 I follow Baethgen's careful consideration of the affair; see especially pp. 23–5. The primary sources on la Cerbaia are published by Fedor Schneider, 'Nachlese in Toscana,' *Quellen und Forschungen aus italienischen Archiven und Bibliotheken*, 22 (1930–1), 31–86.

48 The deed is published by Fedor Schneider, p. 80.

49 The letter is published in *Pierre*, p. 317 ('Pièces justificatives,' no. 17).

50 Baethgen, p. 32 n. 80. The records concerning prosecution of traitors and confiscation of their property are published by Huillard-Bréholles in *Historia diplomatica* V, 435, 564, 756, 767, 805, 833, 835, 910, 915.

51 The text of the letter is edited by Baethgen, pp. 44–7.

52 *Pierre*, p. 79.

53 Kantorowicz, *Kaiser Friedrich* I, 607–10. Kantorowicz calls Pier della Vigna 'Judas' but nowhere notes that Pietro di Dante had used the comparison, nor does he note its implications for the *Divina Commedia*. Petri Allegherii, *Super Dantis Ipsius Genitoris Comoediam Commentarium* curante Vincentio Nannucci (Florentiae: Angelum Garinei 1844), 158–9.

54 Olschki, p. 106.

55 Baethgen, esp. pp. 29–34; Van Cleve, p. 522.
56 Van Cleve, p. 521.

CHAPTER FOUR: AVARICE AND SUICIDE

1 *Fabii Planciadis Fulgentii V.C. Opera Accedunt Fabii Claudii Fulgentii V.C. de aetatibus mundi et hominis et S. Fulgentii Episcopi Super Thebaiden*, recensuit Rudolfus Helm, addenda adiecit Jean Préaux (Stuttgart: B.G. Teubner 1970), 79 (*Mitologiarum liber III*, 11). *Fulgentius the Mythographer*, trans. Leslie George Whitbread (Columbus, Ohio: Ohio State Univ. Press 1971), 98. Pietro Alighieri, Guido da Pisa and the Anonimo allegorize the Harpies after Fulgentius. Petri Alleghierii, *Commentarium*, p. 160; Guido da Pisa, *Commentary*, p. 247; *Commento alla Divina Commedia d'Anonimo Fiorentino del secolo XIV* a cura di Pietro Fanfani (Bologna: Gaetano Romagnoli 1866), I, 319–20.

2 'Phineus igitur, a fenerando dictus, in modum avaritiae ponitur.' *Scriptores rerum mythicarum latini tres, Romae nuper reperti*, ed. Georg Heinrich Bode (Cellis: E.H.C. Schulz 1834), 173; cited hereafter as Bode.

[Pseudo-Bernardus Silvestris], *The Commentary on the First Six Books of the Aeneid of Vergil Commonly Attributed to Bernardus Silvestris*, ed. Julian Ward Jones and Elizabeth Frances Jones (Lincoln and London: Univ. of Nebraska Press 1977), 73, line 24; all quotations are taken from this edition (their pagination usefully reflects earlier editions).

3 'Arpage enim Grece rapina dicitur – ideo virgines, quod omnis rapina arida sit et sterilis, ideo plumis circumdatae, quia quicquid rapina invaserit celat, ideo volatiles, quod omnis rapina ad volandum sit celerrima. Aello enim Grece quasi edon allon, id est alienum tollens, Oquipete id est citius auferens, Celenum vero nigrum Grece dicitur, unde et Homerus prima Iliados rhapsodia: ... "Statim niger tuus sanguis emanabit per meam hastam" – hoc igitur significare volentes quod primum sit alienum concupisci, secundum concupita invadere, tertium celare quae invadit.' *Mitologiarum liber I*, 9 (Helm, pp. 21–2; Whitbread, pp. 52–3). Pietro Alighieri, pp. 161–2; Guido da Pisa, *Commentary*, p. 247; Anonimo, I, 319–20.

4 Bode, p. 173. In Bode, see also the First Vatican Mythographer, 27 (pp. 9–10); and the Second, 13, for the harpies, and 142, for Phineus (pp. 78–124).

5 Fulgentius, *Mitologiarum liber III*; pseudo-Bernardus Silvestris, *Commentum*, p. 74: I read 'rapacitas' for Jones' 'capacitas.'

6 Benevenuti de Rambaldis de Imola, *Comentum super Dantis Aldigherij Comoediam* curante Jacopo Philippo Lacaita (Florentiae: Barbèra, 1887), I, 427, 447. Francesco D'Ovidio, after expressing his own difficulty in seeing the connection between the Harpies and suicide, patronizingly mocks Benvenuto's gloss that they symbolize avarice: 'Benvenuto, sedotto da vere e da supposte etimologie, fa le Arpie simboli di avarizia, e arzigogola artificiosi rapporti tra questa e il suicidio'

(p. 179). Vincenzo Presta similarly fails to see the intimate moral and artistic unity which the harpies have with the rest of the canto: 'Proprio a canto finito ci si accorge di come la *imitatio virgiliana* delle Arpie non sia più che una semplice suggestione culturale che, pur se investita da contenuto allegorico, non supera la mera enunciazione e resta quindi senza un vero sviluppo narrativo.' 'In margine al canto XIII dell'*Inferno,*' *Dante Studies,* 90 (1972), 15.

7 See above, n. 6.

8 'Omnem suam substantiam perdidit.' Fulgentius, *Mitologiarum liber III,* 3 (Helm, p. 62; Whitbread, p. 85). Bode, pp. 103, 198–9. For Renato Serra ('Su la pena dei dissipatori,' *Giornale Storico della Letteratura Italiana,* 43 [1904], 278–98), the chase in Hell was drawn from the 'wilde Jagd' legends of folklore.

9 For 'canes Jovis' see n. 4 above. For Actaeon's 'Harpyia' see *Metamorphoses* III, 215. Ed. and trans. Frank Justus Miller, *LCL* (Cambridge, Mass.: Harvard Univ. Press; London: William Heinemann 1966), 2 vols.

10 See, for example, William J. Kennedy, 'Irony, Allegoresis, and Allegory in Virgil, Ovid and Dante,' *Arcadia: Zeitschrift für vergleichende Literaturwissenschaft,* 7 (1972), 115–34, esp. pp. 123–9. Kennedy follows the conventional interpretation of the cantos in which the Poet exonerates and rehabilitates Pier della Vigna, the innocent victim of the emperor's unjust persecution.

11 Salimbene, *Cronica* I, 288, 635–6; Van Cleve, p. 522.

12 The pseudo-Bernardus Silvestris, *Commentum,* pp. 18–19.

13 Dante has Virgil say expressly:

's'elli avesse potuto creder prima,'
    rispose 'l savio mio, 'anima lesa,
    ciò c'ha veduto pur con la mia rima,
non avrebbe in te la man distesa.'

(*Inf.* XIII, 46–9)

14 'Cum sorores Phaetontis plangerent eius mortem: subito *in arbores sunt conversae.* ... *Talis mutatio videtur quotidie in avaris* ... processu temporis: ipsi efficuntur arbores id est avari: terrae admodum arboris adhaerentes. Nam pes id est affectio efficitur radix inquantum in terra id est in bonis terrenis infigitur per amorem. Cortex etiam exterioris malae conversationis et malae consuetudinis eos operit: et sic in arbores id est viros incompatientes et insensibiles diabolus eos vertit. Unde isti sunt sicut arbor mala quae non facit fructus bonos: quae merito comburi praecipitur [Matth. 3:10].' Petrus Berchorius [Ovidius Moralizatus], *Reductorium morale, Liber XV, cap. ii-xv: 'Ovidius Moralizatus' naar de Parijse druk van 1509,* ed. Joseph Engels (Utrecht: Instituut voor Laat Latijn der Rijksuniversiteit 1962), 50. My italics.

15 *Moralia* xx, 21 (*PL* 76, col. 150). The *Liber floridus Lamberti* gives an illustration of the effects of avarice: 'cupiditas' is shown as the root; and the works of the flesh (Gal. 5:19–23) are depicted as the evil fruits (Katzenellenbogen, *Allegories*

of the Virtues and Vices, 65–6, plate 65). Concerning the thorns of the juniper as temptations see, among the *dubia* of Hugh of St Victor, *Allegoriae in Vetus Testamentum* VII, 14 (*PL* 175, col. 711).

16 See the interesting comments in Van Cleve, pp. 100–2, 120, 125, 162–3, 180, 241, 260, 412, 538; *De Mon.*, esp. Lib. III.

17 'Esium nobilem Marchie civitatem, insigne originis nostre principium, ubi nos diva mater nostra eduxit in lucem. ... Bethleem nostra terra Cesaris et origo pectori nostro ... Bethleem, civitas Marchie non minima, es in generis nostri principibus.' *Historia diplomatica* v, pt. 1, p. 378. On Frederick's *christomimesis*, on the theory of the Emperor as 'sol iustitiae,' father and son of Justice, and on the theory of the king as 'animate law' ('lex animata,' 'lex viva'), see Ernst H. Kantorowicz' chapter 'Frederick the Second' in *The King's Two Bodies* (Princeton: Princeton Univ. Press 1957), esp. pp. 97–143.

18 'dum translato quasi vivifice crucis mysterio de partibus transmarinis in Regnum, tanquam iterum in Apulia crucifixus sit Christus. ...' *Historia diplomatica* VI, pt. 2, pp. 710–13. Kantorowicz, *Kaiser Friedrich* I, 607; Ergänzungsband, p. 245.

19 Baethgen edits the letter, p. 46. *Historia diplomatica* VI, pt. 2, pp. 700–1. One cannot help but wonder, of course, at Frederick's apparent naivety at comparing himself to the Pharaoh (=the Devil?!) and his empire to Egypt – blind, grandiose vanity? Given the traditional exegesis on the Exodus, however, could not this be grounds for considering the letter as a Church forgery? Papal documents use precisely such metaphors *against* Frederick II. These are questions which I cannot begin to answer here.

20 'Achitofel alterum, cujus consilio contemptis principibus majestas imperatoria regitur et respublica gubernatur.' *Le Liber Censuum de L'Eglise Romaine*, ed. Paul Fabre, Bibliothèque des Ecoles Françaises d'Athènes et de Rome (Paris: Albert Fontemoing 1905), I, 28, col. 1.

21 St Augustine, *In Joannis Evangelium*, Tractatus L, 9–10 (*PL* 35, col. 1761–2). My italics. St Augustine, *Homilies on the Gospel According to St. John and his First Epistle*, A Library of Fathers of the Holy Catholic Church Anterior to the Division of the East and West (Oxford: John Henry Parker 1849), II, 674–5. My italics.

22 Chrysostomos continues: 'Audite avari, cogitate quae ille passus sit; quomodo pecunias amiserit, et scelus perpetraverit; quomodo avaritiae fructum non tulerit, et animam perdiderit. Talis est avaritiae tyrannis: nec argento fruitur, nec praesenti vita, nec futura: sed omnia confertim amisit, malamque nactus apud illos famam, laqueo gulam fregit.' *In Matthaeum*, Homil. LXXXV (al. LXXXVI), 2 (*PG* 58, col. 760). Concerning Judas' 'Motive of Avarice' see Roman B. Halas, *Judas Iscariot*, Dissertation, Faculty of the School of Sacred Theology of the Catholic University of America (Washington, DC: Catholic Univ. of America Press 1946), 80–1.

23 Halas, p. 81. Cf. Origen, *Commentarius in Matthaeum*, Tomus XI, 9 (*PG* 13,

col. 934). St John Chrysostomos, *Expositio in Psalmum VI*, 6 (*PG* 55, col. 79); *In Epistolam ad Philippenses*, cap. II, Homil. VI, 5 (*PG* 62, col. 225).

24 St John Chrysostomos, *In Matthaeum*, Homil. LXXXI (al. LXXXII), 3 (*PG* 58, col. 733); Homil. XXVIII (al. XXIX), 4 (*PG* 57, col. 356); Origen, *Commentarius in Matthaeum* XI, 9 (*PG* 13, col. 934); XVI, 3 (*PG* 13, col. 1390); St Cyril, *Cathechesis* XIII, 6 (*PG* 33, col. 779); Rabanus Maurus, *Commentaria in Libros duos Paralipomenon*, Lib. II, 27 (*PL* 109, col. 406); St Thomas Aquinas, *ST* II–II, qu. 118, art. 8; Halas, p. 81.

25 'Caeterum quomodocumque interpretatus fueris, merces interpretatur et pretium.' *Breviarium in Psalmos: Psalm. CVIII* (*PL* 26, col. 1157). *Homily 35 on Psalm 108* in *The Homilies of Saint Jerome* I, trans. Sister Marie Liguori Ewald, The Fathers of the Church, 48 (Washington, DC: Catholic Univ. of America Press 1964), 260. Similarly, in his *Commentaria in Evangelium S. Matthaei* I, 10: 'Vel a vico aut urbe in quo ortus est, vel ex tribu Isachar vocabulum sumpsit: ut quodam vaticinio in condemnationem sui natus sit. Isachar enim interpretatur "merces," ut significetur pretium proditoris' (*PL* 26, col. 62). Cf. Isidore of Seville: 'Issachar enim interpretatur *merces*, et significaretur pretium proditoris, quo vendidit Dominum' (*Etymologiarum*, lib. VII, cap. ix, 'De Apostolis,' *PL* 82, col. 290). See Halas, pp. 11–21.

26 *ST* II–II, qu. 118, art. 8 (italics added). In his commentary on *Inf.* XIII, Benvenuto da Imola writes: 'Avaritia et prodigalitas maxime inducunt hominem ad desperationem' (*Comentum* I, 447). Cf. *Purg.* XXVIII, 82–4. The 'daughters of avarice' were often depicted as the 'mala arbor' or 'arbor vitiorum'; see n. 26 on the 'mala arbor' above.

27 For a useful discussion of the conflicting reports of Judas' death in Matthew 27:4–5 and Acts 1:18 and how various Church writers reconciled them, see Halas, pp. 145–70, bibliography, pp. 193–206.

28 *Breviarium in Psalmos: Psalm CVIII* (*PL* 26, col. 1157). *Homily 35 on Psalm 108* (*Homilies*, pp. 258–9).

29 *Moralia* XI, 12 (*PL* 75, col. 959). *Morals* II, 9. For Judas' own *contrapasso* see the discussion in the excellent article by Ronald B. Herzman, 'Cannibalism and Communion in *Inferno* XXXIII,' *Dante Studies*, 98 (1980), esp. pp. 68–9.

30 Pietro Alighieri, *Commentarium*, pp. 158–9 (my italics).

31 Schiller, *Iconography* II, 76–8. Reference to hanging appears not only in Pier della Vigna's speech but also in that of the second suicide, *Inf.* XIII, 151. Giotto's frescoes for the Scrovegni Chapel of the Arena in Padua depict *desperatio* as a hanging woman accompanied by a winged devil. *L'Opera completa di Giotto*, presentazione di Giancarlo Vigorelli, apparati critici e filologici di Edi Baccheschi (Milan: Rizzoli 1966), 107.

It might be mentioned here that the medieval 'lives' of Judas Iscariot – merely elaborations on the legendary tales of Moses, Ruben, Oedipus, and Secundus the Silent Philosopher – were of absolutely no influence upon Dante's episode of the suicides. For a review of such tales see Edward Kennard Rand, 'Medieval Lives of Judas Iscariot,' *Anniversary Papers by Colleagues and Pupils of George Lyman Kittredge* (Boston and London: Ginn 1913), 305–16.

32 André Grabar, *Christian Iconography: A Study of Its Origins*, Bollingen Series XXX, 10 (Princeton, NJ: Princeton Univ. Press 1968), 137; plate 337.

33 Schiller, *Iconography* II, plate 279.

34 Schiller, II, plate 15.

35 Schiller, II, plate 280.

36 Peter Brieger, Millard Meiss, and Charles S. Singleton, *Illuminated Manuscripts of the Divine Comedy*, Bollingen Series LXXXI (Princeton, NJ: Princeton Univ. Press 1969), I, 276–9 [Madrid ms.], 316–18; II, plate 171a [Paris ms.]; the authors unfortunately do not publish this crude but important Madrid illustration.

37 Absalom also may be related to the image of the suicides after the Last Judgment. After his defeat in battle by David's army, Absalom flees into the forest on a mule; his hair is caught in an oak tree so that he dangles from it 'adhesit caput eius quercui et illo suspenso inter caelum et terram' [II Regum (Samuel) 18:9]) and is transfixed by Joab's spear. My acute research assistant, Miss Nona Flores, kindly pointed out to me that Bertran de Born's reference to Ahithophel in *Inf.* XXVIII is also reflected in the line 'e'l capo tronco tenea *per le chiome*' (121). Like Ahithophel, Bertran parted father from son.

38 St Jerome, *Breviarium in Psalmos*, Psalm. CVIII (*PL* 26, col. 1155); *Homily 35 on Psalm 108* [*109*], (*Homilies*, p. 255).

39 St Augustine, *Enarratio in Psalmum CVIII* [*CIX*], 1 (*PL* 37, col. 1431). See also *Enarratio in Psalmum VII* (*PL* 36, col. 97).

40 '"Achitophel etiam consiliarius regis." Quid per Achitophel, qui quondam David consiliarius fuit, et postea, cupiditate depravatus, cum Absalon de nece ipsius tractabat, nisi Judas Scarioth, qui de apostolatus culmine in proditionis foveam cecidit, insinuatur? Quod bene vocabulum Achitophel exprimit; interpretatur enim "frater meus cadens," sive "irruens," seu "tractans." Hic enim inter caeteros apostolos familiaritatis locum cum ipso Salvatore habuit; sed postea cum Judaeis avaritia seductus, mortem Domini meditando, perpetuo mortis sibi ruinam ascivit. Unde et Achitophel (sicut in libro Regum narratur [II Reg. 17]) videns suum consilium infatuatum, in domo propria laqueo vitam finire elegit. Similiter et Judas, Evangelio testante, videns quod Jesus ad mortem damnatus esset, poenitentia ductus retulit triginta argenteos principibus sacerdotum et senioribus, dicens: "Peccavi tradens sanguinem justum. At illi dixerunt: Quid ad nos? tu videris. Et projectis argenteis in templo recessit, et abiens laqueo se suspendit" (Matth. 27).' Rabanus Maurus, *Commentaria in Libros duos Paralipomenon*, Lib. II, 27 (*PL* 109, col. 406).

41   The thirteenth-century Moralised Bible, ms. Oxford, Bodl., 270b, fol. 158; Alexan-
dre de Laborde, *La Bible moralisée illustrée conservée à Oxford, Paris, et Lon-
dres*, Société française de reproductions de manuscrits à peintures (Paris: Pour les
membres de la Société 1911–27), I, plate 158.
     Artists' depictions of a hanging Judas with pendent viscera reflected a conflation
of the differing accounts of the betrayer's death in the Vulgate (Matt. 27:5, and
Luke's account in Acts 1:18: 'Suspensus crepuit medius et diffusa sunt omnia
viscera eius'). See Giotto's depiction, plate 22.

42   Such as those in the Österreichische Nazionalbibliothek, Vienna, Codex 1179, f.
109ᵛ (Laborde, IV, plate 681), Codex 2554, f. 47ᵛ (Laborde, IV, plate 755), and the
Codex of Toledo Cathedral, I, f. 126 (Laborde, IV, plate 628).

43   The British Library, Harley 1527, f. 56 (Laborde, III, plate 527).

44   *PL* 196, col. 1360.

45   *ST*, III, qu. 81, art. 2.

46   'Equitatis virgam vertebat in colubrum.' Guido da Pisa, *Commentary*, p. 249.
Frederick's letter to the Count of Caserta is published in Baethgen, p. 46.

47   Following St Augustine, Dante recognized *cupiditas* or greed as the antithesis of
justice 'quod iustitia maxime contrariatur cupiditas' (*De Mon.* I, 11).

48   *L'Ottimo Commento della Diviña Commedia* a cura di Alessandro Torri, vol. I
(Pisa: Niccolò Capurro, 1927), 258. While the second suicide's role as a representative of *all* of Florence (Jacopo Alighieri, Jacopo della Lana, Boccaccio, Leo Spitzer)
cannot be completely ruled out, he was obviously meant to be recognizable
personally to his contemporaries. As Manfredi Porena aptly puts it, 'Non è un X
qualunque.' *La Divina Commedia* (Bologna: Zanichelli 1951), I, 125). Graziolo
de' Bambaglioli glosses v. 151: 'Iste florentinus fuit dominus Loctus iudex de Aglis
de Florentia, qui secundum quod fertur, ex dolore prenimio cuiusdam false
sententiae quam protulerat, ... se ipsum suspendit.' *Il Commento dantesco dal
'Colombino' di Siviglia con altri codici raffrontato*, contributi di Antonio Fiam-
mazzo all'edizione critica (Savona: s.n., 1915), 39. On Lotto degli Agli see Guido
Zaccagnini, 'Personaggi danteschi in Bologna,' *Giornale Storico della Letteratura
Italiana*, 64 (1914), 1–47, esp. pp. 24–5. Ferdinando Neri, '*Il suicida fiorentino*,'
Studi medievali, n.s. 2 (1929), 205–7. On Rocco de' Mozzi: Gino Masi, 'Fra savi e
mercanti suicidi del tempo di Dante,' *Il Giornale dantesco*, 39, n.s. 9, (1938),
199–238. Eugenio Chiarini, 'Mozzi, Rocco,' *Enciclopedia dantesca* IV, 1052. R.
Kay, 'Rucco di Cambio de' Mozzi in France and England,' *Studi danteschi*, 47
(1970), 49–57. Vincenzo Presta, 'In margine al canto XIII dell'*Inferno*,' *Dante
Studies*, 90 (1972), 13–24.
     To base the identification upon the gallicism 'gibetto' and to affirm that Rocco
de' Mozzi's claim is better because of French family and business connections is
nonsense. The word 'gibetto' is not used by the *historical* Lotto or Rocco but by

the historical Poet, Dante Alighieri. It might be added that the present writer often uses 'hara kiri' and 'kaputt' in allied contexts but this in no way suggests that he has Japanese or German commercial associations, regrettably.

49 Origen, *In Matthaeum Commentariorum Series*, 78 (*PG* 13, col. 1727).

50 Halas, pp. 22–3. It is possible that Dante meant to echo the idea of suffocation also in his use of the verb 'soffiare' (it derives from Latin *subflare*, **sufflare*); the word applies to both suicides:

Allor *soffiò* il tronco forte, e poi
si convertì quel vento in cotal voce

(Inf. XIII, 91–2)

Chi fosti, che per tante punte
soffi con sangue doloroso sermo?

(Inf. XIII, 137–8)

51 For a full identification of the Tree as justice see Singleton's note to *Purg.* XXXII, 37–9 (*Purgatorio: Commentary*, pp. 784–5). See also n. 4 above.

CHAPTER FIVE: THE *GRAN VEGLIO*

1 The critics' incomprehension of the episode is frankly admitted. Michele Barbi concluded: 'Il preciso significato del simbolo bisogna confessare che non riesce né interamente chiaro né sicuro.' *Problemi fondamentali per un nuovo commento della Divina Commedia* (Florence: Sansoni 1955), 139–40. In 1920, Bendetto Croce had also confessed his incomprehension of the Canto: 'Il significato allegorico di questa immaginazione è al solito disputato e non si riesce a determinarlo con sicurezza (è la storia del genere umano? è quella dell'Impero?); nondimeno, quella statua non è priva di una singolare efficacia, mezza com' è tra la figura e il geroglifico che, pur nel suo chiuso aspetto, s'impone al sentimento e dice qualcosa all'anima, mormorando, senza che si riesca a percepirla distintamente, una storia lontana, e accennando a un misterioso destino.' *La Poesia di Dante*, 7th ed. (Bari: Laterza 1952) 80–1. Umberto Bosco expressed his bewilderment thus: 'Concludendo: io non so, e lo confesso candidamente, se Dante nel delineare il suo Veglio abbia avuto un preciso schema ideologico a cui abbia fatto aderire i particolari della sua figurazione.' 'Il Canto XIV dell'*Inferno*,' *Nuove letture dantesche*, vol. II, Casa di Dante in Roma, anno di studi 1966–7 (Florence: Le Monnier 1968), 73.

The following articles are helpful and, though not cited in later notes, are recommended to the reader: Antonio Lubin, *Allegoria, morale, ecclesiastica, politica nelle due prime cantiche della Divina Commedia*, dissertation, University of Graz (Graz: G.A. Kienreich 1864), esp. pp. 65–9; G.G. Vaccheri and C. Bertacchi, *Il Gran Veglio del Monte Ida*, tradotto nel senso morale della Divina Commedia (Turin: Candeletti 1877); Giacomo Poletto, *Alcuni studi su Dante come Appendice al Dizionario dantesco* (Siena: Tipografia San Bernardino 1892), 191–9;

Michele Scherillo, 'Il Canto xiv dell'*Inferno*,' *Lectura Dantis*, 14 (Florence: Sansoni 1900); Isodoro del Lungo, 'Le lacrime umane del male nell'*Inferno* dantesco (*Inf.* xiv, 76–119),' *Rassegna Nazionale* (il 1° luglio, 1904), 3–11; reprint, 'Canto Decimoquarto,' in *Lectura Dantis genovese: i canti XII–XXIII dell'Inferno*, vol. ii (Florence: Le Monnier 1906), 77–120; Giuseppe Finzi, 'L'Episodio di Capaneo,' in *Saggi e Conferenze* (Florence: Le Monnier 1907), 221–41; Emanuele Ciafardini, 'Capaneo nella *Tebaide* e nella *Divina Commedia*,' in *Due saggi danteschi* (Naples: Tipografia degli Artigianelli 1925), 25–60; Luigi Pietrobono, 'Allegoria o arte?' *Giornale dantesco*, 37, n.s. 7 (1936), 95–134, esp. pp. 120–3; see also his earlier essay, 'Il Canto xiv dell'*Inferno*,' *Giornale dantesco*, 30 (1927), 133–41; Salvatore Santangelo, 'Il Veglio di Creta,' *Studi letterari: miscellanea in onore di Emilio Santini* (Palermo: U. Manfredi 1956), 113–23; Mario Apollonio, 'Il Canto xiv dell'*Inferno*,' *Lectura Dantis Scaligera*, vol. i (Florence: Le Monnier 1961), 451–78; Bruno Nardi, *Saggi e note di critica dantesca* (Milan-Naples: Riccardo Ricciardi 1956; reprint 1966), esp. pp. 154–6; Ettore Paratore, 'Il Canto xiv dell'*Inferno*, ' *Tradizione e struttura in Dante* (Florence: Sansoni 1968), 221–49; Fortunato Matarrese, 'Capaneo,' in *Interpretazioni dantesche* (Bari: Tipografia Due Stelle n.d.), 281–300; Giovanni Reggio, 'Veglio di Creta,' *Enciclopedia dantesca*, v, 901–3. I have been unable to consult C. di Mino's 'La visione di S. Francesco e il Veglio de Creta,' in *L'Italia francescana*, 27 (1952), 284–99.

2 Benedetto Croce, *La Poesia di Dante*, 7th ed. (Bari: Laterza 1952), 80–1. Compare Claudio Varese's neo-Crocean remarks: 'Ci sono piuttosto elementi poetici che non di poesia' ('Il Canto xiv dell'*Inferno*,' *Letture Dantesche*, ed. Giovanni Getto [Florence: Sansoni 1962] 251, 265). It is clear, however, that such an approach is not merely that of Crocean critics. Giovanni Busnelli speaks of the 'digressione sul Veglio di Creta.' For him the passage is merely an unpoetic filler. *Il Virgilio dantesco e il Gran Veglio di Creta*, 2nd ed. (Rome: Civiltà cattolica 1919), 160–1. Bruno Nardi speaks of 'l'intermezzo del Veglio di Creta dopo l'episodio di Capaneo' (*Saggi e note di critica dantesca* [Milan-Naples: Ricciardi 1966], 156). See also Niccolò Tommaseo, *Divina Commedia* (Turin: UTET 1944), i, 168–9. Along very different lines from my argument is Emilio Bigi's 'Un caso concreto del rapporto di struttura e poesia (Il Canto xiv dell'*Inferno*),' *Cultura e Scuola*, 4 (1965), 455–70; reprint *Dante nella critica d'oggi*, ed. Umberto Bosco (Florence: Le Monnier 1965), 455–70.

In a very curious, unconvincing essay, Vittorio Vettori believed he saw the poetic unity of the Canto in the fact that the raging Capaneus was merely the erudite Guido Cavalcanti but thinly disguised. 'Il Canto di Capaneo,' in *Letture dell'Inferno* a cura di Vittorio Vettori (Milan: Marzorati 1963), 140–54.

3 It is not too great an exaggeration to say that little satisfying progress concerning the solution of the puzzle has been made since Giovanni Pascoli's fundamental

chapter, 'Le rovine e il Gran Veglio,' in *Sotto il Velame*, 2nd ed. (Bologna: Nicola Zanichelli 1912), 179–302; here, pp. 198–9, some eighty years ago. In this essay the poet-critic made the following assertions: the *fessura* of the Veglio recalls mankind's *vulneratio naturae* resulting from the Fall according to the explanation of the Venerable Bede and St Thomas Aquinas. The Acheron, logically, symbolized original sin, both in its role as the river of death and because it flows from the wound in the statue. The figure's stance, erect more on the foot of clay than on the foot of iron, symbolizes the abnormality of man. For Pascoli this meant that the usurpation of the Papacy over the temporal realm had eclipsed the sun of temporal order. Instead of standing on both feet, upon the spiritual and temporal equally, the statue stands on the weaker foot, that of *terracotta*.

Luigi Valli generally followed Pascoli, and, in a blend of acumen and error, added some opinions of his own. The statue brings to mind the image of the Wayfarer in the Prologue scene who, according to Pietro Alighieri, makes his way over the desert shore 'claudus,' that is, with one halting foot. The Veglio, Valli believed, is not, therefore, to be interpreted as if Mount Ida were its fixed and permanent location; but rather, since the statue is erect, it must be seen 'come ad un certo punto del suo cammino.' The Veglio is in Crete because it has been 'surprised' in that position by the fact of having one foot infirm. Crete stands halfway between Jerusalem and Rome. Damiata, 'meaningless historically,' is of mere necessity behind the Veglio's back as he gazes upon Rome from where he awaits the 'redemption of the eagle' (p. 122). Valli's thesis, untenable theologic-ally, was that the Veglio represented mankind 'half redeemed,' 'redenta dalla Croce sì, ma dall'Aquila no' (p. 136). Clearly, however, the symbolic Veglio can be in no way redeemed; indeed, as we will show, the statue symbolizes unredemption, the *poena* and *culpa* of sin incurred through rejection of the Deity.

See the dissertation of Giuseppe Mazzotta, esp. his chapter 'The Old Man of Crete and Cato,' in 'Dante's Theology of History' (unpublished dissertation, Cornell University 1969), 6–48, now in *Dante, Poet of the Desert: History and Allegory in the Divine Comedy* (Princeton, NJ: Princeton Univ. Press 1979), esp. ch. 1, 'Opus Restaurationis,' pp. 14–65. Mazzotta realized that 'the Old Man of Crete is represented in the context of the theology of the sin of pride,' but he did not see the intimate relation of this idol to perfect blasphemy; his major problem was that he identified the statue not with Jove-Zeus, but with Cronos.

Without making any connections with Crete, Zeus, and idolatry, Luigi Valli, following Capetti, usefully points out that on their voyages to Rome both Aeneas, bearer of the Empire, and St Paul, bearer of the Church, went *off course* at Crete. The episodes recounted in the *Aeneid* II, 134–65 and in Acts 27 bear great similarities to one another. Both Aeneas and Paul are overtaken at Crete by misfortune: pestilence besets Aeneas' men; Paul, a prisoner aboard a Roman galley, is caught in a storm. Both gain divine aid through a dream: Aeneas from the

Penates; St Paul from an Angel; to both, help and security are assured. Both are told to continue their voyages and not delay in Crete: Aeneas is forbidden to colonize the island; Paul is told that he is preordained to arrive in Rome. Valli concludes untheologically, 'Creta è il luogo dello smarrimento nella mezza redenzione degli uomini.' Luigi Valli, *Il Segreto della Croce e dell'Aquila nella Divina Commedia* (Bologna: Nicola Zanichelli 1922), 119–38. Mazzotta follows Valli, *Dante, Poet*, pp. 28–9. The reader should also consult the *Companion to the Divine Comedy*, commentary by C.H. Grandgent, ed. Charles S. Singleton (Cambridge, Mass.: Harvard Univ. Press 1975), 63–4.

4 Giovanni Busnelli, *L'Etica nicomachea e l'ordinamento morale dell'Inferno di Dante con un'appendice: la concezione dantesca del Gran Veglio di Creta* (Bologna: Nicola Zanichelli 1907); Busnelli's *Il Virgilio dantesco e il Gran Veglio di Creta*, 2nd ed. (Rome: Civiltà cattolica 1919) is a response to Tito Bottagisio's 'Il Gran Veglio di Creta: Fonte storica – simbolismo,' *Il VI° centenario dantesco* (Ravenna), 4 (1917), 71–7, 89–95.

5 Richard of St Victor, *De Eruditione hominis interioris libri tres, occasione accepta ex somnio Nabuchodonosor apud Danielem* (PL 196, col. 1229–1366); Philip of Harveng, *De somnio regis Nabuchodonosor* (PL 203, col. 585–92). Mazzotta, 'Dante's theology,' follows Busnelli, pp. 6–48; see also *Dante, Poet*, pp. 14–65.

6 Francesco Flamini, *Avviamento allo studio della Divina Commedia* (Livorno: Giusti 1916), 58–9; Busnelli, *Il Virgilio*, p. 173.

7 Busnelli, *Il Virgilio*, p. 161.

8 Busnelli (*Il Virgilio*, p. 167) was not correct on this point: 'Il luogo e i fiumi richiamano idee pagane; mentre la statua e le ferite ci riconducono alla Bibbia e alla scolastica.' As I will later demonstrate, however, the Bible and Patristics not only directed the choice of location, Crete, but, more especially, Dante's concept of the rivers. Mazzottta, 'Dante's Theology,' incorrectly considers the colossus in Daniel as 'the weeping statue' (p. 13).

9 H. Theodore Silverstein, 'The Weeping Statue and Dante's *Gran Veglio*,' *Harvard Studies and Notes in Philology and Literature*, 13 (1931), 165–84.

10 In verses 8 and 9, for example, 'une landa / che dal suo letto ogne pianta rimove' Dante again echoes and inverts the baptismal terms, 'plantare' and 'conplantare' expressing the 'planting' of the Christian in the Vineyard of the Lord (the Church) at baptism, as we noted in a similar instance in chapter 3.

11 Silverstein, pp. 177–9. See Paul A. Underwood, 'The Fountain of Life in Manuscripts of the Gospels,' *Dumbarton Oaks Papers*, 5 (1950), 41–138. The weeping and bleeding of the Veglio associate the statue not only with Christ, but also with Satan and his bloody drool as a Christological inversion at the bottom of Hell (*Inferno* xxxiv, 53–4). This latter association stresses the negativity of the statue on earth – a symbol, as I hope to show, of vehement denial of the Godhead.

12 Busnelli (*Il Virgilio*, p. 97) notes the biblical passage but ignores the vast iconographical and exegetical tradition which grew from it.

13 Hugo Rahner, 'Flumina de ventre Christi: Die patristische Auslegung von Joh. 7:37–38,' *Biblica*, 22 (1941), 367–403.

14 Cited by Rahner, p. 368. See *Commentaire sur Daniel*, introd. Gustave Burdy, ed. and trans. Maurice Lefèvre, Sources chrétiennes (Paris: Editions du Cerf 1947), 86.

15 It has been shown that the reading 'peccatrici' (not 'pectatrici') is the correct reading of the verse. See Guido Mazzoni, 'Le peccatrici del Bulicame e le pectatrici di Viterbo (*Inf*. XIV, 79–80),' in *Almae luces, malae cruces* (Bologna: Nicola Zanichelli 1941), 239–66; Michele Barbi and A. Duro, 'Peccatrici o pectatrici?' *Studi danteschi*, 28 (1949), 11–43. 'Peccatrici' is accepted by Petrocchi and Singleton. Baptismal typology and doctrine similarly bear this out in allegory: in baptism the *sinner* is figuratively washed 'in the blood of the Lamb.' Philip of Harveng uses the term 'massa peccatrice' in his commentary on Nebuchadnezzar's dream (*De Somnio regis Nabuchodonosor; PL* 203, col. 585).

16 Cf. 1 Corinthians 10:6–7.

17 It is important to note that St Paul's words here pertain directly to the subject of Dante's Canto, which is, as we will show, not merely blasphemy but *perfect* blasphemy and idolatry. The rock in the desert is a figure of Christ: 'Now these things that were done [i.e. the works of Moses] in a figure of us, that we should not covet evil things, as they also coveted. *Neither become ye idolaters. ...*' (1 Corinthians 10:6–7).

18 *In Psalmum 45 Enarratio*, 45, 12 (*PL* 14, col. 1138–9). Similarly, he urges the faithful as he explains Psalm 1 (*In Psalmum I Enarratio; PL* 14, col. 940): 'Bibe Christum quia petra est quae vomuit aquam, bibe Christum, quia fons vitae est, bibe Christum quia flumen est, cujus impetus laetificat civitatem Dei, bibe Christum, quia pax est, bibe Christum, quia flumina de ventre ejus fluent aquae vivae.' Tertullian had used the same language (*Adversus Judaeos*, 13; *PL* 2, col. 635; *De Baptismo*, 9 and 20; *CSEL* 47, pp. 202, 210). Rufinus echoes the same concepts in his *Commentarius in symbolum Apostolorum*, 23 (*PL* 21, col. 361). Isidore of Seville makes a direct connection of Christ's wound with baptismal waters: 'Item de eadem aqua, quae ex latere ejus profluit, propheta alius dicit: "Flumina aquae viventis egredientur de ventre illius," aquae scilicet baptismatis, quae credentes vivificant et quae sitientibus largiuntur' (*De fide catholica contra Judaeos* I, 48, 2; *PL* 83, col. 490–1). The depiction of Moses striking the rock was immensely popular in early Christian art. In the Catacomb of Priscilla in Rome alone, the episode is depicted no less than seventy-three times.

19 As Jesus went down into the water, fire kindled in the Jordan; and while He came out of the water, the Holy Spirit, like a dove, hovered over Him.' Justin, *Dialogus cum Tryphone Judaeo*, 88 (*PG* 6, col. 686). See also Carl-Martin Edsman, *Le Baptême de feu*, Acta Seminarii Neotestamentici Upsaliensis, IX (Leipzig and

Uppsala 1940), esp. pp. 182–6; Jean Daniélou, *The Bible and the Liturgy*, ed.
Michael A. Mathis, Liturgical Studies (Notre Dame, Indiana: Univ. of Notre Dame
Press 1956), 107. More to the point is the fact that the baptism of Christ fulfilled
the sacrifice of Elias-Elijah in the Old Testament, in which fire descends upon the
holocaust. On the Spirit descending at Christ's Baptism, see Matthew 3:16; Mark
1:10; Luke 3:22; John 1:29–34. In the following pages on baptismal typology I
follow both Daniélou's study and that of Per Lundberg, *La Typologie baptismale
dans l'ancienne Eglise*, Acta Seminarii Neotestamentici Upsaliensis, x (Leipzig and
Uppsala 1942). Since these two works deal in the main with only very early
Christian sources, I have supplemented the points with later medieval quotations.
Most typologies are conveniently, though partially, outlined in St Ambrose, *De
Sacramentis* II (*PL* 16, col. 423–30), in Hugh of St Victor, *De Sacramentis* II, vi
(*PL* 176, col. 460), and St Augustine, *Contra Faustum Manichaeum* xix, 12 (*PL* 42,
col. 355). The types listed in John Damascene are cited by St Thomas Aquinas in
ST III, qu. 70, art. 1, reply obj. 2, and in *ST* III, qu. 6, art. 11, reply obj. 3.

20 Daniélou, *Bible and Liturgy*, pp. 13, 107 et passim. The fact that the fire is
quenched above the bloody stream also enables Dante to pass unscathed, thus in a
sense fulfilling Isaias 43:19: 'I will make a way in the wilderness and rivers in the
desert.' Merely the red colour is sufficient for Hugh of St Victor to identify the Red
Sea with the blood of Christ: 'The form of baptism already preceded once in the
flood. ... Similarly also in the Red Sea where the water proclaimed baptism and *the
redness blood.' De Sacramentis* II, vi, 15 (*PL* 176, col. 460); *On the Sacraments
of the Christian Faith*, trans. Roy J. Deferrari (Cambridge, Mass.: Mediaeval Academy of America 1951), 301–2. Hugh is, of course, following a tradition stretching back even beyond Isidore's *Quaestiones in Vetus Testamentum: in Exodum 19*:
'Quid mare Rubrum, nisi baptismus est Christi sanguine consecratus?' (*PL* 83,
col. 296).

21 Edsman, esp. pp. 87, 200. Compare Gregory of Nyssa, *In baptismum Christi*:
'The Spirit, vivifying, burning, inflaming, which consumes the impious and illuminates the faithful' (*PG* 46, col. 592).

22 2 Peter 3:3–10; Daniélou, *Bible and Liturgy*, pp. 77–9.

23 See the number of texts adduced in Daniélou, *Bible and Liturgy*, pp. 70–98.

24 Compare, for example, Isidore of Seville, *Quaestiones in Vetus Testamentum: In
Exodum 19*: 'Hostes sequentes cum rege, qui a tergo moriuntur, peccata sunt
praeterita, quae delentur, et diabolus, qui in spirituali baptismo suffocatur' (*PL* 83,
col. 296); and St Bernard of Clairvaux, *Sermo 39 super Cantica Canticorum*, 5: 'Et
prosequere modo mecum singula proportionis membra. Ibi populus eductus de
Aegypto, hic homo de saeculo; ibi prosternitur Pharao, hic diabolus.' *Sermones
super Cantica Canticorum 36–86, Opera*, II, 21. See also Hugh of St Victor, *De
Sacramentis* II, vi, 8 and 15 (*PL* 76, col. 460–2); *On the Sacraments*, pp. 296,
301–2; St Thomas Aquinas, *ST* III, qu. 66, art. 11, esp. reply to obj. 3.

25 Daniélou, *Bible and Liturgy*, esp. p. 77.

26 Daniélou, *Bible and Liturgy*, p. 77.

27 Whether Virgil himself is supposed to comprehend this fact fully can only be the subject of speculation. Did Virgil learn of this at Christ's *descensus*? Virgil we know is all too aware of the Christian faith's existence and herein lies his pathos and tragedy. On Virgil's knowledge of Christian dogma, see the comments of Busnelli in *Il Virgilio*, esp. pp. 23–52.

28 The meaning of the Veglio in *Inferno* xiv is precisely the significance ascribed to the *vetus homo* in the *Glossa Ordinaria*: '*Vetus homo*. Id est, veteres actus sunt crucifixi, id est, mortui. Vetustas nostra et maledictio in duobus consistit, scilicet, in culpa et poena. Christus autem sua simpla vetustate nostram duplam consumpsit. In sepulcro enim uno die et duabus noctibus quievit. Per unum diem simpla ejus vetustas signatur, per duas vero noctes gemina nostra; unde: *Culpam* nostram Christus delevit praesentem, praeteritam, et futuram. Praeteritam remittendo, praesentem ab ea retrahendo, futuram ut vitaremus gratiam conferendo. *Poenam* quoque similiter consumpsit, gehennalem prorsus delendo, ut eam vere poenitentes non sentiant. Temporalem vero non penitus quidem tulit: manet enim fames, sitis, mors et hujusmodi; sed regnum et dominium ejus dejecit, et in novissimo penitus exterminabit' (*PL* 114, col. 488). On the effects of baptism and the *poena* and *culpa* of sin here and in the hereafter, see St Thomas, *ST* iii, qu. 69, art. 3 and 7.

29 The barrators in their boiling tar fulfil Isaias 34:9–10: '[Hell's] streams will be turned to burning pitch. Its smoke will go up from generation to generation and it will be waste forever.'

30 For the mosaics of Torcello, see Antonio Niero, *La Basilica di Torcello e Santa Fosca* (Venice: Ardo n.d.), 33–4. On Christ and the Ancient of Days, see Peter the Archdeacon, *Quaestiones in Danielem*, 43–4 (*PL* 96, col. 1354) and Rupert of Deutz, *In Danielem*, cap. xiii–xiv (*PL* 167, col. 1514–16). See also Edsman, *Le Baptême de feu*, p. 88; see pp. 92–3 for the iconography in Christian art.

31 1 Corinthians 15:21–2 and 45–9; Romans 5:12–21. See Busnelli, *Appendice*, pp. 172–6; Busnelli, *Il Virgilio*, pp. 79–93. On the Adamic myth see also Paul Ricoeur, *The Symbolism of Evil*, trans. Emerson Buchanan (Boston: Beacon Press 1969), 232–305.

32 *Commentariorum in Danielem Prophetam*, 40 (*PL* 25, col. 504).

33 *In Danielem*, cap. vi (*PL* 167, col. 1505).

34 The Church Fathers used other passages, such as Zacharias 3:9, to bolster this identification of 'lapis' with Christ.

35 After the tenth century, in Christian iconography, Christ at his baptism is often depicted beneath a 'Wasserberg,' or Mountain of Water. See the illustrations in Schiller, *Iconography* i, 137; plates 362, 363, 364, 365, 370, 371, 372, 375, 382. Gregory of Nyssa in his *In Baptismum Christi*, for example, following St Paul (Romans 6:3–6), identifies the water of baptism as the earth of burial: 'We, when

we receive Baptism, do so indeed in the image of our Lord and Master, but *we are not buried in the earth*, for this will be the dwelling of our body when it is dead. But *we are buried in the water, the element which is akin to the earth*. And in doing so three times, we imitate the grace of resurrection' (*PG* 46, col. 586).

36 *De eruditione* I, 22; 26 (*PL* 196, col. 1266; 1274). See also Mazzotta, 'Dante's Theology,' p. 14.

37 '[Christ] had these defects – not that He contracted them but that He assumed them.' St Thomas, *ST* III, qu. 14, art. 3 and 4.

38 'Tot autem in nostro ruinoso et pleno rimarum pariete invenit foramina, quot nostrae infirmitatis et corruptionis in suo corpore sensit experimenta.' *Sermo 56 super Cantica Canticorum, Opera*, II, 115. The Ottimo comments that the right foot is 'di terra cotta *a modo di mattone*' (*Commento*, p. 270; my italics). In speaking of the Incarnation, the Church Fathers conventionally adduced Isaias 53:4: 'Surely he hath borne our infirmities' and Romans 8:3: 'God sent His own Son in the likeness of sinful flesh.'

39 St Thomas, *ST* III, qu. 15, art. 1, reply 2.

40 *Commentariorum in Danielem Prophetam*, 31–40 (*PL* 25, col. 503–4); Peter the Archdeacon, *Quaestiones* I, 1 (*PL* 96, col. 1347); Rupert of Deutz, *In Danielem*, cap. 6 (*PL* 167, col. 1506); Peter Comestor, *Historia scholastica: Historia libri Danielis* (*PL* 198, col. 1447–9). St Cyril of Jerusalem in his *Catachesis* XII, 18 (*PG* 33, col. 747; *The Works of St. Cyril of Jerusalem*, vol. I, trans. Leo P. McCauley and Anthony A. Stephenson, The Fathers of the Church, vol. 61 [Washington, DC: Catholic Univ. of America Press 1969], 238), concerning Psalm 2:9, states that the iron part of the statue in Nebuchadnezzar's dream represents the Romans: ' "You shall rule them with an iron rod." I have already said that the rule of the Romans is clearly called "an iron rod"; but what is still wanting concerning this point let us call to mind from Daniel. For in declaring and interpreting the image of the statue of Nabuchodonosor, he tells also his whole vision concerning it; and that "a stone hewn from a mountain without a hand being put to it," that is to say, not produced by man's contrivance, would overpower the whole world.' Most important for Dante's *Commedia* and the *De Mon.* is that Nebuchadnezzar's vision foretells the coming of Christ.

Also see Busnelli, *Il Virgilio*, pp. 91–3. On the six ages see Eusebius, *Chronicon Liber* I [*Historia ecclesiastica*] (*PG* 19, col. 101–315); Isidore of Seville, *Etymologiarum Liber* VIII, 'De diis gentium,' 11 (*PL* 82, col. 314–20); Ado of Vienne, *Chronicon in aetates sex divisum* (*PL* 123, col. 23–138). Mazzotta also deals briefly with hexaemeric literature ('Dante's Theology,' esp. pp. 15, 21; *Dante, Poet*, pp. 30–40), but not in the context of baptismal imagery.

41 St Augustine, *DCD* XXII, xxx; *LCL* VII, 383. On the five ages of the world also see Daniélou, *Bible and Liturgy*, pp. 276–8.

The crack in the Veglio passes through the clay, iron, brass, and silver of the body, but not through the golden head. Notably it is the four-part *body* of the Veglio which is split by the *fessura*; the golden head representing the Golden Age of primal innocence is unscathed.

42 *DCD*, ibid. On such number symbolism and its connection to baptism, see Vincent Foster Hopper, *Medieval Number Symbolism* (New York: Columbia Univ. Press 1938), 86; Underwood, *The Fountain of Life*, pp. 86–7; Daniélou, *Bible and Liturgy*, p. 284 et passim.

43 *DCD*, ibid. Augustine, naturally, followed the tradition of St Ambrose's *Hexaemeron* (*PL* 14, col. 123–359; *The Six Days of Creation [Hexaemeron]*, trans. John J. Savage, Fathers of the Church, vol. 42 [New York: Fathers of the Church 1961], 3–83), and is followed in his chronology by such writers as Isidore of Seville (*PL* 82, col. 314–20), and Ado of Vienne (*PL* 123, col. 23–138). See also J.D. Cooke, 'Euhemerism: A Medieval Interpretation of Classical Paganism,' *Speculum*, 2 (1927), 396–410, and Jean Seznec, *The Survival of the Pagan Gods*, trans. Barbara Sessions, Harper Torchbooks: The Bollingen Library (New York: Harper and Row 1961).

44 *De Somnio regis Nabuchodonosor* (*PL* 203, col. 586).

45 *Contra Faustum Manichaeum* xii, 8 (*PL* 42, col. 257); *Reply to Faustus the Manichaean*, in *A Select Library of the Nicene and Post-Nicene Fathers*, ed. Philip Schaff, first series, vol. iv (New York: Charles Scribner's Sons 1887; reprint Grand Rapids: Eerdmans 1974), 185–6. See also *De Genesi contra Manichaeos* ii, 24 (*PL* 34, col. 216); *Tractatus* xv, 4 (*PL* 35, col. 1513).

46 Underwood, pp. 86–8; the number eight is also majorly connected to baptism, of course, but that is outside our present argument.

47 *PL* 38, col. 1196–1201.

48 *De Sacramentis* ii, vi, 8 (*PL* 176, col. 455); *On the Sacraments*, p. 296.

49 St Thomas Aquinas, *ST* iii, qu. 69, art. 3; Daniélou, *Bible and Liturgy*, p. 77; Underwood, p. 87. 'Old age' as 'sin' is a common metaphor in the Church Fathers. See, for example, St Augustine, *Enarratio in Psalmum* vi, 9. Hugh of St Victor, *De Sacramentis* ii, vi, 11, states that the Christian 'is washed of the stains of age with a threefold immersion' (*On the Sacraments*, p. 299). St Thomas Aquinas, *ST* iii, qu. 69, art. 1: 'By Baptism man dies unto the oldness of sin, and begins to live unto the newness of grace. *But every sin belongs to the primitive oldness.* Consequently every sin is taken away by Baptism.' See also Busnelli, *Il Virgilio*, p. 18.

50 *PL* 36, col. 91. St Augustine is echoed in this, for example, by Hugh of St Victor, whose works Dante knew well: 'For the body too do they assign its number "four." ' In the same paragraph Hugh continues: 'And this is the number four of the body, in which it is given to be understood that everything which is composed of divisibles, or solubles, is itself also divisible or *dissoluble*.' *Didascalicon de studio legendi*, ed. Charles Henry Buttimer, The Catholic University of

America Studies in Medieval and Renaissance Latin, x (Washington, DC: Catholic Univ. of America Press 1939), II, v, p. 29; *The Didascalicon of Hugh of St. Victor: A Medieval Guide to the Arts*, tran. and introd. Jerome Taylor (New York and London, Columbia Univ. Press 1961), 66. Italics added. The Veglio, as we note, is cleft only in his four body parts; he also reflects the 'dissolubility' of the statue in the dream of Nebuchadnezzar.

51 Daniélou, *Bible and Liturgy*, p. 77.

52 Daniélou, *Bible and Liturgy*, p. 72.

53 *De Baptismo*, 3 (*PL* 1, col. 1197–8); *Treatise on Baptism* in *Baptism: Ancient Liturgies and Patristic Texts*, ed. André Hamman, trans. Thomas Hatton (Staten Island, NY: Alba House 1967), 32. That Christ's death is also a baptism (Luke 12:50; Romans 6:4) has many doctrinal ramifications.

    Just as the Flood annihilated the predeluvian sinners, so, in imitation of the death of Christ, the sinful body which Christ also had assumed is annihilated in the baptismal 'waters of death.' Christ himself arose from the Jordan as the 'first born of the new creation,' just as Christians too, upon their emergence from the baptismal font, become members of that new creation (Daniélou, *Bible and Liturgy*, p. 77).

54 St Justin Martyr, *Dialogus* CXXXVIII, 2–3, cited in Daniélou, *Bible and Liturgy*, pp. 78–9.

55 *DCD* xv, 1; *LCL* IV, 412.

56 *Ad Inquisitiones Januarii: Epistola LV* II, 3 (*PL* 33, col. 205). See also XIV, 24 (*PL* 33, col. 215). Underwood, p. 86.

57 John 3:5; 2 Corinthians 5:17; Daniélou, *Bible and Liturgy*, p. 72. St Augustine always speaks of the *gradual* coming of the sixth age: 'Coepimus esse sub gratia; iam commortui sumus cum Christo, et consepulti illi per baptismum in mortem / We have begun to be under grace [and] we are already dead together with Christ, and buried with Him by baptism unto death.' Cited in Underwood, p. 87. *De Genesi contra Manichaeos* II, 24 (*PL* 34, col. 216); see also *Tractatus* xv, 4 (*PL* 35, col. 1513).

58 See note 35 above.

CHAPTER SIX: THE IDOLATERS

1 Singleton, *Inferno: Commentary*, pp. 242–3. For Juvenal, Ettore Paratore, 'Il Canto XIV dell'*Inferno*,' *Lectura Dantis romana*, 14 (1959), 25–6; reprinted in his *Tradizione e struttura in Dante* (Florence: Sansoni 1968), 241.

2 'When a mountain in Crete was cleft by an earthquake, a body standing sixty-nine feet high was found, which some believed to be that of Orion, and others of Otus.' See Tito Bottagisio, 'Il Gran Veglio di Creta,' p. 72; Claudio Varese, 'Il Canto XIV dell'*Inferno*,' *Letture dantesche*, ed. Giovanni Getto (Florence: Sansoni

1962), 261; Singleton, *Inferno: Commentary*, p. 242. For the Christian belief in the extraordinary height and longevity of prediluvian man, see *DCD* xv, 9.

3 H. Theodore Silverstein, 'The Weeping Statue and Dante's *Gran Veglio*,' *Harvard Studies and Notes in Philology and Literature*, 13 (1931), 167.

4 Nebuchadnezzar believed himself God's equal. St Jerome, *Commentariorum in Danielem* (*PL* 25, cols. 514–15).

5 Peter Comestor, *Historia scholastica: Liber Danielis*, cap. III, *Secunda visio Danielis*: 'Porro Nabuchodonosor fecit statuam auream altitudine cubitorum sexaginta, latitudine sex, et statuit eam in campo Dura, fluminis scilicet cujusdam, juxta quem gigantes aedificaverunt turrim' (*PL* 198, col. 1449). Nebuchadnezzar became the medieval type of the idolatrous man punished by madness (in the tradition also of Saul, 1 Kings [Samuel] 15–16). See Penelope B.R. Doob, *Nebuchadnezzar's Children* (New Haven and London: Yale Univ. Press 1974), 2.

6 *PL* 25, col. 505. My emphasis. Of the idolatry and blasphemy of the Children of Israel see St Thomas, *ST* II–II, qu. 14, art. 3.

7 *De Trinitate: In Danielem*, cap. VI (*PL* 167, col. 506).

8 Ovid, *Metamorphoses*, ed. Frank Justus Miller, *LCL* (Cambridge, Mass.: Harvard Univ. Press; London: William Heinemann 1966), vol. I, p. 300.

9 *Metamorphoses* vol. I, p. 308.

10 *Arnulphi Aurelianensis Allegoriae super Ovidii Metamorphosin* in Fausto Ghisalberti, 'Arnolfo d'Orleans, un cultore di Ovidio nel secolo XII,' *Memorie del Reale Istituto Lombardo di Scienze e Lettere*, 24 (1932), 217.

11 *Ovide moralisé, poème du commencement du quatorzième siècle*, ed. C. De Boer, vol. II, in *Verhandelingen der Koniklijke Akademie van Wetenschappen te Amsterdam*, 21 (1920), 311–12.

12 *Ovide moralisé, Verhandelingen*, 21, pp. 320–1. See also *Ovide moralisé en prose*, vol. 61, no. 2 (1954), 192.

13 Petrus Berchorius, *Ovidius moralizatus*, ed. J. Engels (Utrecht: Instituut voor Laat Latijn der Rijksuniversiteit 1962), 103. My emphasis.

14 St Thomas, *ST* II–II, qu. 164, art. 3.

15 *ST* II–II, qu. 94, art. 3, reply obj. 2.

16 *ST* II, qu. 13, art. 1.

17 I should note that Battus, in Ovid's *Metamorphoses* II, 676–707, is changed into a flint. So far I have found no moralizations in any medieval mythographer which would make the tale applicable to the theme of idolatry or perfect blasphemy.

18 Singleton, *Inferno: Commentary*, pp. 230–1.

19 See St Augustine, *DCD, LCL* III, 24, n. 2. This follows Euhemerus ca 300 BC, known chiefly through Ennius' *Euhemerus* or *Sacra Historia* summarized by Lactantius in prose. Rupert of Deutz, *De victoria Verbi Dei* (*PL* 169, cols. 1397–1410). See also George Cary, *The Medieval Alexander* (Cambridge: Cambridge Univ. Press 1956; reprint 1967), esp. pp. 90–5, 104, 154, 290.

20 *Quod idola dii non sint*, 3 (*PL* 4, col. 568).

21 St Augustine confused the name of the priest with the real author of the spurious but influential letter, and was thus unaware that it had been written by Leon of Pella toward the end of the fourth century or the beginning of the third century BC (*DCD* VIII, 5; *LCL*, III, 24–5; also *DCD* VIII, 27 and XII, 11). See also Minucius Felix, *Octavius*, 21:3, ed. G. Quispel (Leiden: Brill 1949), 44; Clement of Alexandria, *Cohortatio ad gentes* (*PG* 8, col. 152).

22 Strabo, *Geography*, 17, 1, 43, ed. H.L. Jones, *LCL* (Cambridge, Mass.: Harvard Univ. Press; London: Wiliam Heinemann 1932), VIII, 112–17. *Oxford Classical Dictionary* (Oxford: Clarendon Press 1949; reprint 1968), 32–4, 'Alexander III.'

23 St John Chrysostom (*PG* 49, col. 221–40); *The Twelfth Instruction*, 57 in *Baptismal Instructions*, trans. and ed. Paul W. Harkins, Ancient Christian Writers, 31 (Westminster, Md.: Newman Press; London: Longmans Green 1963). On the adoration of Alexander see Jean Seznec, p. 11: 'The superhuman career of Alexander, and above all his expedition to India – where he became the object of adoration similar to that which, according to the myth, had once greeted Dionysus there – had suddenly thrown light upon the origin of the gods.' Dante condemns Alexander in the *De Mon.* II, 8, 10.

24 Lucan, *De bello civili* (*Pharsalia*) in *Lucan*, trans. J.D. Duff, *LCL* (London: William Heinemann; New York: G.P. Putnam's Sons 1928), 544–9. Dante refers to *Pharsalia* IX also in the *Convivio* III, v, 12. On Cato and Ulysses, see John A. Scott, *Dante Magnanimo* (Florence: Olschki 1977), esp. pp. 146–93.

25 Dante cites Cato's words (*Pharsalia* IX, 580: 'Jupiter is whatever thou seest, wherever thou goest') in the *Letter to Can Grande* together with citations from Jeremiah concerning the ubiquitousness of God. On the temptation of God, see St Thomas Aquinas, *ST* II–II, qu. 97, art. 1–4.

26 See particularly Charles S. Singleton's observations on *Purg.* II, in *Elements*, pp. 19–29.

27 Concerning the revelatory, retrogressive ways of the poem, see Charles S. Singleton, 'The Vistas in Retrospect,' *Atti del Congresso Internazionale di Studi Danteschi* (Florence: Sansoni 1965), 279–304; reprint *Modern Language Notes*, 81 (1966), 55–80. Robert Hollander uses the references to Cato to demonstrate 'verbal figuralism' in the Poem: see *Allegory in Dante's Commedia* (Princeton, NJ: Princeton Univ. Press 1969), 124–9. See also E. Proto, 'Nuove ricerche sul Catone dantesco,' *Giornale Storico della Letteratura Italiana*, 59 (1952), 223; Mazzotta, 'Dante's Theology,' p. 38. In the *Conv.* IV, xxviii, Dante asks and affirms: 'Quale uomo terreno più degno fu di significare Iddio, che Catone? Certo nullo.' *Il Convivio*, ed. G. Busnelli and G. Vandelli, 2ª edizione, ed. Antonio Enzo Quaglio (Florence: Le Monnier 1964), pt. 2, p. 359.

28 Also *Inf.* XIV, 60, 63–6.

29 *The Apocryphal New Testament*, pp. 522–3; see also pp. 514, 516. In the

Apocalypse of Mary there is a river of fire and boiling pitch (pp. 563–4). Elias-Elijah is the prefiguration and final fulfilment of John the Baptist (Matt. 17:10–13; Mark 9:13; Luke 1:17); see St Augustine, *In Joannis Evangelium*, Tract. IV, cap. 4 (*PL* 35, col. 1407); compare the punishment of the Egyptian idolaters in Wisdom (Sapientia) 16:16: 'For the ungodly ... were ... utterly consumed by fire.'

30 St Gregory of Nyssa, *In diem luminum* (*PG* 46, col. 591); *Sermon for the Feast of Lights* in *Baptism: Ancient Liturgies and Patristic Texts*, ed. André Hamman, trans. Thomas Hatton (Staten Island, NY: Alba House 1967), 132–3. My emphasis. See also St Basil's *Great Protectic on Holy Baptism*; Hamman, *Baptism*, p. 79 (*PG* 31, cols. 424–44).

It is a curious fact that the sanctuaries of the idolatrous Cretan Zeus were superseded by shrines of Elijah, 'Saint Elias,' in Christian times. See A.B. Cook, *Zeus: A Study in Ancient Religion*, 3 vols. (Cambridge: Cambridge Univ. Press 1914, 1925, 1940); here, II, 163–86 (pages are numbered consecutively through all volumes). See my text below for the legends of Zeus Cretagenes and chapter 5, n. 19. Elijah is the prefiguration of St John (Baptism), and the type of the enemy of idolatry (his sacrifice).

31 *ST* II–II, qu. 13, art. 4.

32 *ST* II–II, qu. 14, art. 3.

33 *Statius*, trans. J.H. Mozley, vol. II, *LCL* (Cambridge, Mass.: Harvard Univ. Press; London: William Heinemann 1957), 390–1.

34 We noted that the Veglio both reflects Christ's image *and* is the image of 'corruptible man.' The impossible thesis that the sinners of *Inf.* xv are not sodomites was defended by André Pézard in his otherwise erudite and thorough work, *Dante sous la pluie de feu* (Paris: J. Vrin 1950), and it has been taken up again by Richard Kay in *Dante's Swift and Strong: Essays on Inferno XV* (Lawrence, Kansas: Regents Press of Kansas 1978).

35 *ST* II–II, qu. 94, art. 3, reply to obj. 3.

36 *Commentum*, p. 20. Notably for the Canto, Bernardus also identifies Crete as 'divine judgment,' for 'the nature of the flesh ill-judges divine matters when it places them after temporal things.'

37 St Gregory of Nyssa writes, for example: 'By the "flesh" I mean the "old man" who may be taken off by those who desire to wash themselves in the bath of the Word' (*PG* 44, col. 1003). Antonino Pagliaro's view, in *Ulisse: ricerche semantiche sulla Divina Commedia*, vol. II (Messina-Florence: Casa Editrice G. D'Anna 1967), 525, is completely erroneous: 'La statua del Veglio di Creta non ha in sé nessun riferimento necessario alla storia umana che vuole rappresentare; né alcun legame naturale esiste fra la sua ubicazione e posizione è quello che essa vuole significare ... l'allegoria rimane autonoma e quasi estranea al contesto. ...'

38 The classical and medieval sources disagree on the exact place of Zeus' birth

and rearing on the island. Hesiod assumes Zeus was born in Crete and reared in a cave on Mount Aegeum (*Theogonia*, 468–84 in *Hesiod: the Homeric Hymns and Homerica*, trans. Hugh G. Evelyn-White, LCL [Cambridge, Mass.: Harvard Univ. Press; London: William Heinemann 1959], 114–15). Diodorus Siculus declares that he was born on Dicte in Crete and brought up on Mount Ida (*The Library of History* III, 61:1–4; v, 64:3–7 in *Diodorus of Sicily*, trans. C.H. Oldfather et al., *LCL* [London: William Heinemann; Cambridge, Mass.: Harvard Univ. Press 1933–67], II, 282–3; III, 271–7). Apollodorus (*The Library*, trans. Sir James George Frazer, vol. I, *LCL* [Cambridge, Mass.: Harvard Univ. Press; London: William Heinemann 1961], 6–9) names Dicte as the place of Zeus' childhood as does Virgil in the *Georgics* IV, 153 (in *Virgil*, trans. H. Rushton Fairclough, *LCL*, vol. I [Cambridge, Mass.: Harvard Univ. Press; London: William Heinemann 1965], 206–7), and as does Servius (*Servii Grammatici ... in Vergilii Carmina Commentarii*, ed. Georg Thilo and Hermann Hagen, vol. I [Leipzig: Teubner 1881], 359–60). Dicte is also the place of Zeus' rearing in the Three Vatican Mythographers (in *Scriptores rerum mythicarum latini tres Romae nuper reperti*, ed. Georg Heinrich Bode [Cellis: 1834], *Myth*. I, 104 [p. 34], *Myth*. II, 16 [p. 79]).

Mount Ida is supported by Càllimachus, *Hymn* I, 51 (in *Callimachus and Lycophron*, ed. and trans. A.W. Maier, and *Aratus*, ed. and trans. G.R. Maier, *LCL* [London: William Heinemann; New York: G.P. Putnam's Sons 1921], 36–7). Ida also is Ovid's choice in his *Fasti* IV, 207 (Ovid's *Fasti*, ed. and trans. Sir James George Frazer, *LCL* [Cambridge, Mass.: Harvard Univ. Press; London: William Heinemann 1959], 202–3), and Lactantius Placidus in his *Commentary on Statius' Thebaid* IV, 784 (in Lactantii Placidii *Commentarios in Statii Thebaida*, ed. Richard Jahnke [Leipzig: Teubner 1898], 253).

See also Hyginus, 'Curetes,' *Fabulae*, no. 139, ed. H.I. Rose (Leyden: Sythoff, 1963), 101–2, and his *Astronomica* II, 13, ed. Bernhard Bunte (Leipzig: Weigel 1875), 46–9; and Lucretius, on 'Curetes' in *De Rerum natura* II, 633–9, ed. and trans. W.H.D. Rouse (Cambridge, Mass.: Harvard Univ. Press; London: William Heinemann 1966), 130–1. See esp. Cook, *Zeus*, p. 157 n. 4; pp. 940 ff.

Failure to see the connection between verses 102 and 103 and their relation to euhemerism led Busnelli to state: 'Quando vi fosse messa quella statua, se prima o dopo la nascita di Giove, e avanti l'apparizione degli uomini sulla terra, il poeta nol dice.' *Il Virgilio dantesco e il Gran Veglio di Creta*, 2nd ed. (Rome: Civiltà cattolica 1919), 164. The following pages of this chapter show that the Poet does indeed give us this information: the statue was set in position certainly *after the birth of the idolater, Jove*; indeed, as we will see, during Jove's maturity and, consequently, far, far later than the creation of mankind.

Bottagisio also realized the importance of contemporary archaeology on Crete

('Il Gran Veglio,' pp. 71–3), but he limited his inquiry to Pliny's statements about the statue in the *Historia Naturalis* I, vii, ch. 16. Bottagisio goes on to show that the Bible states that giants actually inhabited the Earth. He thus missed the essential poetic connections in Dante's Poem.

On the birth of Zeus-Jove the reader should consult D.G. Hogarth, 'The Birth Cave of Zeus,' *Monthly Review* (1901), 47–64; Cook, 'The Mountain as Birthplace of Zeus,' *Zeus*, pp. 148–54; and Martin P. Nilsson, *The Minoan-Mycenean Religion and Its Survival in Greek Religion*, 2nd ed. rev. (Lund: C.W.K. Gleerup 1950), 461, 534, 543–7, 553–4, 565). See also R.F. Willetts, *Cretan Cults and Festivals* (London: Routledge and Kegan Paul 1962), 219 and notes (clearly all derivative and confused from those of Cook).

Writing on Felix Faber's *Evagatorium* (1483), the British scholar R.M. Dawkins, in 'The "Gran Veglio" of *Inferno* XIV,' *Medium Aevum*, 2 (1933), 95–107, drew the completely unwarranted conclusion that Faber's description of a buried Veglio was not derived from Dante but from another (merely posited and unidentified) source: 'The conclusion to be drawn is that Dante and Felix Faber are based on some common source' (p. 100). Even the most cursory comparison between the two authors, however, reveals that such is *not* the case. The word parallels and the derivative concepts, as well as chronology, prove beyond any doubt that Dante is Faber's ultimate source.

It is an amusing coincidence that modern archaeologists exploring the Idaean cave discovered 'numerous objects in bronze, silver and gold.' 'The floor is covered to a depth of several feet with a layer of ashes and charcoal in which were found many terra cotta lamps.' Cook, *Zeus*, p. 937.

39 Willetts, p. 202.

40 Julius Firmicus Maternus, *De errore profanarum religionum*, 6 (*PL* 12, col. 995–7); *The Error of the Pagan Religions*, trans. Clarence A. Forbes, Ancient Christian Writers, 37 (Newman Press: New York, NY and Paramus, NJ 1970), 54–6. William Keith Chambers Guthrie, *Orpheus and Greek Religion* (London: Methuen 1935; reprint 1952), 111. Willetts, pp. xi, 44, 49–50, 204–6, 213–14, and esp. pp. 219–21.

41 Antoninus Liberalis, *Les Métamorphoses*, ed. Manolis Papathomopoulos (Paris: Société d'Edition 'Les Belles Lettres' 1968), XIX. Arthur Bernard Cook, 'The European Sky-God,' *Folk-Lore*, 15 (1904), 388–9. Cook, *Zeus*, pp. 928–9. For Boios, also see Willetts, p. 217.

The themes of death and resurrection eerily present in this pagan myth were recognized as being close to Christian truth by early Church writers; see text below. The burial beneath a mountain (parallel to the Mountain of Water or 'Wasserberg' in artistic depictions of Christ's baptism) and the blood issuing from a mountain cave also bear an odd similarity to Dante's Canto.

42 J. Rendel Harris, 'The Cretans Always Liars,' *Expositor* (1906), 305–17, here, p. 307.

'Cretans were branded the liars of antiquity for showing on one hill the tomb of Zeus.' Hogarth, 'The Birth Cave of Zeus,' p. 47. Cook, *Zeus*, p. 926 n. 1.

43 *Callimachus and Lycophron*, pp. 36–7. Cf. Apollodorus I, 4: 'The Curetes in arms, guarded the babe in the cave, clashing their spears on their shields in order that Cronus might not hear the child's voice' (*The Library* I, 6–9).

44 A most interesting piece of folklore dating from an early period concerns the ridge of Mount Juktas of the Ida complex in Crete. There, far more than in other places on earth, the mountain peaks assume a convincing anthropomorphic appearance forming the striking shape of a gigantic head and shoulders. (I thank my friend and colleague in Classics, David Bright, for showing me slides of this phenomenon.) In the *Palace of Minos at Knossos*, Sir Arthur James Evans wrote: 'The long ridge of the mountain rising in successive peaks has given rise to a widespread belief in the island that it reproduces the profile of the native Zeus.' Cited by Cook, *Zeus*, p. 940. A. Trevor Battye also described the same phenomenon: 'Rocks and mountains often bear the likeness to human lineaments; every traveller can recall many such resemblances, but none that I have seen have the convincing dignity of the face on Iuctas' (Cook, *Zeus*, p. 939). Twentieth-century travellers and scholars continue to repeat even in popular magazines an observation made over five hundred years ago by the Florentine priest, Cristoforo Buondelmonte in 1415: 'Ad meridiem viam capiendo ad montem hodie Juctam devenitur per periculosissimam viam. Hic mons a longe faciei effigiem habet, in cuius fronte templum Jovis usque ad fundamenta deletum invenitur; in naso tres ecclesiae sunt congestae. ... Versus austrum, prope Ideum montem, ubi est barba, sub monte atro, Tegrinnum castrum inexpugnabile videtur.' Emile Legrand, *Description des Iles de l'Archipel grec par Christophe Buondelmonti florentin du XVe siècle* (Paris, 1897; reprint Amsterdam: Philo Press 1974), 148; see also Cook, *Zeus*, p. 158 n. 2. It is safe to assume that Buondelmonti's was not the first traveller's report, for, as I noted, modern photographic evidence still attests his truthfulness startlingly. Perhaps indeed many voyagers, treasuring the memory of Dante's *Veglio*, have sought visible corroboration in the mountains of Crete. But Buondelmonti's 'Descriptio Cretae,' like many others cited, nowhere mentions Dante's poem; it is indeed an odd omission for a cleric from Florence. We must turn to Crete and to the literary and religious fortunes of its legends of Jove to seek out Dante's meaning in *Inf.* xiv. We must also bear in mind that in Dante's time Crete was *Italian*, a possession of Venice.

45 *In Epistolam Pauli ad Titum* I (*PL*, 26, col. 573).

46 St John Chrysostom, *In Epistolam ad Titum Commentarius* (*PG* 62, col. 676–7); *Homily III: Titus I:12–14*, ed. and trans. Philip Schaff, Nicene and Post-Nicene Fathers, 1st series, vol. XIII (New York: Charles Scribner's Sons 1905), 528.

47 *Inf.* XIV, 15. In Lucan's *Pharsalia* IX, 511–86, it is Jupiter who has the devotion of Cato.

48 Lactantius, *Divinae institutiones* I, 11 (*PL* 6, col. 178–9); *Divine Institutes*, p. 52.

49 *Divinae institutiones* V, 5 (*PL* 6, col. 565); *Divine Institutes*, p. 339.

50 *Divinae institutiones* V, 5 (*PL* 6, col. 566–8); *Divine Institutes*, p. 340. Concerning the concepts of original and personal justice in the *Purgatorio* see Charles S. Singleton, *Journey*, especially ch. 11, 'Virgo or Justice,' pp. 184–203. Crete as the site of the first human civilization is also alluded to in the *Aeneid* III, 105, 'gentis cunabula nostrae'; it is also the place of the first primal innocence of the Age of Gold.

51 *Divinae institutiones* V, 5 (*PL* 6, col. 567); *Divine Institutes*, p. 341.

52 *Divinae institutiones* V, 6 (*PL* 6, col. 568); *Divine Institutes*, p. 342. Contrast the origins of idolatry in Wisdom (Sapientia) 14:12. See also *Divinae institutiones* I, 22 (*PL* 6, col. 248–9); *Divine Institutes*, pp. 91–2. Compare the *Ovide moralisé* I, 859–62:

> Jupiter fu, selonc l'estoire,
> Rois de Crete, et fesoit a croire
> Par l'art de son enchantement
> Qu'il ert dieus. ...

Later in *Purg.* XXVIII, at the meeting with Matelda, Dante makes the connection of the Golden Age with Eden and the Fall far clearer (139–44). The context concerns the origin of the Earthly Paradise and again the source of rivers, this time Lethe and Eunoe (121–6). The unstable statue, the source of the rivers of sin, standing on one cracked foot of clay, must there be contrasted with that which is strength in the Christian universe, the Will of God, expressed again in a baptismal image as 'la fontana salda e certa' (124).

53 Plotinus, *Enneads* III, 6 in *Plotinus*, trans. and ed. A.H. Armstrong, *LCL* (Cambridge, Mass.: Harvard Univ. Press; London: William Heinemann 1967), III, 242–3.

54 Jean Daniélou, *Platonisme et théologie mystique* (Paris: Aubier 1944), p. 224. In the *Enneads* IV, 7, 10, Plotinus himself had linked the image of a statue to the same concept: 'By reentering into herself, in thinking herself in her primitive condition ... [the soul] clears up and recognizes in herself the divine statues, soiled by the rust of time.' *On the Immortality of the Soul*, in Plotinus, *Complete Works*, ed. and trans. Kenneth Sylvan Guthrie, vol. I (Alpine, NJ: Platonist Press 1918), 81.

55 St Gregory of Nyssa, *De Virginitate, PG* 46, col. 367–8; *On Virginity,* in *Ascetical Works,* p. 41. Daniélou, *Platonisme,* p. 225.

56 The *Allegoriae in Sacram Scripturam* interprets: 'Speculum est fides, ut in Paulo: "Videmus nunc per speculum et in aenigmate," id est, per fidem. ... *Speculum,* favores saecularium, ut in Isaia: "Auferet Dominis a filiabus Sion specula," quod in reprobis, in quibus delectantur, destruet saecularis' (*PL* 112, col. 1050).

57 *PG* 46, col. 89; *On the Soul and Resurrection,* in *Ascetical Works,* trans. Virginia Woods Callahan, The Fathers of the Church, 58 (Washington, DC: Catholic Univ. of America Press 1967), 237–8. Jean Daniélou, *Platonisme,* esp. 'Le miroir de l'âme,' pp. 223–35, here p. 224.

58 Cf. St Gregory of Nyssa, *On the Soul and the Resurrection,* p. 238; *De anima et resurrectione dialogus, PG* 46, col. 90–1.

59 In the thought of St Augustine there were two significant Empires into which the world had been divided, the Assyrian (i.e. Babylonian) Empire and the Roman. In the *City of God* he states: '*Sed inter plurima regna terrarum, in quae terrenae utilitas vel cupiditas est divisa societas* – quam civitatem mundi huius universali vocabulo nuncupamus – *duo regna cernimus longe ceteris provenisse clariora, Assyriorum primum, deinde Romanorum,* ut temporibus, ita locis inter se ordinata atque distincta. Nam quo modo illud prius, hoc posterius, eo modo illud in Oriente, hoc in Occidente surrexit' (*LCL* v, 366–7; my emphasis). Rome indeed is equated to Babylon, 'the first Rome.' 'We must name the Assyrian kings when the occasion arises, *to show how Babylonia, as the first Rome, runs its course aside the City of God in its pilgrimage in this world*' (p. 371). Rome itself is thus identified as the Earthly City. Busnelli (*Il Virgilio,* pp. 123–30) discussed the significance of 'Roma' but fails to see the connection with idolatry.

60 *PL* 167, col. 506.

61 Cf. Busnelli, *Il Virgilio,* p. 123.

62 See the comments on Platonic metaphors in Daniélou, *Platonisme,* pp. 223–35. Damietta (or 'Damiata') is also an integral part of the theme for it was the entrance port to the East, the place of the heathen for contemporary Christian pilgrims; in the Poem it figures 'Egypt,' the place of Idolatry. From Damietta Palmers followed the Exodus route to Jerusalem and the Holy Sepulchre. St Francis, for example, returned by way of Damietta in 1219 with his missionaries after preaching the Gospel and condemning the Koran. See also M. Margaret Newett, *Canon Pietro Casola's Pilgrimage to Jerusalem in the Year 1494* (Manchester: Manchester Univ. Press 1907), esp. p. 6 and the preface to P. Amat di S. Filippo, *Biografia dei viaggiatori italiani* (Rome: Società Geografica Italiana 1882). On the question of pilgrimage and the *Comedy,* see John G. Demaray, *The Invention of Dante's Commedia* (New Haven and London: Yale Univ. Press 1974).

63 *ST* II–II, qu. 163, art. 2.

64 *ST* II–II, qu. 163, art. 3.

65 *ST* II–II, qu. 94, art. 4, reply obj. 1.

66 Ibid. My emphasis. St Thomas also deals with the five ages of the *saeculum* and the four of idolatry: first comes the Golden Age when God was worshipped; the sixth age dispels the sin of the previous four: 'There was no idolatry in the first age, owing to the recent remembrance of the creation of the world, so that man still retained in his mind the knowledge of one God. In the sixth age idolatry was banished by the doctrine and power of Christ, who triumphed over the Devil' (*ST* II–II, qu. 94, art. 4).

67 The assumption of mankind as a single moral or spiritual body is axiomatic in both the classics and in Christianity. Cf. *De Mon.* I, 3 (pp. 356–8). It is the assumption behind Aristotle's concept of justice in the *Nicomachaean Ethics* v, ii. The identity of all men in the fleshly disorder of Adam is St Paul's whole metaphorical basis in 1 Corinthians 15:21–2 and especially v. 39. 'One is the flesh of all men.' St Thomas cites Porphyry: 'All men born of Adam may be considered as one man, inasmuch as they have one common nature which they receive from their first parents. ... Indeed Porphyry says that "by sharing the same species, many men are one man." Accordingly, the multitude of men born of Adam are so many members of one body' (*ST* I–II, qu. 81, art. 1). Adam, sinning, incurred the stain of mankind 'peccò tota nel seme suo':

> dannando sé, dannò tutta sua prole
> Onde l'umana specie inferma giacque
> Giù per secoli molti in grand' errore.

(Par. VII, 27)

68 Origen, *In Librum Jesu Nave, Homilia (Homilies on Joshua)* IV, i (*PG* 12, col. 843). See also 1 Corinthians 10:6–7.

69 *PG* 33, col. 1088–9. My emphasis. Daniélou, *Bible and Liturgy*, p. 118. By baptism man regains his likeness to God. Tertullian, *De baptismo* 5 (*PL* 1, col. 1206).

70 *PG* 3, col. 403–4. Daniélou, *Bible and Liturgy*, pp. 46–7. St Thomas (*ST* III, qu. 66, art. 3) cites St John Chryostomos' *Hom. XXV in Joannem* iii:5: '"Unless a man be born again," etc. When we dip our heads under the water, just as in a grave, the old man is buried, and, being submerged, is entirely hidden below; then when we emerge, the new man rises again.' See also *ST* III, qu. 66, art. 7, esp. reply to obj. 2, and *ST* III, qu. 68, art. 5.

71 *ST* III, qu. 1, art. 2. St Thomas later cites Dionysius' definition of baptism that it 'confers our most sacred and Godlike regeneration' (*ST* III, qu. 66, art. 1).

CHAPTER SEVEN: ULYSSES

1 A complete bibliography is impossible here; at last count there were some 350 modern books and articles. See my 'Ulisseana: A Bibliography of Dante's Ulysses to 1981,' Italian Culture, 3 (1981), 23–45.

For the romantic view see: Francesco De Sanctis, Lezioni e saggi su Dante in Opere di F. De S. (Milan: Einaudi 1955), 262–94, 424, 427, 442–54; Storia della letteratura italiana a cura di Benedetto Croce, 8th printing (Bari: Laterza 1964), I, 192; and esp. Mario Fubini, Il peccato di Ulisse e altri scritti danteschi (Milan-Naples: Ricciardi 1966). Even Antonino Pagliaro reiterates the view: 'L'Ulisse dantesco è l'immagine a livello epico, dell'amore per il sapere'; see Ulisse: ricerche semantiche sulla Divina Commedia (Messina-Florence: D'Anna 1967), I, 403. Alfredo Bonadeo has recently repeated that certain sinners 'rise above' the infernal system of punishments; such cases, affirms Bonadeo untenably, evince heterodoxy on Dante's part ('Punizione e sofferenza nell'Inferno dantesco,' Proceedings, Pacific Northwest Council on Foreign Languages, 28, part I [21–3 April 1977], 74–7). Mario Fubini's views are enshrined in the Enciclopedia dantesca (sub voce) together with his short, tendentious bibliography.

Among those on the revisionist side, Bruno Nardi ('La tragedia di Ulisse,' in Dante e la cultura medievale, 2nd ed. [Bari: Laterza 1949], 153–65), Rocco Montano ('Il folle volo di Ulisse,' Delta n.s. 2 [1952], 10–32), and, more recently, Amilcare A. Iannucci ('Ulysses' "folle volo": The Burden of History,' Medioevo romanzo, 3 [1976], 410–45), have all, correctly I believe, seen Ulysses' sin as reflective of the Fall. Others have seen fraudulence in Ulysses' oration to his men, among them: A. Mori, L'ultimo viaggio di Ulisse (Milan: Pirola 1909), 12; André Pézard, Dante sous la pluie de feu (Paris: Vrin 1950), 290; W.B. Stanford, The Ulysses Theme (Oxford: Blackwell 1954; reprint 1963), 181; Giorgio Padoan, Il pio Enea, l'empio Ulisse: Tradizione classica e intendimento medievale in Dante (Ravenna: Longo 1977), 196 et passim; John A. Scott, Dante magnanimo: Studi sulla 'Commedia' (Florence: Olschki 1977), 117–93. Scott noted that St Augustine condemned vain curiosity and the libido experiendi noscendique in the Confessions x, 8, 15, and x, 35, 55, and that the saint distinguished between the wisdom of the Earthly City and the true Wisdom of God in the DCD xvi, 9. Richard Kay, 'Two Pairs of Tricks: Ulysses and Guido in Dante's Inferno xxvi–xxvii,' Quaderni d'italianistica, 1 (1980), 107–24.

Mario Trovato, in 'Il contrapasso nell'ottava bolgia,' Dante Studies, 94 (1976), 47–59, approaches the problem in a way quite different from my study.

2 Guido da Pisa, Expositiones et Glose super Comediam Dantis: Commentary on Dante's Inferno, ed. Vincenzo Cioffari (Albany, NY: State Univ. of New York Press 1974), 520.

3 St Gregory, *Moralium* I, 21 (*PL* 75, col. 536); *Morals*, I, 42. *Allegoriae in Sacram Scripturam* (*PL* 112, col. 905): 'Culex est Barrabas latro, ut in Evangelio: "Liquantes culicem," quod Judaei sibi dimitti postulabant latronem.'

4 In *Virgil*, ed. and trans. H. Rushton Fairclough, *LCL* (Cambridge, Mass.: Harvard Univ. Press; London: William Heinemann 1969), II, 370–403.

5 Dante's description of Cerberus in *Inf.* VI, 11–31 owes more to the 'Culex' than to the *Aeneid* VI, 417–25. Specifically the detail of red eyes is calqued on the mock-heroic poem (cf. vv.220–3).

6 As in, for example, St Augustine's *DCD* XXII, 30. For St Ambrose in the *De Trinitate Tractatus*, cap. xvi (*PL* 17, col. 529), the number five signifies the cities of Egypt and thus the slavery of the flesh: ' "Erunt quinque civitates in terra Aegypti, loquentes lingua Chanaan (Isaias XIX, 18)," hoc est, quinque sensus carnales, qui miserae animae tenebris Aegypti oppressae loquuntur.'

7 In an excellent article, Joan M. Ferrante noted the contradiction in Ulysses' very words, but to different effect: '[Ulysses] describes his desire to gain experience of the world and of vice and valor (v. 98) as so strong that no bonds can hold him back, though the destination of the voyage turns out to be the "mondo sanza gente" *where such experience could not be had.*' 'The Relation of Speech to Sin in the *Inferno*,' *Dante Studies*, 87 (1969), 33–46, here p. 41 (my italics). Harvey D. Goldstein, in 'Enea e Paolo: A Reading of the 26th Canto of Dante's *Inferno*,' *Symposium*, 19 (1965), 316–27, concludes that the vice recognized and fought in *Inf.* XXVI is the Poet's tendency to make bad use of his poetic genius, to enjoy his own eloquence and become simply a writer of 'alti versi' – and, thus, a fraudulent counsellor; the meeting with Ulysses exorcises this tendency. Giuseppe Mazzotta adopts Goldstein's position in 'Poetics of History: *Inferno* XXVI, '*Diacritics*, 5 (1975), 37–44. James Truscott attends intelligently to the rhetoric of both Guido da Montefeltro and Ulysses in 'Ulysses and Guido (*Inf.* XXVI–XXVII),' *Dante Studies*, 91 (1973), 47–72. See also John Freccero, 'Dante's Prologue Scene,' *Dante Studies*, 84 (1966), 1–25.

Ulysses' exhortation reads like a parody of Proverbs 4:5: 'Get wisdom, get prudence: forget not, neither decline from the words of my mouth.' I thank Anthony L. Pellegrini for pointing this out to me.

I do not find 'manhood' a totally imprecise translation for 'virtù' in this context, although it is, perhaps, too anachronistic and limiting for the Poet's irony.

8 The various conflicting views of admiration and indictment expressed by critics, of course, had their roots in the diverse reactions of the earliest commentators, some of whom expressed a rather non-committal approval of the Greek hero, while others censured him. Dante's sons, Jacopo and Pietro, the Ottimo, Jacopo della Lana, and Benvenuto da Imola floated confusedly in a vague approval of a search for virtue and knowledge. The Pisan friar, Francesco da Buti, however, put

forth a severer view: Ulysses' oration was an act of fraud, and his last voyage an act of pride. Clearly, da Buti's view is more compatible with Dante's tropological portrayal of the deceptiveness of sin. Theology, common sense, and artistic consistency demand such an interpretation.

Jacopo Alighieri, *Chiose alla cantica dell'Inferno di Dante Alighieri scritte da Jacopo Alighieri* a cura di G. Piccini (Florence: Bemporad 1915); Petri Allegherii, *Super Dantis ipsius genitoris Comoediam Commentarium* a cura di Vincenzo Nannucci (Florence: Garinei 1844); *L'Ottimo commento della Divina Commedia* a cura di Alessandro Torri, 3 vols. (Pisa: Capurro 1827–9); Jacopo della Lana, *Comedia di Dante degli Allagherii col commento di Jacopo della Lana bolognese* a cura di L. Scarabelli, 3 vols. (Bologna: Tipografia Regia 1866); Benevenuti de Rambaldis de Imola, *Comentum super Dantis Aldigherij Comoediam* a cura di J.F. Lacaita, 5 vols. (Florence: Barbèra 1887); Francesco da Buti, *Commento di Francesco da Buti sopra la Divina Commedia* a cura di C. Giannini, 3 vols. (Pisa: Nistri 1858–62).

9 *ST* II-II, qu. 118, art. 8. As we noted in chapter 3, the daughters of avarice (*cupiditas, avaritia*) and pride were often depicted as the 'arbor mala' or 'arbor vitiorum.' Adolf Katzenellenbogen, *Allegories of the Virtues and Vices in Medieval Art* (New York: Norton 1964), 63–8, plates 64–7.

10 I find the late Professor Hatcher's position that Ulysses is not punished for fraudulent counsel untenable (Anna Granville Hatcher, 'Dante's Ulysses and Guido da Montefeltro,' *Dante Studies*, 88 [1970], 109–17). Both he and Guido burn in the same *bolgia*, and the black cherub makes it quite clear what the crowning sin is in verses 115–16 of *Inf.* XXVII: 'Venir se ne dee giù tra i miei meschini / perchè diede'l *consiglio frodolente.*' James G. Truscott disputed Professor Hatcher's challenge in his essay 'Ulysses and Guido,' especially p. 61. I also personally believe that Ulysses is punished for his ultimate and inveterate sin of fraudulent counsel, and I seek here to show how Ulysses is exemplary of that sin and to explain the cruxes I list.

Dante informs us at the end of *Convivio* I, vii that he knows of no Latin translation of the *Iliad*, but it is interesting to ponder whether some of the tradition of the *Ilias latina* (first century AD) had not subsequently influenced him. That work, known for centuries, and used by abecedarians, renders two epithets for 'Ulixes': he is a man of *consiliis illustris* (v. 139) and a *fraudis commentor* (vv. 527, 579). See the edition by Frédéric Plessis (Paris: Hachette 1885). Would such knowledge, known to every schoolboy for over a millenium previous to Dante, remain unmentioned in secondary literary works and *florilegia*? Some commentators believe Dante knew the Homeric version in some way: see, for example, Benvenuto da Imola, *Comentum* II, 293–4.

11 'Evil is augmented and amassed by the practice of evil, and it exists without

moderation of limit, it fights through guile and deceit and is revealed by its deeds.' St Ambrose, *De fuga saeculi* VII, 39 (*PL* 14, col. 587); *Flight from the World*, in St Ambrose, *Seven Exegetical Works*, trans. Michael P. McHugh (Washington, DC: Catholic Univ. Press in association with Consortium Press 1972), 311. My position here is close to that of Mario Trovato in his essay, 'Il contrapasso nell'ottava bolgia,' *Dante Studies*, 94 (1976), 47–60.

12 *ST* II-II, qu. 118, art. 8.

13 *Allegoriae in Sacram Scripturam, PL* 112, col. 905.

14 Anthony K. Cassell, 'Failure, Pride and Conversion in *Inferno* I: A Reinterpretation,' *Dante Studies*, 94 (1976), 1–24. See also Rudy S. Spraycar, 'Dante's *lago del cor*,' *Dante Studies*, 96 (1978), 1–19.

15 *On Christian Doctrine*, trans. D.W. Robertson, Jr, Library of Liberal Arts (New York: Liberal Arts Press 1958), 39.

16 *On Christian Doctrine*, p. 39.

17 It was originally the fiftieth day after Passover.
   The Greeks' scorning of Dante's speech reverses the gift of glossolalia and its generous use by the Apostles, whose preaching everyone heard in his native language (Acts 2:4, 6, 8).

18 S. Fulgentii Episcopi, *Super Thebaiden* in Fabii Planciadis Fulgentii V.C. *Opera*, ed. Rudolf Helm, add. Jean Préaux (Stuttgart: Teubner 1970), 183; *Fulgentius the Mythographer*, trans. Leslie George Whitbread (Columbus, Ohio: Ohio State Univ. Press 1971), 241.

19 As Robert Hollander puts it: 'Dante brings in the Elijah-Elisha story (II Kings 2:11–12, 23–34) to set up a negative typology for Ulysses: as Dante is like Elisha, who was also the bearer of the true record of an ascent to God because he was singled out for this privileged vision, so Ulysses, the great voyager, is *not* like Elijah (whom Dante shall himself ultimately resemble), for his awesome voyage was precisely the inversion of the divine voyage, taking him and his men to perdition.' *Allegory in Dante's Commedia* (Princeton, NJ: Princeton Univ. Press 1969), 117. For Ulysses as an anti-Aeneas, see H.D. Goldstein's excellent essay, 'Enea e Paolo,' p. 322, and David Thompson's 'Dante's Ulysses and the Allegorical Journey,' *Dante Studies*, 85 (1967), 35–58, reprinted in his *Dante's Epic Journeys* (Baltimore and London: Johns Hopkins Univ. Press 1974). Amilcare Iannucci has recently re-examined the relation and contrast between the journey of Dante Wayfarer and that of Ulysses; see 'Ulysses' "folle volo": The Burden of History,' pp. 410–45.

20 Rupert of Deutz, *De victoria verbi Dei* V, cap. xiv (*PL* 169, col. 1328). (Cited hereafter as *De victoria*.) Concerning the *contrapasso*, Pietro Alighieri cites James 3:6: 'And the tongue is a fire, a world of iniquity. The tongue is placed among our members, which defileth the whole body and inflameth the wheel of our nativ-

ity, being set on fire by Hell.' The Epistle continues (3:8): 'But the tongue no man can tame, an unquiet evil, full of deadly poison' (*Commentarium*, p. 231). The human tongue contrasts with the pure tongue of the Holy Spirit.

21 *De victoria* v, cap. xvi (*PL* 169, col. 1329).

22 *De victoria* v, cap. x (*PL* 169, col. 1324), v, cap. xi (col. 1325). See also Rupert's *Commentum in Apocalypsim* vi, xi (*PL* 169, cols. 1026–7).

23 *De victoria* v, cap. xi (*PL* 169, col. 1325). 'Verbum ipsius quasi facula ardebat [Ecclesiasticus (Sirach) 48:1].' Giuseppe Mazzotta, following Robert Hollander (*Allegory in Dante's Commedia*, p. 117), recognized this inverted typology: 'Elijah is the explicit anti-type of Ulysses, and, like Ulysses in *Inferno* xxvi, is conventionally described "as a fire, and his word burned like a torch" [Ecclesiasticus (Sirach) 48:1].' However, Mazzotta did not note that Ulysses inverted Elijah in many other ways ('Poetics of History,' p. 41; see also Mazzotta's chapter 'Rhetoric and History' in *Dante, Poet*, pp. 66–106).

24 St Gregory the Great, *Homilarium in Ezechielem*, lib. ii; *Homil.* xxxix, 5 (*PL* 76, col. 1216). In the same context St Gregory alludes to the legend of Elijah's translation to the Earthly Paradise, the same ultimate destination where Ulysses meets destruction, 'some secret region of the earth' (col. 1216).

25 St Ambrose, *De fuga saeculi* vi, 34 (*PL* 14, col. 585); *Flight*, p. 307.

26 Cf. *Purgatorio* xix, 22–4; Joseph Mazzeo, *Medieval Cultural Tradition in Dante's Commedia* (Ithaca, NY: Cornell Univ. Press 1960), 209–12. For Jezebel as 'the outpouring of vanity,' see St Ambrose, *De fuga saeculi* vi, 34 (*PL* 14, col. 585); she is 'the impurity of the flesh' mentioned, among the *dubia* of Hugh of St Victor, in the *Allegoriae in Vetus Testamentum* vii, 14 (*PL* 175, col. 710). Elijah is 'the victorious contemptor of worldly vanity' in Rupert of Deutz' *De victoria* v, xiv (*PL* 169, col. 1327).

27 *De victoria* v, cap. ix, x (*PL* 169, cols. 1325–6).

28 2 Kings 17:17–24, see St Augustine, *De mirabilibus Sacrae Scripturae* ii, 23 (*PL* 35, col. 2183). *De victoria* v, cap. x (*PL* 169, col. 1324).

29 See, for example, Hugh of St Victor's exegesis on this passage, *Miscellanea* iii, cvi (*PL* 177, col. 690). Elijah's curse in 4 [2] Kings 1:10, as Hugh quotes it, 'If as you say I, as a man of God am a prophet, heavenly flames will burn against you now, and against those who are with you,' is fulfilled in Hell. Cf. St Augustine, *De mirabilibus* ii, 20 (*PL* 35, col. 2182).

30 *Moralia* xxvi, 58 (*PL* 76, cols 583–4); *Morals* iii, pt. 1, p. 178.

31 *Moralia* xxvi, 60–2 (*PL* 76, cols. 384–6); *Morals* iii, pt. 1, pp. 180–1. The paradigms of fraud are found under the terms hypocrisy, fraudulence, and dissimulation in the Church Fathers; notably the terms 'simulator' and 'hypocrita' are used interchangeably. St Thomas cites Isidore's *Etymologies* x: ' "Hypocrite" is a Greek word corresponding to the Latin "simulator," for whereas he is evil within,

he shows himself outwardly as being good; ὑπὸ denoting falsehood, and κρίσις judgment' (*ST* ii–ii, qu. 111, art. 2). Most usefully, for our understanding of Geryon and Ulysses, St Thomas adds: 'We must conclude, therefore, that hypocrisy is dissimulation ... *when a sinner simulates the person of a just man.*' In *ST* ii–ii, qu. 111, art. 3, obj. and reply 3, St Thomas cites St Gregory's *Moralia* xviii, 13: 'A hypocrite, or as the Latin has it, a dissimulator, is a covetous thief: for through desire of being honoured for holiness, though guilty of wickedness, he steals praises for a life which is not his.' Hypocrisy for St Thomas included guile in words and fraud in deed. Dante may be stressing the generic sense of 'ipocresia' for fraudulence when he places it first in the *terzina* and first in the list which Virgil gives of the sins of Malebolge in *Inf.* xi, 57–60:

... nel cerchio secondo s'annida
ipocresia, lusinghe e chi affattura,
   falsità, ladroneccio e simonia,
   ruffian, baratti e simile lordura.

Given the long patristic tradition behind the meaning of the word, it is difficult to ally 'ipocresia' only to the *bolgia* of the 'ipocriti tristi.' St Gregory the Great contrasts Elijah with dissemblers in his *In septem psalmos poenitentiales expositio: Psalm. III*, vers. 9 [10] (*PL* 79, col. 573).

32 Critics and commentators generally agree that the punishment in the eighth *bolgia* is a Hellish inversion of the Pentecost. See André Pézard, *Dante sous la pluie de feu*, p. 283 et passim; Terence P. Logan, 'The Characterization of Ulysses in Homer, Virgil and Dante: A Study in Sources and Analogues,' *Eighty-Second Annual Report of the Dante Society* (1964), 42; Hollander, *Allegory*, p. 118, n. 12. What has not been examined before is that Elijah *is* the prefiguration of the Gift of Tongues to the Apostles.

33 St Ambrose, *De Isaac vel anima* viii, 77 (*PL* 14, col. 531); *Isaac or the Soul* in *Seven Exegetical Works*, p. 61. Emphasis added.

34 *De Isaac* viii, 78; *Isaac*, p. 62. The 'wings of fire' are also the flames of divine Scripture. See also *De fuga saeculi*, passim.

35 John Freccero, 'Dante's Prologue Scene: Section ii, "The Wings of Ulysses,"' *Dante Studies*, 84 (1966), esp. pp. 13–14. Of interest also are Mark Musa's 'Le ali di Dante (e il Dolce stil novo), *Purg.* xxiv,' *Omaggio a Dante*, issue of *Convivium*, 34 (1966), 361–7; and Hugh Shankland's two articles, 'Dante aliger,' *Modern Language Review*, 70 (1975), 764–85, and 'Dante *Aliger* and Ulysses,' *Italian Studies*, 32 (1977), 21–40. Cf. *Par.* ii, 57; xi, 3; xv, 53–4.

36 *Moralia* xxxi, 11 (*PL* 76, col. 581); *Morals* iii, 433.

37 *PL* 112, col. 856–7.

38 Anna Dolfi, 'Il Canto di Ulisse: Occasione per un discorso di esegesi dantesca,' *Forum Italicum*, 7, no. 4; 8, no. 1 (1974), 22–45, here, p. 27. Except for this

misconception, Professor Dolfi's article is excellent, and especially useful for its synopsis of criticism.

39 *De eruditione* III, cap. xii (*PL* 196, col. 1359): 'Vultis adhuc plenius nosse quales alas soleat fraudulentia habere? Ut igitur breviter exprimam quid sentiam: Una dicatur simulationis, alia dissimulationis, tertia ostentationis, quarta excusationis.' This work was familiar to Dante.

40 *De eruditione* III, cap. xiii (*PL* 196, col. 1360): 'Scimus autem quia hypocritarum fraudulentia in omni eo quod actitat ad honoris sui promotionem anhelat. Omne enim quod agit, vel agendo intendit, ambitioni deservit. *Nihil autem aliud est ambitio quam honoris affectatio.* Prima autem species hujus mali est affectatio libertatis, secunda affectatio dignitatis, tertia affectatio auctoritatis, quarta affectatio potestatis.'

41 *De eruditione* III, cap. xiii (*PL* 196, col. 1360): 'Ecce quomodo ambitio in quattuor se capita dividit, cui omnis, ut dictum est, hypocritarum actio subservit. Libertatis affectatio est, quando jam quis subterfugitat aliis subesse. Dignitatis affectatio est superiora ambiendo semper de gradu in gradum anhelare. *Auctoritatis affectatio est, cum jam ambit quis vir magni consilii et sanctitatis omnibus apparere et statuenda quaeque, vel diffinienda ab ejus consilio vel arbitrio pendere.* Potestatis affectatio est, cum jam ambit aliis praeesse. Videmus saepe illos etiam qui voluntariam obedientiam professi sunt, quam libenter, quam desideranter molestas satis et onerosas occupationes suscipiunt, ut exeundi, loquendi, agendi majusculam libertatem ex administrationis suae occasione obtineant. Quid agit hoc, quaeso, nisi libertatis ambitio?' Ironically, Homer praises Odysseus as 'the equal of Zeus in counsel' (*Iliad* II, 169), but such knowledge would not become known in Italy until after 1362, with Leontius Pilatus' translation.

Hercules is elsewhere treated as a positive, superhuman character in the *Commedia*; compare *Inferno* IX, 97–9, where Dante treats him as a *figura* of Christ, paralleling their *descensus ad inferos* and Harrowing by implication. Niccolò Pisano carved Hercules as Fortitude on the pulpit in the Baptistry of Pisa, 1260. Erwin Panofsky, *Renaissance and Renascences in Western Art* (New York and Evanston: Harper and Row 1960), fig. 48.

42 Giuseppe Mazzotta comes close to the same conclusion in 'Poetics of History: *Inferno* XXVI,' and in *Dante, Poet*, pp. 93–4.

43 Compare, for example, St Thomas Aquinas, *ST* II–II, qu. 111, art. 1, and St Gregory the Great, *Moralia* XXXI, 20 (*PL* 76, col. 584). The implicit contrast between the faithless Ulysses and 'pius Aeneas' has been made forcefully many times before and I see no useful purpose in discussing it again here. (See Padoan, *Il pio Enea*, pp. 170–204; John Scott, *Dante magnanimo*, pp. 117–93.) I might note, however, that Macrobius' *Commentary on the dream of Scipio* I, viii, 6, gives the pattern to be followed by the righteous, the opposite of that followed by

Ulysses: 'Man has political virtues because he is a social animal. By these virtues *upright men devote themselves to their commonwealths, protect cities, revere parents, love their children, and cherish relatives.*' Ed. and trans. William Harris Stahl (New York and London: Columbia Univ. Press 1952), 121.

44 *Moralia* xxxi, 20 (*PL* 76, col. 584); *Morals* iii, pt. 2, p. 441. Emphasis added.

CHAPTER EIGHT: SATAN

1 See Charles S. Singleton, 'In exitu Israel de Aegypto,' *Seventy-eighth Annual Report of the Dante Society* (1960), 1–24.

2 See John Freccero, 'The Sign of Satan,' *Modern Language Notes*, 80 (1965), 11–26; and my earlier essay, 'The Tomb, the Tower and the Pit: Dante's Satan,' *Italica*, 56 (1979), 331–51.

Other useful studies, not otherwise mentioned in the notes, are: Arturo Graf, 'Demonologia di Dante,' in his *Miti, leggende e superstizioni del Medio Evo* (Turin: Chiantore 1925; reprint, Bologna: Arnaldo Forni 1965), ii, 79–139; Bruno Nardi, 'L'Ultimo canto dell' *Inferno*,' *Convivium*, 25 (1957), 141–8; Aleardo Sacchetto, 'Chant xxxive de l'*Enfer*,' *Bulletin de la Société d'Etudes Dantesques du Centre Universitaire Méditérranéan*, 8 (Nice 1959), esp. p. 39; André Pézard, 'Le dernier chant de l'*Enfer*,' in the same journal, 11 (1962), 47–66; Vittorio Rossi, 'Il canto xxxiv dell'*Inferno*,' in *Letture dantesche*, ed. Giovanni Getto (Florence: Sansoni 1962), 653–65; Giorgio Petrocchi, 'Il canto xxxiv dell'*Inferno*,' *Lectura dantis scaligera* (Florence: Le Monnier 1967), 1–24; reprint in *Itinerari danteschi* (Bari: Adriatica 1969), 295–310; Aldo Vallone, 'Il canto xxxiv dell'*Inferno* e l'estremo intellettualismo di Dante,' *Nuove letture dantesche*, 3 (Florence: Le Monnier 1969), 189–208; Aulo Greco, 'Il canto xxxiv dell'*Inferno*,' in *Inferno: Letture degli anni 1973–76*, Casa di Dante in Roma (Rome: Bonacci 1977), 803–21; Andrea Ciotti, 'Lucifero,' *Enciclopedia dantesca, sub voce*. Many critics, such as Rudolf Palgen, 'La *Visione di Tundalo* nella *Commedia* di Dante,' *Convivium*, 37 (1969), 129–47, have seen the influence of the *Vision of Tundale* on the Poem; Palgen's essay is most thorough. He shows that Dante's Satan is a *contaminatio* of several literary sources: that of Lucifer and 'Acherons' in the *Visio Tnugdali*, of the magic mechanical devil of Genus in the *Roman des sept sages*, ed. Jean Misrahi (Paris: Droz 1933), 66, and Polyphemus (*Ovide moralisé*, vol. v, ed. C. de Boer in *Verhandelingen der Koninklijke Nederlandsche Akademie van Wetenschappen, Afdeeling Letterkunde*, n.s. 43 [1938], 61). See also V.G. Vetrugno, 'La genealogia e lo sviluppo del Lucifero dantesco,' *L'Alighieri*, 11 (1970), 16–42.

For the question of Satan's fall and the authenticity of the *De situ et forma aque et terre*, see the edition and brilliant introduction by Giorgio Padoan (Florence: Le Monnier 1968), with his extensive bibliography of the matter.

3 The submersion of human reason into bestiality is figured by the centaurs in the

circle of the tyrants. Charles Singleton observes that the centaurs' joining, where the human waist meets the equine breast, receives triple emphasis in *Inf.* XII, 70, 84, 97. *Inferno: Commentary*, pp. 192–5.

For other recent essays loosely connected with the concept of submersion to the waist see Kleinhenz, 'Towering Giants'; Mark Musa, 'Aesthetic Structure in the *Inferno*, Canto XIX,' *Essays on Dante*, ed. M. Musa (Bloomington: Indiana Univ. Press 1964), 170; Mark Musa and Anna Granville Hatcher, 'Lucifer's Legs,' *PMLA*, 79 (1964), 191–9. For the 'fiumana' of *Inf.* II and its intimate connection to baptismal typology, see the thought-provoking essay by John Freccero, 'The River of Death: *Inferno* II, 108,' in *The World of Dante*, ed. S. Bernard Chandler and Julius A. Molinaro (Toronto: Univ. of Toronto Press 1966), 25–42.

It is important for the concept of the *contrapasso* that the half-buried stance of the simonist popes and of Judas inversely reflects the swallowing of Jonah head-first by the whale; this biblical story also appeared frequently in early Christian art, particularly on sarcophagi. It echoed Christ's identification of himself as the 'new Jonah.' Jonah's three days in the whale prefigured Christ's death and resurrection, and mankind's salvation. See the many illustrations in Josef Wilpert, *I Sarcofagi cristiani antichi* (Rome: Pontificio Istituto di Archeologia Cristiana 1929–36), 3 vols.; and Friedrich W. Deichmann, *Repertorium der christlich-antiken Sarkophage* (Wiesbaden: F. Steiner 1967).

4　Such references in the Church Fathers are legion. See, for example, Leo the Great's letter to the Bishops of Sicily: 'Proprie tamen in morte crucifixi, et in resurrectione mortui, potentia baptismatis novam creaturam condit ex veteri: ut in renascentibus et mors Christi operetur ... dum in baptismatis regula, et mors intervenit interfectione peccati, et sepulturam triduanam imitatur trina demersio, et ab aquis elevatio, resurgentis instar est de sepulcro.' *Epistola* XVI, iii, *Ad Universos Episcopos per Siciliam Constitutos*; *PL* 54, col. 698. St Cyril, *PG* 33, cols. 1077–80; Gregory of Nyssa, *PG* 44, col. 1003; *PG* 46, col. 420. Daniélou, pp. 37–9, 77, 79, 89 et passim.

5　For the concept of baptism by fire as the judgment of God, see Carl-Martin Edsman, *Le Baptême de feu*, Acta Seminarii Neotestamentici Upsaliensis, IX (Leipzig: Alfred Lorentz; Uppsala: A.-B. Lundequist; Almquist and Wiksell 1940). The Poet uses immersion, especially to the waist or chest, as a sign of God's judgment over evil many times through the first canticle.

6　Gertrud Schiller, *Iconography of Christian Art*, vol. I, trans. Janet Seligman (Greenwich, Conn.: New York Graphic Society 1971), 136–7. Schiller gives the significance *in malo*, and she is undoubtedly correct; it is also the one most appropriate in the context of Satan in the present essay. There is, however, the symbolic sense *in bono* which she omits. Christ as 'ichthys' or 'fish' was one of the earliest Christian symbols; at baptism novices become 'pisciculi,' 'little fishes' immersed in the waters, a tradition attested to as early as Tertullian: 'But we, little fishes, according to the example of our *ichthus*, Jesus Christ, are born in water, nor have we safety [salvation] in any other way than by remaining permanently in the water' (*PL* 1, col. 1197). The Perebleptos fresco (see plate 28) shows both human forms and fish beneath the waves of the Jordan.

Among the scores of references to the Pharaoh as the Devil, see, for example, St Bernard of Clairvaux, *Sermo 39 super Cantica Canticorum*, 5: 'Et prosequere modo mecum singula proportionis membra. Ibi populus eductus de Aegypto, hic homo de saeculo; ibi prosternitur Pharao, hic diabolus.' *Sermones super Cantica Canticorum 36–86*, ed. J. Leclerq et al., *Opera*, vol. II (Rome: Editiones Cisterciensis 1958), 21. For the Flood, see Hugh of St Victor, *De Sacramentis* II, 6, viii; *On the Sacraments of the Christian Faith*, trans. Roy J. Deferrari (Cambridge, Mass.: Medieval Academy of America 1951), 296. Per Lundberg, *La Typologie baptismale dans l'ancienne église*, Acta Seminarii Neotestamentici Upsaliensis, x (Leipzig: Alfred Lorentz; Uppsala: A.-B. Lundquist 1942). See Jean Daniélou, *The Bible and the Liturgy*, ed. Michael A. Mathis, Liturgical Studies (Notre Dame, Ind.: Univ. of Notre Dame Press 1961), esp. pp. 70–98. See also Freccero, 'The River of Death,' p. 34 and n. 22.

7 Schiller, *Iconography* I, plate 363. Concerning the Chantilly codex (Musée Condé 697, f. 221) of the *Divina Commedia*, Millard Meiss describes the souls depicted around Satan: 'The traitors do not seem frozen in ice but rather floating in transparent water.' 'An Illuminated *Inferno* and Trecento Painting in Pisa,' Art Bulletin, 47 (1965), 21–34; here, p. 28.

8 Schiller, I, plate 375.

9 Singleton, *Elements*, pp. 39–42.

10 *Treatise on the Trinity*, ST I, qu. 26, art. 1: 'Procession, therefore, *is not to be understood* from what it is in bodies, either *according to local movement*, or by way of a cause proceeding forth to its exterior effect; as, for instance, like heat proceeding from the agent to the thing made hot. *Rather* it is to be understood *by way of an intelligible emanation*, for example, of the intelligible word which proceeds from the speaker, yet remains in him. In that sense the Catholic Faith understands procession as existing in God.'

11 For the tradition see Carl-Martin Edsman, *Le Baptême de feu*, esp. pp. 182–6.

12 The blessing of the font's waters and the Paschal taper took place on the eve of Holy Saturday, the very time of Dante's arrival and departure from Lucifer in the Poem.

Compare the *Missal* of Isidore of Seville as preserved in the *Liturgia mozarabica*: at the *Benedictio aque*, the exorcism of Satan from the waters includes the casting of salt and a triple insufflation by the priest: 'Hic faciat sacerdos signum crucis in ipso sale, et *insufflet tribus vicibus*: et postmodum dicat hunc sequentem exorcismus: "Exorcizo te, creatura salis ..." ' (*PL* 85, col. 105). Compare also the *Benedictio* text (*Missale mixtum secundum regulam B. Isidori dictum Mozarabes, PL* 85, col. 465). P. de Puniet in his article on 'La Bénédiction de l'eau' in *Dictionnaire d'archéologie chrétienne et de liturgie*, ed. Fernand Cabrol, tome 2ᵉ, 1ᵉ partie (Paris: Létouzey et Ané 1910), 685–713, states that the ceremony of the benediction was fixed from the seventh century in the *Gelasian Sacramentary*, and compares texts of ancient Syrian and Byzantine liturgies, translating the priest's directions into Latin: 'Insufflat in aquas'; 'Insufflat in aquam' (p. 698).

In the twentieth century, according to the *Missale romanum*, the priest performed this triple breathing *twice*, probably reflecting a conflation of several liturgies; the rite reads as follows (*Sabbato: De benedictione aquae baptismalis*): The priest first breathes three times in the form of a Cross upon the water ('*halat ter* in aquam in modum crucis') saying: 'Do [O God] with your mouth bless these clear waters (simplices aquas), that *besides their natural power of cleansing the body, they may also be effectual for the cleansing of minds.*' The priest next plunges the Paschal candle three times into the font, singing: 'May the power of the Holy Spirit descend into the fulness of this font.' He then breathes three times again over the water ('*sufflans ter* in aquam') and sings: 'And make the whole substance of this water fruitful for the effecting of regeneration.' *Missale romanum* (Ratisbon: Pustet 1963), 239–48. A triple spiration effecting the *death* of the soul is one of Dante's most ingenious doctrinal and poetic *trovate.*

13 Daniélou, *Bible and Liturgy*, p. 107. The baptism of Christ fulfilled the sacrifice of Elias-Elijah in the Old Testament, in which fire descends upon the holocaust. On the Spirit descending at Christ's Baptism, see Matthew 3:16; Mark 1:10; Luke 3:22; John 1:29–34. On baptismal *epiclesis*, see Daniélou, *Bible and Liturgy*, pp. 13, 107, et passim.

14 Compare *ST* III, qu. 39, art. 1; also n. 12 above; and the rite of Milan: '(*Exorcismus*) Exorcizo te creatura aquae in nomine dei patris omnipotentis, et in nomine iesu christi filii eius domini nostri, et in virtute spiritus sancti, ut fias aqua exorcizata *ed effugandam omnem potestatem inimici et ipsum inimicum eradicare et explantare valeas cum angelis suis apostatis* per virtutem eiusdem domini nostri iesu christi qui venturus est iudicare vivos et mortuos et seculum per ignem. Amen.' *Missale romanum mediolani, 1474*, ed. Robert Lippe, Henry Bradshaw Society, XVII (London: Harrison and Sons 1899), I, xxv. See B. Neunheuser, 'De benedictione aquae baptismalis,' in *Ephemerides liturgicae*, 44 (1930), 484–91; *Dictionnaire de spiritualité ascétique et mystique: doctrine et histoire*, fondé par M. Viller et al., tome IV, pt. 1 (Paris: Beauchesne 1960), 24. In the context of baptism, the iconography of Satan, and Dante's constant satire of the Florentines, it is well to remember the triform figure of Satan in the frescoes of the Florentine Baptistry, and Dante's desire to be crowned as a poet in that very 'bel San Gio-

vanni.' As, in the next few pages, we treat the iconography of Joseph betrayed by his brothers, we should keep in mind that it may also be no coincidence that Dante, betrayed by Florence and accused as traitor, would wed his poetic symbolism to the sacrament and sanctuary closest to his heart.

15 'Quis est ille quem parentes et fratres adoraverunt super terram, nisi Christus Jesus?' *De Joseph*, 2:8 in *Sancti Ambrosii Opera*, ed. Karl Schenkel, CSEL, 32, 2 (Prague, Vienna, Leipzig: Tempsky and Freytag 1897), 76; *PL* 14, cols. 637–72.

16 'Et ut scias verum hoc esse mysterium, ipse de se Dominus ait: "Posuerunt me in lacu inferiori et in umbra mortis" (Psalm 87:7 [88:6])' (*PL* 14, col. 644). Usefully, for the 'lago' of Cocytus, St Ambrose equates the well or pit, 'puteus,' with 'lacus' and 'piscina'; cf. *PL* 14, col. 512.

17 *Moralia* xxxiii, 45 (*PL* 76, col. 702); *Morals* iii, 599; St Gregory is discussing Job 41:4: 'Who can go into the midst of his mouth?'

18 Dante may have calqued his description on the cow-like unconcern of Satan described by St Gregory: 'Before the coming of the Redeemer of the world, [Satan] drank up the world without wondering. ... even after the knowledge of the Redeemer, he seizes many with his open mouth.' *Moralia* xxxiii, 12 (*PL* 76, col. 677–8); *Morals* iii, 565–6. 'The Redeemer of mankind Who not only restrained us from falling into the mouth of Leviathan but granted us also to return from his mouth.' *Moralia* xxxiii, 22 (*PL* 76, col. 686); *Morals* iii, 577. Both passages are important for the 'hydraulic system' of Hell ending with Satan.

19 *Moralia* xxxiii, 22 (*PL* 76, col. 700–1); *Morals* iii, 577.

20 *PL* 112, col. 1073–4.

21 *Moralia* ii, 53: 'Ventus autem vehemus quid aliud, quam tentatio fortis accipitur?' (*PL* 75, col. 582); *Morals* i, 104.

22 *Moralia* xxix, 57–61, esp. p. 59 (*PL* 76, col. 509–12); *Morals* iii, 343–6, esp. p. 345.

23 *Moralia* xxix, 58 (*PL* 76, col. 570); *Morals* iii, 343. Many critics, and, most persuasively, Palgen, in '*La Visione di Tundalo*,' have ascribed the lake of ice to Tundale; however, I believe that Dante saw in the *Visione* merely a *corroboration* for the biblical doctrine, and that he may perhaps have seen it even as an historical reaffirmation.

24 *Moralia* xxxii, 18, 'Fenum sicut bos comedet' (*PL* 76, col. 646–7); *Morals* ii, 524.

25 St Ambrose, *De Interpellatione Iob et David*, lib. ii, 5:18, in *Sancti Ambrosii Opera*, ed. Karl Schenkel, CSEL, 32:2 (Prague, Vienna, Leipzig: Tempsky and Freytag 1897), 244. St Ambrose, *The Prayer of Job and David*, in St Ambrose, *Seven Exegetical Works*, trans. Michael P. McHugh, The Fathers of the Church, 65 (Washington, DC: Catholic Univ. of America Press, in association with Consortium Press 1972), 364. See also Walafrid Strabo, *Glossa ordinaria* (*PL* 114; col. 339), and Rabanus Maurus, *De universo* xxii, 7 (*PL* 111, col. 603).

26 *Moralia* xi, 60, 'Homo quasi folium et stipula tentationis vento movetur' (*PL* 75, col. 980); *Morals* ii, p. 37.

27 H.D. Austin, in his brief essay '*Mola* in Dante's Usage,' *Speculum*, 19 (1944), 127–9, totally disregarding Satan's holocaust of souls in history, was only concerned with showing that Dante refers to a *horizontal* millstone rather than a *vertical* movement of heavenly dance.

28 One should note that the 'towers' of Satan's City and Tomb are also chimeras (Cassell, 'The Tomb,' p. 340). For the common image of Satan's teeth as temptation and trial see also *Moralia* xiii, 12 (*PL* 75, col. 1022–3); *Morals* ii, 94; *Moralia* xxxiii, 47 (*PL* 76, col. 703; *Morals* iii, 600).

29 Alois Thomas, 'Mystische Mühle, in *Lexikon der christlichen Ikonographie*, vol. iii, ed. Engelbert Kirschbaum (Rome, Basel, Freiburg and Vienna: Herder 1971), 297.

30 St Ambrose, *Expositio Evangelii secundum Lucam* viii, 48 (*PL* 15, col. 1779); St Paulinas of Nola (*PL* 61, col. 193); Maximus of Turin, *Homilia* 111 (*PL* 57, col. 514); Rabanus Maurus, *De Universo* xxii, 7 (*PL* 111, col. 603); Rupert of Deutz, *Commentum in Matthaeum* x (*PL* 168, col. 1556).

31 St Ambrose, *Expositio* xlii–xliii (*PL* 15, col. 1781).

32 *Expositio* xlviii (*PL* 15, col. 1779).

33 *Expositio* l (*PL* 15, col. 1780). The erring mind (*mens*) is purified at baptism, the sacrament of initiation. After the journey, Dante has 'la mente che non erra.'

34 *Expositio*, li (*PL* 15, col. 1780).

35 *Moralia* xxv, 19 (*PL* 76, col. 331); *Morals* iii, 108–9. Although Satan is the main subject of our enquiry into the *contrapasso* of this episode, I should remark in passing that Judas' punishment in particular is based on Job 34:24, where God makes Satan do his bidding: 'He shall break in pieces many and innumerable, and shall make others to stand in their stead.' This prediction of Judas' replacement by Matthias is fulfilled in Acts 1:20–6. St Gregory, however, contrasts the thieving Judas with the Good Thief crucified with Christ: 'For what man could suppose that Judas, even after the ministry of the apostleship, would lose his portion in life? And who would believe, on the other hand, that the thief would find a means of life even at the very instant of his death? But the judge secretly presiding, and discerning the hearts of these two persons, mercifully established the one, and justly *crushed* the other (Judas).' *Moralia* xxv, 19 (*PL* 76, col. 331); *Morals* iii, 108–9.

We might recall here that the end of the paradigm of the 'daughters of covetousness (*cupiditas*),' after descending through violence, falsehood, perjury, and fraud, then evolves into treachery against persons, 'treachery, as in the case of Judas, who betrayed Christ through covetousness' (*ST* ii–ii, qu. 118, art. 8). There is obviously no question about the fitting union in Cocytus of Lucifer, traitor to God the Father in Heaven, with Judas, betrayer of Christ, the Son on Earth.

36 *ST* II, qu. 69, arts., 1 and 2; qu. 79, arts. 1, 4 and 5.

37 *Moralia* XXXIII, 22 (*PL* 76, col. 686); *Morals* III, 577. Palgen suggests an intriguing parallel between Dante's escape, climbing Lucifer, and Ulysses' escape from the cave of the Cyclops, clinging to the shaggy wool of a sheep; hairiness is, of course, a conventional iconographic attribute of demons and devils (Dante's Charon, Cerberus, and others all show a maximum degree of hirsuteness). See 'La visione di Tundalo,' esp. pp. 143–4.

38 Rupert of Deutz, among the hundreds of examples which one could cite, compares Christ's passion to wheat ground in a mill (*Commentarium in Matthaeum*, *PL* 168, col. 1556). See also Emile Mâle, *The Gothic Image*, trans. Dora Nussey (New York and London: Harper and Row 1958), 171–2; and, especially, Alois Thomas, 'Die mystische Mühle,' *Christliche Kunst*, 31 (1934–5), 129–39, and his article 'Mystische Mühle,' pp. 297–9; both his articles have fundamental information and an extensive bibliography. See also Gertrud Schiller, *Ikonographie der christlichen Kunst*, vol. IV, 1 (Gütersloh: Gerd Mohn 1976), 61–2. For St Paul as the miller, see D.W. Robertson, Jr, *A Preface to Chaucer: Studies in Medieval Perspectives* (Princeton: Princeton Univ. Press 1962), 290.

Behind the figure of Lucifer's dark satanic mill lies the same pattern which will come to full devotional and iconographic fruition over a century after Dante, that of Christ in the 'mystic mill.' The Redeemer, prefigured by the manna in the desert and incarnate as the Bread of Life (John 6:26–58), was then depicted in art as the literal product of the 'Mill of the Cross': grain, and the tortured Christ, poured in at the top of the Mill, issued, in most pictorial examples, as Communion wafers below.

In Dante's 'basso inferno' Christ is there only in parody and as judge: Satan himself is forced to act out the divine punishment as a winnowing mill, grinding the decayed grain of bloody souls unproductively, and forever.

German scholars, particularly, have been most active in regard to the doctrine of the 'mystic mill,' but not exclusively. See the illustrations in Remigius Boving, 'Zur Theologie eines Altarbildes aus der ehemaligen Franziskanerkirche Göttingen,' *Franziskaner Studien*, 5 (1918), 26–38, esp. p. 27; F. De Lasteryrie, 'Notice sur quelques représentations allégoriques de l'Eucharistie,' *Mémoires de la Société des Antiquaires de France*, 39 (1878), 82; Joseph Braun, *Der christliche Altar*, vol. II (Munich: Günther Koch 1924), 507; Karl Künstle, *Ikonographie der christlichen Kunst*, vol. I (Freiburg im Breisgau: Herder 1928), 193; Heinrich Schulz, 'Die mittelalterliche Sakramentsmühle,' *Zeitschrift für bildende Kunst*, 63 (1929), 208–16. Religious art of the late Middle Ages allied the Mill of the Host, or Mystic Mill, to the Mystic Winepress, following Christ's own identification of himself with a vine (see the extensive treatment above in chapter 3), and conflating it with the verses in Isaias 63:1–6: 'I have trodden the wine press alone.' See, in this regard: L. Lindet, 'Représentations allégoriques du moulin et du pressoir dans l'art chrétien,' *Revue archéologique*, 36 (1900), 402–13; Arthur Van Gramberen, 'Le pressoir mystique,' *Bulletin des métiers d'art*, 12 (1913), 129–32; Alois Thomas, *Die Darstellung Christi in der Kelter: eine theologische und kulturhistorische Studie*, Forschungen zur Volkskunde (Düsseldorf: L. Schwann 1936), esp. pp. 163–9, for the 'mystic mill.'

39 The text is published in *PL* 186, col. 1237, and, with negligible variations, in Julius von Schlosser, *Quellenbuch zur Kunstgeschichte des abendländischen Mittelalters* (Vienna: Carl Graeser 1896), 280.

40 See the illustrations in Thomas, 'Mystische Mühle,' p. 298.

41 St Eucherius, *Formulae spiritalis intelligentiae*, 7, *CSEL* 31 (1894), 42: 'mola vitae conversio.'

42 Compare, on this subject, the excellent chapter by Robert Hollander in *Studies in Dante* (Ravenna: Longo 1980), 91–105, esp. p. 94 (reprinted from *Italica*, 52 [1975], 348–63); see once again Charles S. Singleton's fundamental study, 'In exitu Israel,' and its necessary corollary, John Freccero's 'Casella's Song,' *Dante Studies*, 91 (1973), 73–80.

Index

This book

was designed by

ANTJE LINGNER

and was printed by

University of

Toronto

Press